The Cornucopian Stage

Harvard-Yenching Institute Monograph Series 140

The Cornucopian Stage

Performing Commerce in Early Modern China

Ariel Fox

Published by the Harvard University Asia Center
Distributed by Harvard University Press
Cambridge (Massachusetts) and London 2023

Published by the Harvard University Asia Center, Cambridge, MA 02138

The Harvard University Asia Center publishes a monograph series and, in coordination with the Fairbank Center for Chinese Studies, the Korea Institute, the Reischauer Institute of Japanese Studies, and other faculties and institutes, administers research projects designed to further scholarly understanding of China, Japan, Vietnam, Korea, and other Asian countries. The Center also sponsors projects addressing multidisciplinary and regional issues in Asia.

The Harvard-Yenching Institute, founded in 1928, is an independent foundation dedicated to the advancement of higher education in the humanities and social sciences in Asia. Headquartered on the campus of Harvard University, the Institute provides fellowships for advanced research, training, and graduate studies at Harvard by competitively selected faculty and graduate students from Asia. The Institute also supports a range of academic activities at its fifty partner universities and research institutes across Asia. At Harvard, the Institute promotes East Asian studies through annual contributions to the Harvard-Yenching Library and publication of the *Harvard Journal of Asiatic Studies* and the Harvard-Yenching Institute Monograph Series.

This publication was made possible in part by awards from the James P. Geiss and Margaret Y. Hsu Foundation and the Association for Asian Studies First Book Subvention Program.

Material from chapter 2 previously appeared in "Playing against Type: The Moral Merchant on the Early Qing Stage," *Journal of Chinese Literature and Culture* 6, no. 2 (2019), and material from chapter 3 previously appeared in "Exit, Pursued by a Bear: *Dushu sheng* and the Limits of Community in the Early Qing," *Journal of Chinese Literature and Culture* 7, no. 1 (2020). Reprinted by permission of the publisher.

Library of Congress Cataloging-in-Publication Data

Names: Fox, Ariel, 1982- author.
Title: The Cornucopian Stage : performing commerce in early modern China / Ariel Fox.
Other titles: Harvard-Yenching Institute monograph series ; 140.
Description: Cambridge (Massachusetts) : Harvard University Asia Center, 2023. | Series: Harvard-Yenching Institute monograph series; 140 |
Identifiers: LCCN 2023008706 | ISBN 9780674293755 (hardcover)
Subjects: LCSH: Chinese drama--Ming dynasty, 1368-1644--History and criticism. | Chinese drama--Qing dynasty, 1644-1912--History and criticism. | Theater--China--Suzhou Shi (Jiangsu Sheng)--History--17th century. | Money in literature. | Merchants in literature. | Commerce in literature. | Theater and society--China--History--17th century.
Classification: LCC PL2386 .F69 2023 | DDC 895.12/46093553--dc23/eng/20230406
LC record available at https://lccn.loc.gov/2023008706

Index by Vicki Low
♾ Printed on acid-free paper in the United States of America

For Sylvie

Contents

Illustrations

Maps

Plates

Acknowledgments

It is only appropriate to begin a book about abundance by taking stock of all I have received. My deepest debts of gratitude are owed to my advisor at Harvard, Wai-yee Li, and my colleague and mentor at the University of Chicago, Judith Zeitlin; I have been doubly fortunate to have been guided by their wisdom and kindness.

At Harvard, Wilt Idema modeled for me an attention to narrative complexity and the rich world of premodern performance traditions, and Michael Szonyi helped me look beyond the confines of my field. My interest in late imperial Chinese literature was first sparked by taking classes with Shang Wei as an undergraduate at Columbia; working with him, Robert Hymes, and Madeleine Zelin taught me how to read across time and space and opened me to the possibilities of a life in the academy.

I am incredibly lucky to be a part of a community of scholars from whom I have learned so much. This book is better because of generous feedback I have received from Maram Epstein, Andrea Goldman, Alison Hardie, Yuming He, Rania Huntington, Ling Hon Lam, Qiancheng Li, Xiaoqiao Ling, Liu Chiung-yun, Tina Lu, Bruce Rusk, Rivi Handler-Spitz, Catherine Swatek, Sophie Volpp, Stephen West, Ellen Widmer, I-Hsien Wu, and Paola Zamperini. Though technically neither advisor nor mentor, Paize Keulemans has been such a constant and generous interlocutor that it is hard not to think of him as both. Over the years, I have relied on the deep knowledge, friendship, and collaborative energies of Einor Cervone, Scott Gregory, Lulu Hansen, Will Hedberg,

Thomas Kelly, Stacie Kent, S. E. Kile, Casey Schoenberger, Maria Franca Sibau, Brian Skerratt, Josh Stenberg, and Suyoung Sun.

My wonderful colleagues in the Department of East Asian Languages and Civilizations and the Committee on Theater and Performance Studies have given me an intellectual home at the University of Chicago. I thank my chairs, Michael Bourdaghs, Jacob Eyferth, Donald Harper, and Hoyt Long in EALC and David Levin and Ellen MacKay in TAPS, who have been expert guides and advocates, and Dawn Brennan and Vicki Walden, who helped me navigate all manner of administrative complexities. It has been a lovely twist of fate to have ended up in the same place as Chelsea Foxwell, who has been a friend and academic role model since my undergrad days. I am especially grateful for the thoughtfulness and generosity of Kyeong-Hee Choi, Jacob Eyferth, Paola Iovene, Wu Hung, and Judith Zeitlin, who helped me through the difficulties of book-finishing and baby-having during a never-ending pandemic by opening up their homes, offices, and personal libraries to me when the world was shutting down.

My work has been supported by postdoctoral fellowships from the Fulbright U.S. Scholar Program, the Institute of Chinese Literature and Philosophy at Academia Sinica, and the Henry Luce Foundation/ACLS Program in China Studies. Crucial research for this book was made possible by Zhou Qin at Soochow University and Hu Siao-chen at Academia Sinica, who generously hosted me at their institutions and ensured that I benefitted from the rich intellectual and artistic communities they fostered. My thanks to Jiayi Chen, Daniela Licandro, Miguel Llanos de la Guardia, Malcolm Thompson, Yiwen Wu, Yiren Zheng, and Yunjun Zhou, for their indispensible assistance during various stages of research and manuscript preparation, and to Scott Walker for designing the maps. I owe a tremendous debt of gratitude to my editor Kristen Wanner, copyeditor Maura High, and the staff at the Harvard University Asia Center Publications Program for all the time and care they put into bringing this book into being.

I am grateful for the wonderfully nonacademic friendship of Neha Bhardwaj, Annie Chen, Hope Glassberg, Alexandra Magness,

Robyn Mar, Margarita O'Donnell, Chris Sherman, and Erica Wolff. I thank my sister, Marissa Fox, for her indispensable wit and my mother, Karen Fox, for her unflagging support. My husband, Jake Werner, has always had an unreasonable amount of faith in me. This book was made possible by his encouragement, patience, and willingness to read endless versions of the same chapter.

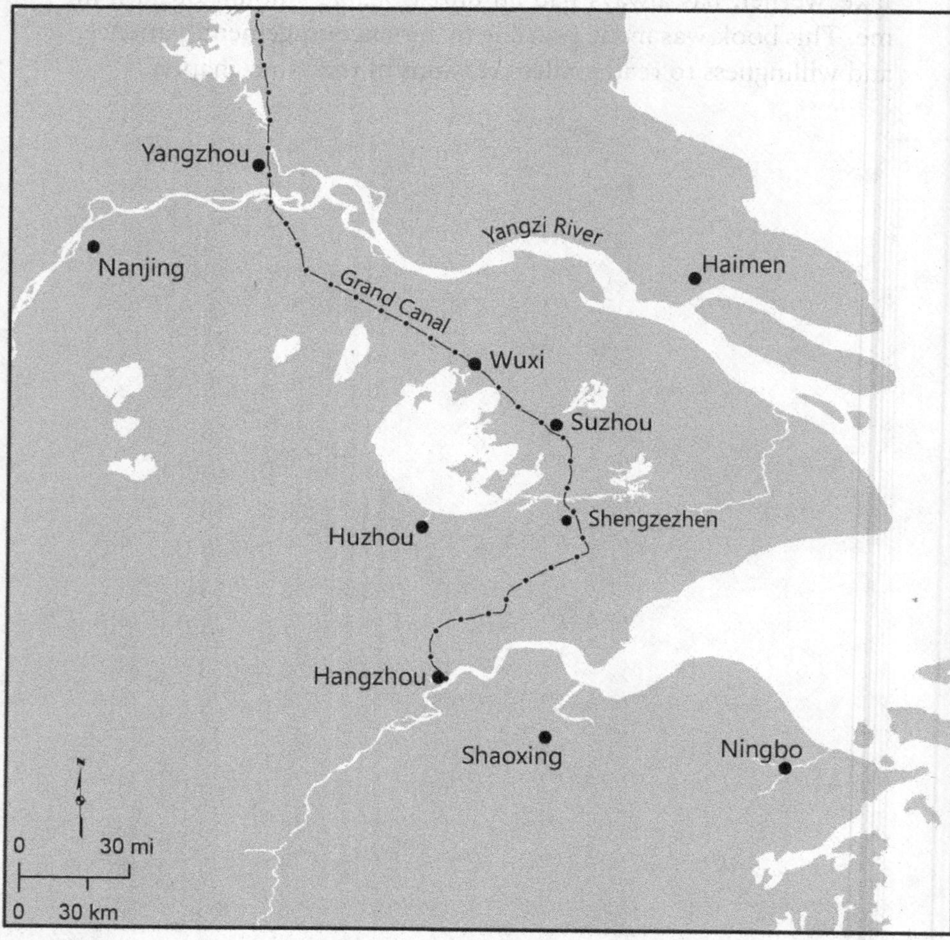

Map 1. Map of seventeenth-century Jiangnan region showing relevant sites.

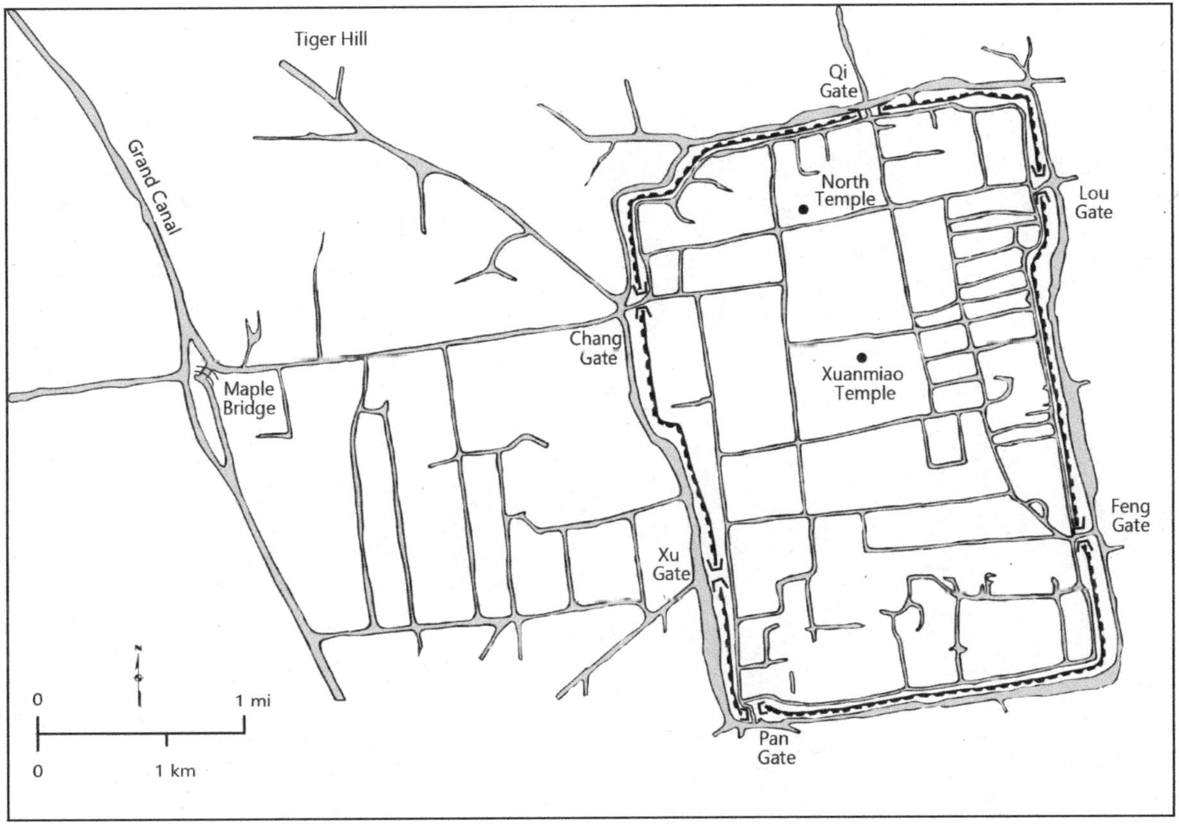

Map 2. Diagrammatic map of seventeenth-century Suzhou and environs showing waterways, city wall, and relevant sites. Based on map in Yinong Xu, *The Chinese City in Space and Time*, 158.

Introduction

Toward the end of the drama *Cornucopia* (*Jubaopen* 聚寶盆), attributed to the playwright Zhu Suchen 朱素臣 (ca. 1620–after 1701), a merchant walks wearily onto the stage.[1] His body and his coffers are exhausted from the vicissitudes of life—a swift and lucky rise, a politically orchestrated downfall. "Money," he declares, "truly is a thing that wears people out" 這錢財竟是累人之物了.[2]

Suddenly he sees two boys, one in silver and the other in gold, silently beckon him over to the west side of the room, where they bow and vanish in a puff of smoke. His wife, concubine, and son enter, having heard the commotion. When the merchant tells them what transpired, they speculate that these mysterious visitors might have left him something of value. He dismisses the idea, but his son hands him a shovel and his wives insist that he

1. Zhu He 朱㿥 is commonly referred to in both contemporaneous and modern scholarship by his *zi* 字 (courtesy name) Suchen 素臣 or his *hao* 號 (pen name) Rui'an 苼庵. The precise dates of his birth and death are unknown, though it is assumed that he was slightly junior to Bi Wei 畢魏 and Ye Shizhang 葉時章, whose names precede his on joint works, and roughly contemporaneous with You Tong 尤侗 (1618–1704) and Wu Qi 吳綺 (b. 1619). The last mention of Zhu's activity appears in a poem by Shen Deqian 沈德潛 (1673–1769) in which he talks about "recalling the *xinsi* year of Kangxi [1701]" 憶惜康熙歲辛巳 and enjoying "new songs" 新曲 composed by Zhu Suchen. Twenty *chuanqi* 傳奇 (southern drama) and three *zaju* 雜劇 (variety plays) are usually attributed to Zhu Suchen; twelve of these *chuanqi* and none of the *zaju* are extant in some form. On Zhu's attributed output, extant and otherwise, see Guo Yingde, *Ming Qing chuanqi zonglu*, 1:635–63, and Li Mei, *Ming Qing zhiji Suzhou zuojia qun yanjiu*, 243–44.

2. Zhu Suchen (attrib.), *Jubaopen*, 41b. The textual history of this play will be discussed in chapter 4. All translations mine unless otherwise indicated; variant characters in the original texts have been standardized throughout.

dig. And lo, in the very spot where the boys stood is a buried cache of silver and gold. "I'm done for," the merchant moans, "my enemy has returned" 完了, 冤家又來了.[3]

His wives try to convince him to keep this unexpected bounty, but it is not human reason he wishes to hear: "Enough, get out of the way! I will talk to it myself and get to the bottom of this matter" 也罷, 你們閃開, 待我對他講個明白.[4] His incredulous wives address each other and an equally incredulous audience as they cry, "You see, he is mad! How can gold and silver speak?" 你看他痴了, 金銀那裡會說話.[5]

But it does speak. "I am your wealth" 是君財 says a voice from offstage.[6] And in so saying, it reveals itself to be not a pile of gold and silver but an animated force connecting humans and gods in a cosmic economy that extends beyond the known world. As the merchant soon learns, he is not a helpless cog, buffeted by fate, but fate itself: the once and future Star of Wealth, reborn on Earth in order to beget the karmic encumbrances that allow him to become that which he has always been.

Like the merchant, this book asks money to speak, to tell us why it takes certain pathways through late imperial pages and stages. Money, the merchants through whose hands it passed, and the markets in which it did so were particularly talkative over the long seventeenth century. The period from the late Ming to the early Qing was a time of tremendous commercial volatility and possibility in China's lower Yangzi region, known as Jiangnan 江南. The integration of urban centers into increasingly global circuits of trade, the expansion of mercantile capital, and the ascendancy of a silver-based economy were implicated in far-reaching changes then appearing throughout Jiangnan society, from the monetization of everyday life to the reorganization of household labor.[7] Across the vast terrain of late imperial liter-

3. Ibid., 42b.
4. Ibid., 43a.
5. Ibid.
6. Ibid.
7. There is a significant body of work on urban Jiangnan's articulation within early modern commercial relations both domestic and global. See, for example, Von Glahn,

ature, from vernacular fiction to poetry and classical anecdotes, the contours of these new everyday repertoires were delimited and articulated.[8]

But it is in plays such as *Cornucopia* that the mutually constituting relation between literary and economic forms could be both acted and enacted. These plays were produced in the literary genre of *chuanqi* 傳奇 (southern drama) and performed in the musical style of *kunqu* 崑曲 (Kun opera)—the predominant mode of theater-making in seventeenth-century Jiangnan—and their tremendous popularity was felt throughout the spaces of everyday life: from the lavish playbooks perused in the scholar's study to the performances of household actors in wealthy residences and of itinerant troupes in the marketplace.

As a form and a practice, *chuanqi* was uniquely situated to articulate connections that were impossible to imagine before. Like the speaking bullion that makes momentarily legible the larger systems of credit and debt in which the individual is enmeshed, *chuanqi* constructs and enacts a social totality. Its content draws from the entire world of text: official and unofficial histories, romances and religious tracts, poetry and local legends. Its form makes use of role types into which all humans and nonhumans could be slotted, of musical modes that traverse north and south, and of a structure that alternates scenes of domestic drama and political crisis. Its production and performance require the collaboration of all legal categories of personhood—the base, the common, the official—as writers and performers, managers and publishers, readers and spectators. The world unfolded by *chuanqi* was a source of fascination for late imperial thinkers, who turned the theatrical into a heuristic: it was through the tropes and conventions of *chuanqi* that literati conceptualized other art forms,

---

Fountain of Fortune; Pomeranz, *The Great Divergence*; Brook, *The Confusions of Pleasure*.

8. On this literature of the early modern everyday, see, for example, Shang Wei on the vernacular novel *Plum in the Golden Vase* (*Jin Ping Mei* 金瓶梅) as the inauguration of "a new type of narrative that captures the rhythms, dynamics, and predicaments of the daily world" as it unfolds in the thoroughfares, inns, brothels, shops, and residences of the late Ming city. Shang, "The Making of the Everyday World," 63.

tested the limits of their moral and metaphysical imaginations, and theorized their own social roles.[9]

The capacious textual, performative, and discursive worlds of *chuanqi* were particularly suited to embed early modern commercial relations within a larger cosmological system through which all people and things flowed. However, the possibilities of these new relations repelled rather than engaged the imaginations of most *chuanqi* playwrights. These playwrights sought instead to bracket and contain the merchant and his money by consigning them to the narrative and moral margins, where they lurk in the wings as sources of suspicion and anxiety that unsettle both value and values, disrupting the economies of sentiment and sociality through which a humane world could be recuperated.

This was the dominant mode of staging commerce in late imperial *chuanqi*, but it was not the only one. In the commercial hub and cultural center of Suzhou, a group of playwrights enlisted the formal possibilities of *chuanqi* to very different ends. In plays about long-distance traders and small-time peddlers, impossible bargains and broken contracts, strings of cash and storehouses of silver, commercial forms are placed not only at center stage but at the center of a new world coming into being.

The body of plays that form the core of this study have received only limited treatment in Chinese-language scholarship, and many have never been discussed at all in Western-language work. These plays were not obscure but of notable popularity and influence in both literati studios and the streets, among actors and elites, and their neglect has impoverished our understanding of the early modern imaginary. My aim is thus to restore this body of work—and the commercial cornucopianism that it articulates—to the center of early modern theatrical life.

What made these plays compelling in their own time and in

9. Over the last couple of decades there has been much work in English on the theatrical imaginary of late imperial China. See, for example, Wai-yee Li, "The Late Ming Moment," in *Enchantment and Disenchantment*; Tina Lu, *Persons, Roles, and Minds*; Volpp, *Worldly Stage*; Lam, *The Spatiality of Emotion*.

ours is also what makes them outliers in the literary histories of late imperial drama: their focus on the economic imaginary of the denizens of urban Jiangnan.[10] But these plays do not merely map the moral and affective terrain of a highly commercialized society; they also provide a framework for making sense of one's place in a social order in flux.[11] If *chuanqi* as a genre provided the conceptual articulation of an early modern subjectivity—in which an agential and autonomous literati subject fashions himself through role-play and performative interiority—the plays of the Suzhou circle made visible and legible the economic character of early modern selfhood. By thematizing the very commercial relations that were being instantiated through acts of performance

10. Such an approach owes a debt to the earlier work of what has been called new economic criticism, though this body of work does not represent a unified theoretical orientation but rather encompasses several diverse approaches to the penetration of economic thinking into the theatrical worlds of the English Renaissance. See Shell, *Money, Language, and Thought*, 47–83; Agnew, *Worlds Apart*; Bruster, *Drama and the Market*; Leinwand, *Theatre, Finance and Society*, 42–80; Woodbridge, ed., *Money and the Age of Shakespeare*.

In recent years, scholars of Ming-Qing literature have begun to conceptualize the late imperial economic imaginary. See Tina Lu, *Accidental Incest, Filial Cannibalism, and Other Peculiar Encounters*; Ning Ma, *Age of Silver*; and Handler-Spitz, *Symptoms of an Unruly Age*. This work largely focuses on vernacular fiction and philosophical writing, where these concerns are more explicitly thematized than in dramatic literature.

11. Sophie Volpp has written perceptively about the intersection of late Ming and early Qing theater and the changing dynamics of late imperial society. Theater, she points out, served as both locus of and metaphor for the social imposture of what she calls the "middle elite," who attempt to turn their commercial profits into cultural capital through their performances of literati identity (including their enthusiastic consumption of theatrical entertainment). While some literati writers turned a critical eye toward this nouveau riche playacting and vulgar consumption of theatrical entertainment, others drew on the language and structure of theatrical spectatorship to make sense of their own place in a social landscape of striving and uncertainty. In both modes of theatrical meaning-making laid out by Volpp, it is the literatus who remains center stage: theater becomes a mode of exposing and critiquing the literati pretenders or of reconciling the literatus to his place in this hypercommercialized terrain through a self-aware embrace of the illusions of stage and social forms. Volpp, *Worldly Stage*, 7–26. My approach here, however, attempts to center the "middle elite" who wrote and feature in these plays (unlike the literati who wrote and feature in the plays discussed by Volpp), which treat the commercial experience not as a form of literati self-actualization that ultimately reinscribes existing social forms, but as the bringing into being of new social possibilities.

and spectatorship, these plays turn everyone—characters and actors, authors and audience—into buyers, sellers, and commodities. Whereas the transformation of everyone and everything into objects of commerce is framed by many contemporaries as a cultural nightmare and a societal dead end, these plays recast money, merchants, and markets as fundamentally productive: the basis for new subject positions, new kinds of communities, and new forms of art.

The Suzhou Circle

The plays that form the core of this study are attributed to playwrights such as Li Yu 李玉 (*zi* Yuanyu 元玉,[12] before ca. 1610–after

12. Li Yu is associated with two courtesy names: Yuanyu and Xuanyu 玄玉. Some scholars have claimed that Li changed his name from Xuanyu to Yuanyu when the Kangxi emperor ascended the throne in 1661 and the characters in his personal name Xuanye 玄燁 were made taboo. See, for example, Kang Baocheng, *Suzhou jupai yanjiu*, 10; Li Mei, *Ming Qing zhiji Suzhou zuojia qun yanjiu*, 278; Pei Xuelai, *Qingdai qianzhongqi Suzhou jutan yanjiu*, 128.

However, the courtesy name Yuanyu is used on the title pages of the Shunzhi-era woodblock editions of *Two of Beard and Brow* (*Liang xumei* 兩鬚眉, preface 1653) and *The Scholar of Meishan* (*Meishan xiu* 眉山秀, preface 1654), as well as in Qian Qianyi's 錢謙益 (1582–1664) preface for the latter. Wu Weiye 吳偉業 (1609–72) refers to Li Yu as Xuanyu in his preface to the Shunzhi-era *Register of the Pure and Loyal*, but the title page of that edition uses Yuanyu. Yuanyu was thus not only a name used by Li Yu prior to the Kangxi era, but it was the primary courtesy name by which he was known to his readers through the end of the Shunzhi reign.

Though less frequently used, Xuanyu is given as Li Yu's courtesy name in some contemporaneous texts, like Shen Zijin's 沈自晉 (1583–1665) ca. 1655 revision of *New Formulary of Southern Songs* (*Nanci xinpu* 南詞新譜) and Gao Yi's 高奕 (fl. ca. 1661) *New Southern Dramas* (*Xin chuanqi pin* 新傳奇品), a catalogue of late Ming and early Qing plays. Shen, *Nanci xinpu*, *canyue xingshi* 參閱姓氏 2a; Gao, *Xin chuanqi pin*, 272. Interestingly, the only Li Yu publication in which "Xuanyu" appears on the title page is the Kangxi-era printing of *Expanded and Standardized Formulary of Northern-Style Lyrics* (*Beici guangzhengpu* 北詞廣正譜), with the final stroke of the character "xuan" omitted to avoid the taboo. However, other errors on the title page suggest that perhaps this edition was carved with limited consultation with its authors or after their deaths (see note 21). And in a strange reversal of *Register of the Pure and Loyal*, Wu Weiye's preface for the *Formulary* instead uses Yuanyu.

One current convention in English-language scholarship is to disambiguate the

1667),[13] Zhu Suchen, Zhu Zuochao 朱佐朝 (*zi* Liangqing 良卿, b. ca. 1620), and Zhang Dafu 張大復 (before 1620–after 1661),[14]

---

two seventeenth-century dramatists named Li Yu by calling the Suzhou circle playwright Li Xuanyu. However, as "Xuanyu" appears in Li Yu's published work only in the two instances listed above, it would make more sense to use the courtesy name Yuanyu, which was the name under which Li Yu was more consistently published throughout his career.

13. Many scholars continue to follow the approximate birth date of 1591 suggested by Wu Xinlei. However, much of the evidence for such a date is tenuous, as it is based on a source written at the turn of the nineteenth century that claims (rather dubiously, as will be discussed later in this introduction) that Li Yu was a servant in the household of the prime minister Shen Shixing 申時行 (1535–1614), as well as a comment in the *Catalogue of Summaries from the Ocean of Song* (*Quhai zongmu tiyao* 曲海總目提要), which was based on material compiled in the early to mid-Qing and first published in the early twentieth century, that *Winning the Prize Courtesan* (*Zhan huakui* 占花魁) was "written by someone during the Wanli period [1572–1620]" 明萬曆間人撰. Wu Xinlei, "Li Yu shengping, jiaoyou, zuopin kao," 47–50. Gu Lingsen makes an argument for Li Yu having been born "before 1600" on the same grounds. Gu Lingsen, "Li Yu lun," 120.

Leaving aside the unreliability of *Ocean of Song*, especially for Li Yu plays (which are almost never attributed to Li Yu in the catalog), such a theory ignores the fact that the vernacular short story on which *Winning the Prize Courtesan* is based was not published until 1627. The earliest extant editions of Li Yu's plays date to the Chongzhen period, and the earliest recorded performance of his plays is in 1643.

The best contemporaneous evidence for Li Yu's birth date is Wu Weiye's description in his preface to Li's *Expanded and Standardized Formulary of Northern-Style Lyrics* of Li as a repeated exam failure prior to the dynastic transition, who only placed on a prefectural honor roll "later in life" 晚幾. As Li Mei has argued, in order for this claim to have been plausible, Li Yu would need to be at least in his thirties at the time of dynastic transition. Li Mei, *Ming Qing zhiji Suzhou zuojia qun yanjiu*, 235. While Li places his birth around 1610, I do not rule out the possibility of an earlier date.

The latest dated evidence of Li Yu's activity is from his 1667 preface to Yuan Yuanke's 袁園客 edition of Ling Mengchu's 凌濛初 (1580–1644) *Three Kinds of Southern Songs* (*Nanyin sanlai* 南音三籟). Some scholars like Li Mei have approximated a death date in the late 1670s or early 1680s, but this is based on estimates of how much more time Li Yu might have required to produce the number of plays attributed to him (many of which are not extant).

14. There is some uncertainty over Zhang Dafu's name(s). Gao Yi's *New Southern Dramas* and *Ocean of Song* both give Zhang's name only as Xinqi 心其, though neither source clarifies if this is a given or courtesy name. The extant manuscript for Zhang's *Drunken Enlightenment* (*Zui puti* 醉菩提) lists Dafu as his given name and Xingqi 星期 as his courtesy name, though this manuscript is undated and of unknown provenance. In modern scholarship, Dafu is more often cited as a given name, as in Li Mei, *Ming Qing zhiji Suzhou zuojia qun yanjiu*, 278, and Zheng Zhenduo, *Chatuben Zhongguo wenxue shi*, 4:1014. However, the most authoritative account of Zhang Dafu's name is in his own aria manual, *Newly Established Southern*

who are often grouped together as members of the so-called Suzhou school (*Suzhou pai* 蘇州派). This appellation, first coined in the early 1980s, follows a long tradition of retrospectively naming schools of thought or artistic style or political factions after the locus of their activities, such as the literary innovators of the Gong'an school 公安派 or the *qin* 琴 musicians of the Yushan school 虞山派.[15] This case, however, is particularly fraught, as none of the playwrights associated with the Suzhou school described themselves as adherents of anything resembling a school. There are no manifestos, no declarations of shared artistic or ideological principles, no articulations of difference between the work produced within and without.

Rather, starting in the mid-twentieth century, scholars began to identify commonalities across the work of a number of playwrights in late Ming and early Qing Suzhou.[16] The earliest such work centered around the affinities (literary, social, and familial) between Li Yu and the brothers Zhu Suchen and Zhu Zuochao, with whom Li Yu sometimes collaborated. The qualities that were identified in the biographical scraps and extant texts of these playwrights came to define the boundaries of this group: a strong personal connection to Suzhou but an otherwise obscure family background, a frequent reliance on contemporary *huaben* 話本 (vernacular short stories) as source material, an attention to the lives of the non-elite, an interest in the recent past and the pres-

---

Scores in the Nine Modes and Thirteen Tones from Cold Mountain Studio (*Hanshan tang Xinding jiugong shisan diao nanqupu* 寒山堂新定九宮十三調南曲譜), as it was edited for publication by his sons and nephew. In this text, Zhang's given name is Yixuan 彝宣 and Dafu 大復 is his courtesy name. Zhang Dafu, *Hanshan tang Xinding jiugong shisan diao nanqupu*, 650.

15. Though Li Yu, Zhu Suchen, and Zhu Zuochao were the subject of literary scholarship starting in the 1920s, the notion that there was some sort of literary school to which they belonged did not emerge until the late 1950s and early 1960s. One of the first scholars to identify commonalities across these playwrights in the 1960s, Wu Xinlei, coined the term *Suzhou pai* in 1981. See Wu Xinlei, "Lun Suzhou pai xiqu dajia Li Yu," 175. As Li Mei points out, Su Ning 蘇寧 first uses the term *Suzhou jupai* 蘇州劇派 the previous year. Li Mei, *Ming Qing zhiji Suzhou zuojia qun yanjiu*, 9n3.

16. For an overview of modern scholarship on the Suzhou circle, see Li Mei, *Ming Qing zhiji Suzhou zuojia qun yanjiu*, 6–10.

ent, and a mistrust of the frequently corrupt and hypocritical agents of the state.

Subsequent work expanded the boundaries of this group to other collaborators or stylistic bedfellows, such as Ye Shizhang 葉時章 and Bi Wei 畢魏, who coedited Li Yu's *Register of the Pure and Loyal* (*Qingzhong pu* 清忠譜) with Zhu Suchen, and Qiu Yuan 邱園 (1617–1690) and Sheng Jishi 盛際時 (fl. mid-seventeenth c.), who supposedly coauthored *Four Grand Celebrations* (*Si daqing* 四大慶) with Ye Shizhang and Zhu Suchen.[17] However, the precise membership of this "school" is a matter of contention, with scholars counting anywhere from nine to twenty-three playwrights.[18]

17. Some scholars attribute authorship of *Four Grand Celebrations* to Zhu Zuochao and not Sheng Jishi on the basis of a comment by Zheng Zhenduo. Although no reasoning is given for this attribution and there is no extant evidence to support this claim, it has been repeated in a number of authoritative sources, such as Wang Yongkuan's 王永寬 entry on the play in Li Xiusheng, *Guben xiqu jumu tiyao*, 444. Rather, as Guo Yingde has pointed out, in the manuscript edition of *Four Grand Celebrations* from Mei Lanfang's 梅蘭芳 (1894–1961) collection, a lyric about the four authors is written into the final scene. These four authors, though written with some character corruption, are clearly Ye Shizhang, Qiu Yuan, Zhu Suchen, and Sheng Jishi, in that order. See Guo Yingde, *Ming Qing chuanqi zonglu*, 1:661; *Fu Si daqing*, sc. 16 n.p.

Another manuscript edition from the collection of the Peking opera actor Cheng Yanqiu 程硯秋 (1904–1958) also contains these author-embedded lyrics in the same order as the Mei Lanfang edition. However, this edition is missing the last page, so the name of the author who appears after Ye Shizhang, Qiu Yuan, and Zhu Suchen is lost. Though hardly definitive, it is worth noting that in the seventeenth-century *New Southern Dramas*, which is arranged chronologically, Ye Shizhang, Qiu Yuan, Zhu Suchen, and Sheng Jishi are listed in that order, with Zhu Zuochao appearing between Ye and Qiu, indicating that he was thought to be older than Suchen and would thus not appear after him on a list.

18. These numbers range from Zheng Zhenduo's (1957) nine, Pei Xuelai's (2020) ten, Gu Lingsen's (1992) eleven, Kang Baocheng's (1993) twelve, Wu Xinlei's (1961) thirteen, Li Mei's (2000) sixteen, Li Jialian's eighteen (2012), and Zhou Chuanjia and Yan Changke's (1985) twenty-three. These lists invariably include playwrights who left behind few or no extant texts or about whom almost nothing is known except their being born in Suzhou and active during the middle decades of the seventeenth century. Kang Baocheng suggests using the term "Suzhou writers' group" 蘇州作家群 for these peripheral or relatively unknown playwrights. Kang Baocheng, *Suzhou jupai yanjiu*, 29. Gu Lingsen makes a similar argument about differentiating a "community" 群落 from a "school" 流派. Gu Lingsen, "Lüelun 'Wumen qupai,'" 86.

This book builds on this body of scholarship while departing from it in several key respects. First, the focus of this study is a thematic orientation that appears across the work of several of these playwrights. This is not meant to be a comprehensive literary biography of the Suzhou school and as such is not concerned with policing the membership rolls of a group that none of its putative members were aware they had joined. But while I am not concerned with the acts of enumeration and definition that have preoccupied others, I am unwilling to dispense with the group as a conceptually useful unit of analysis. The playwrights who appear repeatedly throughout this book formed a network engaged in acts of literary exchange and collaboration that extend beyond the writing of prefaces, dedications, and inscriptions that were de rigueur for the well-connected literatus-author. Instead, they approached playwriting as a shared endeavor, cowriting plays and play cycles,[19] collaborating on anthologies and treatises, and editing, finishing, or proofreading one another's work.[20] Further, these acts of collaboration were potentially a selling point in a crowded literary marketplace: the title page of *Register of the Pure and Loyal* prominently lists the various coeditors, noting they are all from the "same ward" 同里 in Suzhou.[21]

19. There is of course a long history of writing circles that produced collaborative works. On the "talented writers of writing clubs" 書會才人 of the Yuan whose members were most likely professional dramatists rather than literati authors, see Wai-yee Li, "Introduction," in *The Columbia Anthology of Yuan Drama*, 5; on the playwrighting club Nine Mountain Society 九山書會, see Llamas, *Top Graduate Zhang Xie*, 18–21.

20. A number of these plays are recorded as being coauthored works. In addition to *Four Grand Celebrations*, *Four Spectacular Sights* (*Si qiguan* 四奇觀) is attributed to Zhu Suchen, Zhu Zuochao, and two other playwrights who remain unknown; the nonextant *Passing the Examinations* (*Ding changong* 定蟾宮) is attributed to Zhu Suchen, Guo Mengqi 過孟起, and Sheng Guoqi 盛國琦; *A Fine Wine Vessel* (*Yipin jue* 一品爵) and *Pavilion of the Buried Wheel* (*Mailun ting* 埋輪亭) are attributed to Li Yu and Zhu Zuochao. Works attributed to a single author still frequently bear the imprint of multiple hands: *Register of the Pure and Loyal* lists Bi Wei, Ye Shizhang, and Zhu Suchen as coeditors; Zhu Suchen proofread Li Yu's *Expanded and Standardized Formulary of Northern-Style Lyrics*; Zhang Dafu borrowed older texts from Li Yu's private collection when writing his tune manual *Newly Established Southern Scores in the Nine Modes and Thirteen Tones*, in which he also included several of Li Yu's arias.

21. Li Yu, *Qingzhong pu*, 1a. The title page for the Kangxi-era printing of *Expanded and Standardized Formulary of Northern-Style Lyrics*, which Li Yu edited, lists Li Yu

To conceptualize these playwrights not as atomized creators but as a network of cultural coproducers foregrounds the interrelation between commercial modes of theatrical work and the thematic content of that work. Indeed, the move in some scholarship to efface this collaboration by recasting these plays as works of a single author-genius can be seen as an attempt to rescue these playwrights from the ignominy of "professional" or "commercial" playwriting.[22] A network, however, is not a school, and an emphasis on the shared work of these playwrights highlights the unsuitability of a term that implies both an orthodoxy and a hierarchy of transmission. Those who write on the Suzhou school often make such an orientation abundantly clear in their treatment of Li Yu, who is frequently referred to as the "model" 典型, "leader" 領袖, or "nucleus" 核心.[23] Li Yu was indeed one of the most connected and popular of the playwrights, his work published in woodblock editions suitable for the aficionado's study, festooned with inscriptions and prefaces from leading literary figures. He was also one of the older playwrights, born perhaps a decade earlier than playwrights such as Zhu Suchen and Zhu Zuochao. However, no textual evidence suggests that other Suzhou school playwrights or contemporaneous literati saw him

as a native of Wu 吳 county and Zhu Suchen a native of Changzhou 長洲 county (Suzhou was divided, with the western half of the city under the jurisdiction of Wu county and the eastern half under Changzhou). All other contemporaneous sources (including the print edition of Zhu's play *Moon over the Qin Tower* [*Qinlou yue* 秦樓月], which was prepared during Zhu's lifetime by close associates), give Zhu's place of origin as Wu county.

22. This is most apparent in the scholarly discussions of *Register of the Pure and Loyal*. The inclusion of Bi Wei, Ye Shizhang, and Zhu Suchen as coeditors in the early Kangxi woodblock edition indicates a fairly large role in the shaping of the text, and a number of scholars list the play as a "coauthored" 合作 work. However, much scholarly writing on this play treats it as emanating from the singular literary genius and the particular experiences of Li Yu. See, for example, Wu Xinlei, "Shilun Li Yu de daibiao zuo *Qingzhong pu* chuanqi," 165–74.

23. See Gu Lingsen, who argues that the parameters of the school are set by Li Yu: "Li Yu is the core of the Suzhou school, which is to say that the work produced by the Suzhou playwrights must largely accord with the ideology, techniques, and especially artistic style of Li Yu's work" 李玉既是蘇州派的核心,這就是說,蘇州派成員所創作的作品必須與李玉的作品,無論在創作的思想理念、方式方法,尤其是藝術風格上要有較大的共性. Gu Lingsen, "Lun kunqu Suzhou pai," 163.

as a model or leader. And while a number of these playwrights (including Li Yu) published musical manuals, there is no contemporaneous discussion of Li Yu's work serving as a model.

In an attempt to shed these assumptions that confuse Li Yu's stature in modern scholarship with his role in a nonexistent orthodoxy, this book will avoid using "Suzhou school," despite the continuing currency of this term in Chinese-language scholarship. In so doing, I am following scholars such as Li Mei 李玫, who adopts the term "Suzhou writers' group" 蘇州作家群. As Li notes, this is less a departure than a return to the terminology of such earlier scholars as Zhou Yibai 周貽白 (1900–1977), who described not a school but a "playwriting circle" 編劇集團.[24]

These arguments have also found purchase among English-language scholars, who generally use "Suzhou playwrights" in lieu of "the Suzhou school."[25] While there is an appealing simplicity to this terminology, it is a potentially confusing designation in light of the prominent playwrights active in Suzhou at the same time who would never be considered one of the "Suzhou playwrights," such as You Tong 尤侗 (1618–1704). Furthermore, unlike the terminology embraced by Li Mei and others, the term "Suzhou playwrights" obscures the communal work that is one of the defining features of these writers.

For these reasons, I will refer to this group of playwrights as the "Suzhou circle." While "school" implies the vertical transmission from originator to adherents, "circle" connotes a continuous lateral movement without a beginning or a focal point.[26] A "circle"

24. Li Mei, *Ming Qing zhiji Suzhou zuojia qun yanjiu*, 8.

25. For English-language work on these playwrights, see Goldman, *Opera and the City*, 145–74, Keulemans, "Onstage Rumor, Offstage Voices," Wai-yee Li, *Women and National Trauma*, 254–68, Chiung-yun Liu, "Embodied Virtue," Tina Lu, *Accidental Incest*, 1–21, and Guojun Wang, *Staging Personhood*, 92–123. Andrea Goldman uses the term "Suzhou writers' group" (borrowed from Li Mei) in addition to "Suzhou playwrights." Goldman, *Opera and the City*, 146, 309n5.

26. While Li Mei's use of the term "writers' group" 作家群 is also meant to convey a set of commonalities or "shared tendencies" 共同傾向, Li does not delimit her group on the basis of actual cooperation, but rather based on dates of activity, place of residence, status, and playwriting style. Li Mei, *Ming Qing zhiji Suzhou zuojia qun yanjiu*, 14. As a result, Li Mei includes in her group several playwrights who have not

conveys both temporal and physical proximity—emphasizing that these were contemporaries who had meaningful and sustained contact with each other. This terminology thus avoids the imprecision of "Suzhou playwrights" while foregrounding not the nodes but the network.

Between Literatus and Slave

Thinking of these playwrights as a network offers a way out of the biographical fixations that have often occupied scholars more than the plays themselves. This project of excavating a coherent and explanatory biography for any of these writers immediately runs aground on the problems of the archive before it even has a chance to founder on more conceptual shores, as the Suzhou circle has left behind only the most modest of paper trails. This lacuna in the historical record is unusual for authors of *chuanqi*, a genre that required a high level of specialized literary knowledge and was thus largely written by the educated elite. The other major playwrights of the long seventeenth century are known to us in ways the Suzhou circle is not. We know how these other playwrights supported themselves by dint of their official careers and family wealth, as Tang Xianzu 湯顯祖 (1550–1616) and Ruan Dacheng 阮大鋮 (1587–1646) did, or through their publishing concerns like Feng Menglong 馮夢龍 (1574–1646) or patronage networks like Li Yu 李漁 (1610–80, hereafter referred to by his pen name Liweng 笠翁 to avoid confusion with the Suzhou circle playwright).[27] We know these men not merely as playwrights but

had any known contact with the other playwrights. Gu Lingsen's idea of a "community" 群落 approaches this notion of a collaborative circle, but Gu undercuts the possibilities of the term by referring to this group as "the Li Yu community" 李玉群落. Gu Lingsen, "Lun kunqu Suzhou pai," 163.

27. As mentioned in note 12, one convention in English-language scholarship has been to refer to the Suzhou circle playwright as Li Xuanyu, even though most of his publications appeared under the courtesy name Yuanyu or the pen name Yili'an 一笠菴 (Hut of the Bamboo Hat). Using the Suzhou circle playwright's more commonly known given name of Li Yu both avoids this problematic use of his courtesy name and

also as poets, diarists, and partisans—as authors of myriad genres particular to the various literary and social lives of the literati elite. We know their families, what positions their fathers and grandfathers held, and what positions they held, like You Tong's late-in-life ascension to a position in the Hanlin Academy. We know of the Chongzhen emperor's support of Wu Weiye's 吳偉業 (1609–72) early career and of Kong Shangren's 孔尚任 (1648–1718) encounters with the Kangxi emperor. By contrast, Li Yu, the most famous playwright of the Suzhou circle, had a background so obscure and malleable that he has been described as both literatus and slave.

The scraps of biographical narratives about Suzhou circle playwrights often reveal more about the narrators than those whose lives they are narrating. In the case of Li Yu, the only contemporaneous biographical sketch comes from a preface written by Wu Weiye for Li's *Expanded and Standardized Formulary of Northern-Style Lyrics* (*Beici guangzhengpu* 北詞廣正譜). This preface introduces Li as "a literatus deeply interested in studying antiquity" 好奇學古士也, "whose knowledge encompasses the entire world of art" 其學足以囊括藝林. But despite this prodigious talent, official success eluded him:

> He was repeatedly crushed by the examiners. In later years he came close to succeeding, receiving an honorable mention [in the provincial exam]. After 1644, he abandoned the pursuit of an official career. Endowed with Shilang's poetic talent,[28] he followed Qiqing's model and set words to tunes.[29]
>
> 而連厄於有司，晚幾得之，仍中副車，甲申以後，絕意仕進，以十郎之才調，效耆卿之填詞。[30]

asserts for him a more central place in seventeenth-century literary history. The other Li Yu's courtesy name, Liweng, is well known among scholars of Chinese literature and is the name under which he published.

28. A reference to the Tang poet Li Yi 李益 (746–829).

29. A reference to the Song lyricist Liu Yong 柳永 (ca. 987–1053).

30. Li Yu, *Beici guangzhengpu*, *xu* 序 4b–5a.

The "scores of *chuanqi* dramas" 傳奇數十種 that Li Yu wrote are thus situated as a loyalist response to the fall of the Ming, a form of noble *yimin* 遺民 (remnant subject)-style withdrawal that the twice-serving Wu Weiye could not manage himself. Such a framing of Li Yu's playwriting activities is highly dubious at best. Li Yu was already an established playwright prior to the fall of the Ming: *A Fistful of Snow* (*Yi peng xue* 一捧雪), *Between Man and Beast* (*Renshou guan* 人獸關), *Winning the Prize Courtesan* (*Zhan huakui* 占花魁), and *Eternal Reunion* (*Yong tuanyuan* 永團圓) were all published under his name during the Chongzhen period; Qi Biaojia 祁彪佳 (1603–45) writes of seeing a performance of *A Fistful of Snow* in 1643;[31] and *Between Man and Beast* and *Eternal Reunion* were sufficiently popular during the Chongzhen period to merit Feng Menglong's publication of his own edited versions. Beyond fulfilling the expectations of the genre, Wu's insistence here on Li Yu's literati and loyalist credentials reads as a defensive feint that elides those details less befitting the persona of literary genius or loyalist stalwart.

The opposite desire—to excavate some sort of benighted backstory—has led a number of modern scholars to defend the validity of a comment by the Yangzhou philologist and drama aficionado Jiao Xun 焦循 (1763–1820) in his *Discourses on Drama* (*Ju shuo* 劇說) that "Li Yu was a servant of the household of Prime Minister Shen" 元玉係申相國家人, namely, Shen Shixing 申時行 (1535–1614).[32] Jiao asserts that such a background rendered Li "unable to take the civil service examination" 不得應科試, which contradicts the claim made by Wu Weiye that Li sat for the provincial exam in the late Ming.[33] Some scholars have maintained

31. Qi Biaojia, *Qi Biaojia riji*, 3:700. Qi also wrote of seeing a performance of *Eternal Reunion* early in 1645. Ibid., 3:819–20.

32. The scholar Wu Mei 吳梅 (1884–1939) wrote in a comment that Li Yu's father was a slave in the household of Shen Shixing's son Shen Yongmao 申用懋 (presumably to produce a timeline where Jiao Xun's claim makes sense), though no sources are used to buttress this claim. *Li Yu xiqu ji*, 1:2.

33. Jiao Xun concludes with the conventional logic that Li Yu "wrote *chuanqi* to vent his frustrations [about his inability to participate in politics]" 因著傳奇以抒其憤. *Ju shuo*, j. 4, facs. rpt. in *Xuxiu Siku quanshu*, 1758:662–63.

that this does not necessarily discredit Jiao Xun's account of Li Yu's childhood in the Shen household, pointing to exemptions that would have allowed someone of a servant background to sit for the exam.[34] As evidence of Jiao's claims, some have pointed to a lyric that Wu Qi 吳綺 (1619–94) wrote in honor of Li Yu that contains the line, "As is your family tradition, you naturally excel at the 'Clear and Even' tune" 家傳自擅清平調.[35] This tune, a Tang dynasty melody that Li Bai famously set to lyrics, links Li Yu's lyrical production with that of his supposed forebear.[36] However, some scholars have argued that the reference to a "family tradition" also gestures to the role of Li Yu's father in the theatrical entertainments of the Shen household. That writers of his own time omit references to such a background is interpreted as an attempt to spare Li Yu the embarrassment of such low origins.[37]

A similar move can be seen in the treatment of Zhu Suchen. *Moon over the Qin Tower* (*Qinlou yue* 秦樓月), his only published play, is surrounded by the assorted prefatory materials that signal participation in celebrated literati circles and refined aesthetic commitments: high-quality illustrations, a preface by Wu Qi, a commentary and additional scenes by Li Liweng, and inscriptions by You Tong, among others.[38] Many modern scholars, however, begin their discussion of Zhu Suchen with a comment like one that appears in the *Dictionary of Premodern Chinese Dramatic Literature* (*Zhongguo gudai xiqu wenxue cidian* 中國古代戲曲文學辭典): "The facts of his life are difficult to know in any detail; we only know that he was born into straitened circumstances and did not become an official, and he liked composing songs and was good at playing the *sheng* [pipe organ]" 生平事蹟難以詳考，僅知他出身寒

34. Feng Yuanjun, "Zenyang kandai *Yi peng xue*," 270–72.

35. Wu Qi, *Linhui tang ji*, 25:4a.

36. Qian Qianyi, in his preface to Li Yu's *The Scholar of Meishan*, suggests a similar filiation. Li Yu, *Meishan xiu, tici* 題詞 7b.

37. On this debate, see Yan Changke and Zhou Chuanjia, *Li Yu pingzhuan*, 3–5; Li Mei, *Ming Qing zhiji Suzhou zuojia qun yanjiu*, 256–60; Li Jialian, *Qingchu Suzhou juzuojia yanjiu*, 54–58.

38. Zhu Suchen, *Qinlou yue*, *xu* 序 1a–4b, *tiqing* 題情 1a–4b, *xiuxiang* 繡像 1a–6b.

素，未出仕，喜度曲，善吹笙.[39] These details appear verbatim in various authoritative texts and are cited by the leading scholars of late imperial drama.[40]

However, none of these assertions is supported, even by the sources that are occasionally offered, such as the aforementioned preface by Wu Qi, a note in a poem by Shen Deqian 沈德潛 (1673–1769), and a biographical entry in a nineteenth-century gazetteer. The claim that Zhu was born into poverty does not appear in any of these sources, and the reference to Zhu's being good at playing the *sheng* seems to be based on a mistaken reading of his *hao* as Sheng'an 笙庵 (Hut of the Pipe Organ) rather than Rui'an 苼庵 (Leafy Hut).[41] The notion that Zhu did not attain office is based on a biographical detail found in the Daoguang era (1820–50) *Complete Gazetteer of Zhapu* (*Zhapu beizhi* 乍浦備志) that describes a Zhu Suchen who turned to farming after failing to pass the civil service exam.[42] However, as Li Mei has argued, the names, places of residence, literary output, and social sphere given for this Zhu Suchen do not match anything known about the playwright.[43] Indeed, this Zhu Suchen is described as being an elderly recluse living in the mountains in 1635, an impossibility given that Shen Deqian writes of the playwright being alive in 1701, and that it is generally agreed upon that Zhu was born around or after 1620.

The contemporaneous texts that make arguments both explicit and implicit about the playwrights' literary and loyalist bona fides and the twentieth- and twenty-first-century scholarship that embraces shaky backstories of poverty and servitude are merely selling the same product in different markets: the former

39. Wang Yongkuan et al., *Zhongguo gudai xiqu wenxue cidian*, 1041.

40. See, for example, Guo Yingde, *Ming Qing chuanqi shi*, 354–55; Deng Shaoji, ed., *Zhongguo gudai xiqu wenxue cidian*, 1041.

41. Kang Baocheng cites a reference to Zhu playing a different type of wind instrument in a poem that appears in *Collected Poems from Songjiang* (*Songjiang shichao* 松江詩鈔, 1808): "Under the moonlight, listening to Xiang Ziyi sing and Zhu Suchen play the vertical flute" 月夜聽項于儀度曲朱素臣吹簫. Kang Baocheng, *Suzhou jupai yanjiu*, 194.

42. Zhao Jingshen and Zhang Zengyuan, eds., *Fangzhi zhulu Yuan Ming Qing qujia zhuanlüe*, 164–65.

43. Li Mei, *Ming Qing zhiji Suzhou zuojia qun yanjiu*, 264–65.

pitched to the aesthetic and political commitments of early Qing Jiangnan literati consumers of printed editions of the latest dramas, the latter to the academic trends and political discourses that valorize grassroots artistic production.

Biography of a Network

We do not know to what extent these playwrights were scholars or servants—while the plays, corrected scores, and aria formularies compiled by the Suzhou circle reflect a high level of specialized literary knowledge, and while some of these playwrights earned the support and praise of the leading literati of the day, the gaps and biographical scraps they left behind bespeak a humbler pedigree.[44] Unlike others among their contemporaries, such as Feng Menglong and Li Liweng, they have left behind no poems or letters or essays typical of literati playwrights; their operas and their manuals for writing operas alone survive. The only thing that can really be known about these playwrights is that they were unusually successful sellers of culture in the crowded Suzhou marketplace.

Li Yu, the Zhu brothers, and Zhang Dafu were all remarkably productive; according to contemporaneous sources, their collective output totaled over sixty plays at a time when most known playwrights would publish only a handful. This was well known and a selling point: the first page of the woodblock edition of *Moon over the Qin Tower* published in the late 1670s declares itself "the fifteenth play of Rui'an [Zhu Suchen]" 苼菴傳奇第十五種. The commercial impetus of such an output surfaces in contemporaneous accounts that emphasize the popularity and reliable profitability of these plays. In his 1654 inscription for the play *The Scholar of*

44. Such a pedigree or lack thereof is brought to the surface in a biographical sketch of Zhang Dafu that appears in the *Ocean of Song*: "He possessed a rough understanding of the Classics and was good at setting lyrics to music. Unconcerned with making a living, his nature was plain and simple. He was also quite knowledgeable about diction and allusions" 粗知書, 好填詞, 不治生產, 性淳樸, 亦頗知辭典. Dong Kang, ed., *Quhai zongmu tiyao*, 1:797.

Meishan (*Meishan xiu* 眉山秀), the poet-historian-official Qian Qianyi 錢謙益 (1582–1664) offers this assessment of Li Yu:

> Among new music being produced, Mr. Yuanyu's plays like *Winning the Prize Courtesan* and *A Fistful of Snow* truly fill people with admiration. Yuanyu's lyrics permeate all under heaven. Aficionados as far away as Korea vie to play every sheet of paper that falls from his hand.[45] He is like [the Tang poets] Dafu and Changling, who enjoyed great renown in their own time, their verses sung by all of the tavern singing girls.[46]
>
> 而新聲間出，則元玉氏《占花魁》、《一捧雪》諸劇，真足令人心折也。元玉言詞滿天下，每一帋落，雞林好事者爭被管絃，如達夫、昌齡聲高當代，酒樓諸妓，咸歌其詩。[47]

The almost instantaneous transformation of Li Yu's texts into performance appears throughout Qian's preface, as when he quickly shifts from his own solitary experience reading Li Yu's plays in the Humble Administrator's Garden in Suzhou to imagining their musical expression reaching far and wide, high and low, "causing fish to leap out of the water to listen and clouds to cease their movement in the sky" 令魚出聽而雲爲停矣.[48] And while the

45. A reference to the poems of Bai Juyi 白居易 (772–846) being sought by merchants from the kingdom of Silla. While Silla no longer existed (it was defeated by the Koryŏ in the tenth century; by Qian Qianyi's time, the area formerly considered Silla was part of the Chosŏn kingdom), the expression of interest from Silla was still used to indicate widespread literary renown. As will be discussed in more detail below, the plays of the Suzhou circle were in circulation beyond the immediate environs of Suzhou; for example, Li Yu's *Coins of Heavenly Peace* survives in a lavishly copied mid-Qing palace edition. The popularity of these plays across Jiangnan is thematized in Zhu Suchen's *Moon over the Qin Tower*.

46. A reference to the Tang poets Gao Shi 高適 (ca. 702–65) and Wang Changling 王昌齡 (ca. 690–756), who, along with Wang Zhihuan 王之渙 (688–742), famously competed to see whose compositions were most favored by the tavern singing girls.

47. Li Yu, *Meishan xiu*, *tici* 3a–b. Here and in the immediately following reference to Bai Juyi, Qian is using language from Wang Shizhen's 王世貞 (1526–90) *Drunken Words in the Garden of Art* (*Yiyuan zhiyan* 藝苑巵言). Wang Shizhen, *Xinke zengbu Yiyuan zhiyan*, 6:3a.

48. Li Yu, *Meishan xiu*, *tici* 5b. A reference to Huba's 瓠巴 zither playing, as in *Xunzi xinzhu*, 6. Throughout the preface, Qian repeatedly returns to the expansive-

fish are perhaps not paying audience members, Qian intimates the profitability of these performances through the intertextual parallel on which he concludes his preface: "During the Tang dynasty, a girl who could play Bai Juyi's 'Ballad of the Lute' could fetch a price in the ten thousands. This play of Yuanyu's, transmitted to those who appreciate opera, will even further increase his prestige"[49] 昔大曆中女子能按香山《琵琶行》, 至索價十萬。元玉此劇傳諸顧曲者, 又增一番聲價矣.[50]

That Li Yu's plays were texts to be performed, and highly sought-after ones at that, was also remarked upon by Feng Menglong: "[Li Yu's] first play, *Between Man and Beast*, became so popular that whenever actors obtained new scripts to perform, everyone would rush out to buy a copy of the play; as soon as a draft was completed they would snatch it up" 初編《人獸關》盛行, 優人每獲異稿, 競購新劇, 甫屬草, 便攘以去.[51] It is no surprise that under such market pressures the second volume of the play "was completed a bit hastily" 草草速成.[52] These imperfections, and the clamor that produced them in

ness of Li Yu's reach, crossing high and low as in a description of Li "exhausting the elevated diction of the canon and fishing out the low gossip of the streets" 上窮典雅, 下漁稗乘.

49. The word translated here as prestige, *shengjia* 聲價 (lit. "the price of [one's] sound"), explicitly ties reputation to potential for monetization.

50. Li Yu, *Meishan xiu*, *tici* 7b–8a. Qian is again drawing from the wording of Wang Shizhen's *Drunken Words in the Garden of Art*, which references a famous anecdote from Bai Juyi's letter to Yuan Zhen 元稹 (779–831). In both Bai's letter and Wang's essay, the text that increases the value of the courtesan is Bai's "Song of Everlasting Sorrow," not "Ballad of the Pipa." Wang's line is also repeated almost verbatim in the tenth scene of Zhu Suchen's play *The Appearance of the Star of Literature* (*Wenxing xian* 文星現). The substitution of "Ballad of the Pipa" here is particularly apt, as it narrates an encounter with and a performance by a former courtesan who tells of how her skillful playing of the pipa drove up her value among clients.

51. Reading 稿 for 槁. From Feng Menglong's preface to his revision of Li Yu's *Eternal Reunion*. Feng, ed., *Mohanzhai chongding Yong tuanyuan chuanqi*, *xu* 2a–b. Li Liweng gives a similar description of the clamor for his plays in *Casual Expressions of Idle Feeling* (*Xianqing ouji* 閒情偶寄): "Every time I would finish a play, no sooner had my brush left the page than my publishers would snatch it away. The second half would not even be completed by the time the woodblocks for the first half were already cut" 每成一劇, 才落毫端, 即為坊人攫去。下半猶未脫稿, 上半業已災梨. Li Yu, *Xianqing ouji*, 52.

52. Feng, ed., *Mohanzhai chongding Yong tuanyuan chuanqi*, *xu* 2b.

the first place, led Feng to publish his own versions of not only Li Yu's *Between Man and Beast* but also his *Eternal Reunion, A Fistful of Snow*, and *Winning the Prize Courtesan*, as well as the play *Three Debts of Gratitude* (*San bao'en* 三報恩) by Li Yu's collaborator Bi Wei.[53]

In discussing Li Yu's work, both Qian Qianyi and Feng Menglong emphasize materiality (紙, 稿), competition (爭, 競), and acquisition (獲, 購, 攘) in a way that foregrounds the commercial lives of these plays, tracking the path from the act of writing to the production of a saleable commodity to the consumption of a performance. Just as Qian and Feng reveal more about Li Yu through references to the circulation of his work than through the stock expressions of literary biography, this book provides a biography of the Suzhou circle only indirectly and incidentally through their attributed work. Such a biography, like their work, is necessarily collective—it cannot tell the contours of a particular life, but it can give shape to the concerns and fantasies of a group that operated in the space between the amply documented lives of the cultural elite and the performers and spectators of common and mean status lost to the archive.

Manuscripts and Methods

To conceptualize these writers as a circle allows us to account not only for these plays' complex modes of authorship and the biographical lacunae of their authors but also their problematic textual histories. While several of the plays under discussion in this book, such as *Winning the Prize Courtesan*, *Register of the Pure and Loyal*, and *Moon over the Qin Tower*, were printed during their authors' lifetimes, others survive only as manuscripts (see plates 1 and 2). Some of these manuscripts, such as editions of *Three Kinds of Happiness* (*Kuaihuo san* 快活三) and *Fifteen Strings*

53. Feng's revisions of *A Fistful of Snow* and *Winning the Prize Courtesan* are not extant.

of Cash (*Shiwu guan* 十五貫), are marked with early Qing dates that are impossible to verify. Others can be reliably dated to the mid-Qing, such as a palace edition of *Coins of Heavenly Peace* (*Taiping qian* 太平錢, see plate 3), as well as an edition of *Cornucopia* and a number of scenes from Suzhou circle plays that were printed in eighteenth-century collections of opera excerpts like *Coat of Patched Fur* (*Zhuibai qiu* 綴白裘).[54] Some manuscripts, like that of *The Sound of Reading* (*Dushu sheng* 讀書聲), give no indication of when they might have been produced, with their known provenances—from the collections of famous *jingju* 京劇 (Peking opera) actors like Cheng Yanqiu 程硯秋 (1904–58) and Mei Lanfang 梅蘭芳 (1894–1961)—only dating to the late Qing.

But even for those manuscripts that can be reliably dated, it is impossible to attach an author to the words on the page. These texts, which list no author and are often rife with the sort of transcription and homophonic errors that betray a copyist's hand, speak less to authorial intent than to the performance tradition for which they were created. Nevertheless, these manuscripts have been enlisted repeatedly by leading scholars to build claims of individual style within the oeuvre of their putative authors. Li Mei, whose work has been especially influential in English-language scholarship, regularly deploys quotes from the most problematic of these texts to buttress her claims about the supposed value systems of these playwrights, as when she argues, "In *The Sound of Reading*, Zhang Dafu uses his characters [lit. that fall from his brush] to stress that 'the imperial court has abandoned proper ritual and thus has lost its authority'" 張大復在《讀書聲》中，通過他筆下的人物強調「朝廷失禮則不威」.[55] The problems of

54. While Academia Sinica's Fu Ssu-nien Library catalogs this edition of *Coins of Heavenly Peace* as early Qing, the use of taboo word substitutes, as well as formal similarities to other texts, date the manuscript to the Qianlong emperor's reign.

55. Li Mei, *Ming Qing zhiji Suzhou zuojia qun yanjiu*, 18. This, her book's first reference to *The Sound of Reading*, is cited only as "*The Sound of Reading*, scene nine" 《讀書聲》第九出, which presumably is a reference to the manuscript found in the *Guben xiqu congkan* (the only known extant edition of the play). The quote that she cites does not actually appear in this scene; her only other quote from the play inverts the order of two characters and inserts a character that does not appear in the text. Ibid., 201.

asserting that the words that appear in an incomplete, undated performance script are identical to those produced by Zhang Dafu's own hand are never discussed; indeed, throughout her monograph, Li remains unconcerned with textual issues, drawing on the manuscripts included in the *Compendium of Old Editions of Drama* (*Guben xiqu congkan* 古本戲曲叢刊) and elsewhere without reference to which edition she is citing or when it might have been produced.

The elision of problematic attribution and dating has been further aided by high-profile scholarly compilations like the *Collection of Dramas by Li Yu* (*Li Yu xiqu ji* 李玉戲曲集), which includes plays that were printed in the early Qing under Li Yu's name alongside plays that survive only in unsigned and undated manuscripts that the collection's editors have transcribed and corrected. Toward the end of an introduction in which all of the plays are discussed as expressing elements of Li Yu's particular style, there is the briefest of hints of the texts' fundamental indeterminacy: "We must await further research to know if among these plays there are some that are not actually written by Li Yu" 其中某些劇本是否果係李玉所作，尚待考訂.[56] When this collection was first published in 2004, no further research was needed to know which of these texts might be problematic. But the editors do not specify or elaborate; instead, with all of these plays set in identical modern type, they are effectively laundered as equally "dramas by Li Yu."

While attributed authors will be mentioned in the discussion of plays that follows, this book dispenses with the individual playwright as the site of authorship, whether the text be a woodblock edition that passed through the hands of coauthors, editors, and publishers or a manuscript that reflects the emendations and transformations of actors, audience, and copyists. As the argument of this book concerns the uses of early modern theatrical experience in translating and (re)writing commercial experience, the opacity of a play's textual history need not be suppressed in

56. Li Yu, *Li Yu xiqu ji*, 1:7.

service to a tradition of literary scholarship that reifies the literatus author-figure and fetishizes his biography and oeuvre.

Instead, each text will be considered on its own terms with its own modes and sites of production and consumption and as part of a larger ecosystem of early modern theatrical experiences. This will be done by reading both through and around the play: the various extant editions with their paratexts, marginalia, and stage directions; the stories on which they drew; the predecessors and contemporaries through which they were read and understood. Contemporaneous sources like lists of plays, plot summaries, and records of performances serve as supplements and forms of triangulation tethering elements of a play, if not its extant script, to writers, readers, and spectators of seventeenth-century China.

Commercial Acts

This book consists of four chapters, each of which is centered on the staging of a commercial form: the pieces of money that circulate across the stage, the merchants who make that money move, the markets through which those merchants operate, and the modes of capital accumulation that were shaping markets across the world.

The first chapter, "Money Props and the Properties of Money," looks at the silver ingots, copper coins, and paper bills that circulated across the seventeenth-century stage as props and concepts. The plays attributed to the Suzhou circle that foreground forms of money—with titles such as *Coins of Heavenly Peace* and *Fifteen Strings of Cash*—represent a departure from the conventions of late Ming and early Qing drama. Most contemporaneous *chuanqi* are constructed around a priceless, irreproducible object, such as a fan flecked with a courtesan's blood, whose circulation across the stage brings together cultural and political elites who identify the object and in so doing identify with each other. The plays discussed in this chapter, however, place at their center not a singular object whose worth can only be discerned by those in the know, but money, which renders all things commensurate and which wears its value on its face. As it moves between hands, this money maps the contours of an economy in which all beings are enmeshed. Whereas the conventional literati prop encodes a deep anxiety toward the object's commodification, the money prop is not a sign of cultural disorder but a generative force capable of bringing new kinds of social relations into being.

The second chapter, "Every Man a Merchant," explores the literary inscription of commercial identities. In plays that feature characters who make their living in the marketplace, the Suzhou circle recasts the merchant in roles that were usually foreclosed to him: romantic lead, moral exemplar, heroic adventurer. By depicting merchants who act in ways merchants are not expected to act, these playwrights play with the *chuanqi* convention that divides characters into role types that imbricate social status, affect, and narrative import. I place these representations—in which the merchant is recuperated not only as a moral subject but as a universal one—within the context of the increasing slippage of social roles and cultural identities in late Ming and early Qing urban centers that rendered moot any distinction between "literatus" and "merchant." The Suzhou circle playwrights were themselves representative of this phenomenon—with their dubious pedigrees, literary facility, and well-connected friends, they inhabit a liminal space between literatus and merchant as scholars of the marketplace and merchants of culture.

The third chapter, "Ventures over, under, and beyond the Seas," examines how the local, global, and cosmic economies diagrammed in these plays posit an alternative sovereignty to that of the state. I pay particular attention to plays that shift the center of narrative gravity from the imperial court to the vast oceans beyond. Decks of merchant vessels and shores of deserted islands, moorings along the Grand Canal and harbors of foreign lands—all become the sites of exchanges that remake the limits of community and humanity. Just as the previous chapter lays out the recuperation of the merchant as a moral subject, this chapter shows how the imagination of transoceanic trade as generative and salvific recuperates commerce as a moral act. And like the merchant, whose participation in an empire of silver renders his allegiance to the dynastic empire suspect, the communities generated by trade are governed by a logic outside of the control of the imperial court. In this way, the plays gesture back to their own performance contexts that use the spaces of commerce—the bustling temple markets and busy canal waterways—to bring a new kind of community into being. Through its imaginative worlds and physical spaces, the Suzhou stage thus plays a central role in the process through which spectators were made into consumers of goods and ideas both local and global.

The fourth chapter, "Staging the Endless Surplus," traces the literary genealogy of the titular object at the center of the play *Cornucopia*. In a departure from earlier imaginations of treasure-gathering cornucopias, the *jubaopen* 聚寶盆 does not draw together the existing riches of the world. Rather, from the one object placed inside—a grain of rice, a single coin—flows an unceasing, automatic stream of replication. This single investment that produces infinite profit articulates even as it mystifies the ways that capital "works." I argue that through the play's marriage of commerce and divinity *Cornucopia* makes possible a redemptive reading of the infinitely expansive possibilities of mercantile accumulation.

The conclusion, "The Cornucopian Stage," borrows the heuristic of the *jubaopen* to explore the productive possibilities of drama both in Suzhou and across the early modern world. Like a *jubaopen*, the Suzhou stage overflowed with copper coins and silver ingots—dug up from the ground and hidden in the eaves, pushed around in carts or lugged about in sacks or worn around the neck. Here the experience of living through China's "silver century," when the silver extracted from Japanese and New World mines flooded the Jiangnan marketplace, metamorphoses into a fantasy of endless accumulation—a performance of metallic optimism that finds its mirror in a bullion-poor Europe and its theater of debt and loss. The generative capacity of the Suzhou stage was not limited to the literal production of treasures on stage (nor to the profits made offstage by a group of playwrights whose work is often described as "commercial"); rather, the plays of the Suzhou circle show how commercial subjects and objects can be made narratively, morally, and socially productive. I argue that it is in this transformation of the stage into a self-consciously productive space, and the transformation of authors, actors, and audience members into similarly "productive" economic subjects, that the plays of the Suzhou circle expressed an early modern imaginary that was simultaneously being enacted on stages in far-flung but increasingly interconnected commercial centers around the globe.

ONE

Money Props and the Properties of Money

The late imperial stage is a world constructed through a handful of objects.[1] Some of these objects—a whip, an oar—function as signs of an unseen world of horses and boats, locating the story within the material facts of our extratheatrical world while simultaneously calling attention to its position outside of it. Other objects construct not only the world in which the story is situated but also the story itself. These things for which the play is often named—a thorn hairpin, a jade cup, a peach blossom fan—sit at the physical and symbolic center of the drama; as props that move across the stage, they reveal themselves to be simultaneously object and subject, motif and motive force, that which circulates and that which generates.

It is not a coincidence that the generic conventions of *chuanqi* that invest a fan or cup with totemic importance emerged in the late Ming, a period of intensified commercial activity during which the practices of the market came to suffuse the language and structure of everyday life in the urban areas of the Lower

1. Andrew Sofer points to a similar "nonillusionistic" representational tradition on the Elizabethan stage, which also had the effect of emphasizing the physical, symbolic, and semiotic meanings of those objects that did appear on stage. Sofer, *The Stage Life of Props*, 21. It should be noted, however, that the often-cited nonillusionistic nature of the Chinese stage owes much to Qi Rushan's 齊如山 (1875–1962) "national drama" (*guoju* 國劇) interventions and less to the actual material worlds of late imperial theater. See Goldstein, *Drama Kings*, 134–71.

Yangzi region where *chuanqi* were written and performed.[2] Nor were the affective and metaphysical dimensions of this parceling of the world into discrete, saleable objects an experience limited to Jiangnan. As Douglas Bruster's work shows, English Renaissance dramatists grappled with the novelty of merchandise in similar ways, as the obsessive attention paid to moveable props "replicates a larger social fascination with the material" in early modern London.[3] Bruster notes that in the seventeenth century these props become implicated in "the commercial inscription of an identity . . . [that] is constructed by being 'written' into or onto objects."[4] A similar process—in which identity is built, dismantled, and reimagined through material objects—is repeatedly reenacted in the *chuanqi* of the late Ming and early Qing.

But unlike the merchandise that was flooding the Jiangnan marketplace, the objects at the center of most *chuanqi* are not commensurable commodities. Rather, they are literally priceless and irreproducible, invested with a singular history and often marked by the intimate traces of the desired female body for which they serve as eroticized proxies: the fan splattered with Li Xiangjun's blood, the stocking that retains Yang Guifei's scent. This object does not merely get passed around the stage; instead it is subjected to a complex process of valuation and circulation, whereby the literatus-connoisseur elevates it to the vaunted place of a text to be carefully read, interpreted, and inscribed.

The fate of Du Liniang's self-portrait in Tang Xianzu's *Peony Pavilion* (*Mudan ting* 牡丹亭) is instructive. When the student Liu Mengmei discovers a scroll with a portrait of a beautiful woman, he brings it back to his room to carefully examine it, piecing together the identity of the mysterious subject from details like

2. The *zaju* of the Yuan and early Ming are much less frequently named for or centered around objects. Most of the *zaju* that are focused on material objects are Judge Bao plays in which they are treated as clues or evidence of wrongdoing. *Zaju* written later in the mid- to late Ming are increasingly object-focused, as in contemporaneous *chuanqi*.

3. Bruster, *Drama and the Market*, 63. Bruster charts the movement toward props becoming "a focus of interest in themselves" during the period 1590–1620.

4. Ibid., 69.

her tiny shoes. After reasoning that this is probably a self-portrait, Mengmei notices a quatrain written on the upper portion of the painting that he then parses aloud. When he comes to a line that contains characters from his name—"if not by the plum tree [*mei*], then by the willow [*liu*]" 不在梅邊在柳邊—he exclaims in disbelief: "How could she know that I, Liu Mengmei [lit. Willow that Dreams of Plum], would come here?" 怎知俺柳夢梅過.[5] As he studies the painting further, he realizes that though it seems that he is looking at the woman in the painting, it is the painting that is looking at him; though it seems that he is holding the painting, it is the painting that is holding him: "She stares right back at me . . . holding a branch of green plum as if she were carrying me in her hands." 好不回盼小生 . . . 卻怎半枝青梅在手, 活似提掇小生一般.[6] This performance of interpretation is simultaneously a self-assertion of literati hermeneutics and an act of self-discovery—the portrait that seemed to be of a girl is really a portrait about him.

Liu Mengmei's response to reading Liniang's poem is to compose a corresponding verse. It is this impulse to inscribe or reinscribe that, to borrow Bill Brown's formulation, transforms a *thing* with unclear, competing, or surplus meanings into an *object* that exists within a certain relation to the male literatus subject.[7] Such a process is dramatized most explicitly in Kong Shangren's *Peach Blossom Fan* (*Taohua shan* 桃花扇), when the literati painter Yang Wencong decides to paint twigs and leaves on the fan bloodied by the courtesan Li Xiangjun, thereby turning it into "a real peach blossom fan" 真乃桃花扇也.[8] Here the literati interventions of artifice and skill turn these bloodstains—at once abject (in their recollection of the bodily seepage of menses) and erotic (the blood of the deflowered)—from a messy, overdetermined thing, simultaneously repulsive and alluring, into a legible, coherent object.

5. Tang Xianzu, *Mudan ting*, 130. As we learn earlier in the play, "Mengmei" (Dreaming Plum) is a name he has given himself after dreaming of a beautiful young woman (presumably Du Liniang) standing under a plum tree.

6. Ibid., 130.

7. On the distinction between objects and things see Brown, "Thing Theory," 1–22.

8. Kong Shangren, *Taohua shan*, 154.

Once transformed, the fan becomes the site for the performance of connoisseurship and the staging of homosociality, as the assembled men sing Yang's praises: the singing master Su Kunsheng declares, "How marvelous! With only a few strokes of your brush, a branch of peach blossoms" 妙妙，竟是幾筆折枝桃花；[9] the painter Lan Ying later proclaims, "It is painted so brilliantly that you really cannot tell that they were bloodstains" 畫的有趣，竟看不出是血跡來。[10] This marvelous skill serves to reorient the stains from something uncontrolled—from blood that falls how it falls, that lands where it lands, that spreads in unexpected directions—to something that appears to be entirely controlled, intentional, and meaningful. The seeping, spreading edges of an amorphous stain now appear as a hard, intentional limit; the leaking, smelly, wounded body reborn as a fragrant, eternally blooming flower. Through this marvelous skill, the fan is brought into language—it is amenable to being talked about, appreciated, and understood.

By way of these performances of recognition and appraisal, the implicit, amorphous complaint registered by Xiangjun's body on the fan is shaped into a legible narrative by an ever-widening chorus of male literati readers and writers. The discursive object thus molded by literati hands demands an audience; as Yang Wencong tells Xiangjun: "Now that you have this peach blossom fan, you must find someone to appreciate it like Master Zhou appreciated music" 你有這柄桃花扇，少不得個顧曲周郎。[11] That someone is, most immediately, her lover Hou Fangyu; but just as Xiangjun's blood—her inside made outside—is on display, so does her story circulate throughout Jiangnan society. As the fan passes through hands and under admiring eyes, the exquisite beauty of the "peach blossoms" and the pathos of Xiangjun's story turn a private token into a public totem and Xiangjun's suffering into aesthetic spectacle and political metaphor. Like Liu

9. Ibid.

10. Ibid., 185.

11. Ibid., 155; Zhou Yu 周瑜 (175–210) was a general during the Three Kingdoms period and a music connoisseur who was said to always look up at the musician when something was played incorrectly.

Mengmei gazing at Liniang's self-portrait, these literati looked at the Rorschach test of Xiangjun's bloodstain and once again saw themselves.

The literati investments that make the fan such a potent site of meaning produce value without valuation; but that does not mean a price cannot be assigned, and it is this threat of valuation, seemingly against the object's very nature, that preoccupies another famous early Qing *chuanqi*, Hong Sheng's 洪昇 (1645–1704) *Palace of Eternal Life* (*Changsheng dian* 長生殿). Late in the play, an innkeeper named Wang tells how she discovered a silk stocking dropped by the imperial consort Yang Guifei before her death: "Those people from near and far who have heard of the stocking come to have a drink and take a look. In addition to paying for liquor, they also pay to see the stocking; as a result, my business is booming" 但是遠近人家，聞得有錦袜的，都來鋪中飲酒，兼求看袜。酒錢之外，另有看錢，生意十分熱鬧.[12] Like a madam, Innkeeper Wang plies curious patrons with wine and charges them a fee to handle the stocking that still retains Yang Guifei's scent. Li Mo, a former palace musician, mournfully sings: "In olden days in the Golden Palace, no one laid eyes on her tiny steps. How sad that her stocking is now on display in a wineshop, where anyone can carelessly fondle it" 昔在黃金殿，小步無人見。憐今日酒壚邊，等閒攜展.[13] While Li Mo bemoans the way in which the stocking is pimped out by the innkeeper, he nevertheless offers up copper coins to pay for his own fondling session.

Though Li Mo figures the display of the stocking as a violation of the consort's body, this scene dramatizes the way in which the commodification of objects sits in tension with the literati notion of ownership. It is he, Li Mo, who can truly appreciate this relic—his personal relationship with Yang Guifei, his position in the imperial palace, his refined aesthetic and sentimental disposition all mark him as a connoisseur and thus true owner of the object. If the stocking is to be seen and touched and smelled, it

12. Hong Sheng, *Changsheng dian*, 158.
13. Ibid., 160.

should be Li Mo who does so. However, his access to the object is the same as any other patron of the inn with a few coins to spare, an undifferentiated mass of spectators, "a hubbub that draws onlookers" 喧喧引看人[14]—the very antithesis of the individuated literatus—who flock to gape and fondle.[15]

The densely allusive object is thus under threat of disintegration into one of so many interchangeable commodities, and the vehicle of this disintegration is the fistful of coins proffered by cotton weavers, shopkeepers, prostitutes, and sentimental former officials alike. But what happens when all of those coins take center stage?

Considering the aesthetic and moral universe of *chuanqi*, money is an unexpected object to find at its center. Money is not so much an object as the antiobject, the very concept and the sign of commensurability that undoes objects and renders them so many interchangeable things, that makes the real abstraction of commodity exchange concrete. A coin, unlike a stocking or fan, is not a singular object marked with a bodily aura and a knowable history, but a manufactured, reproducible thing that threatens to collapse the distinction between original and copy. And the rarefied, in-group knowledge that invests an apparently worthless thing with value is here displaced by the universal legibility of minted money which often wears its value—or at least a value—on its face.

14. Ibid., 161. This line quotes from Song Zhiwen's 宋之問 (ca. 656–712) poem "Dragon Gate, written on imperial command" 龍門應制, which details Empress Wu's excursion to Longmen; its usage here links Yang Guifei to another problematic female emblem of political turmoil.

15. At the same time, this scene undercuts Li Mo's wistful nostalgia by having the disgruntled old rustic Guo Congjin launch into a searing critique of the fetishized object, the body to which it refers, and those who would define themselves through its aesthetic appreciation and circulation. Guo Congjin declares the stocking a detestable emblem of the folly that led to years of war and suffering and refuses to pay the innkeeper for what he has seen, attempting to extricate himself from the economy in which copper coins are traded for poetic nostalgia and erotic titillation. There is, of course, no way out: the stalemate between Guo Congjin and the innkeeper is broken when Li Mo insists on paying the fondling fee for him. As in the similarly post-Ming *Peach Blossom Fan*, the material fetishism of literati connoisseurship practices is implicated in narratives of late dynastic decadence.

Yet over the course of the long seventeenth century, there was a growing body of plays attributed to playwrights of the Suzhou circle that treated silver ingots, copper coins, and paper bills not as antagonists but as protagonists; plays with titles like *Coins of Heavenly Peace*, *Fifteen Strings of Cash*, and *Dragon and Phoenix Coins* (*Longfeng qian* 龍鳳錢) explicitly placed money at the material, symbolic, and moral center. In these plays, it is money in its various forms that circulates across the stage and through which individuals are brought into the social whole. What is being mapped on stage is not merely a community of connoisseurs or partisans, but an all-encompassing economy of obligations and debts through which all human (and nonhuman and superhuman) relations are organized. If the conventional *chuanqi* prop stages the anxiety of a literati object turned into a commodity, the props of these plays instead rewrite the commensurating power of money as fundamentally generative. If elsewhere the leveling legibility of the money form threatens to devalue or undo the aesthetic-political order, in these plays it can be the basis for new identities and new communities, opening up a space for cultural rejuvenation and political agency.

Penny Dreadful

The staging of the money form as material object and as abstract concept is certainly not limited to the *chuanqi* of the playwrights associated with the Suzhou circle. However, the centering of money as prop and narrative pivot elsewhere in late imperial drama is often deployed as a critique of commercial society and its perversion of the human psyche. A generation earlier, the Suzhou playwright Xu Fuzuo 徐復祚 (1560–ca. 1630) wrote the six-act *zaju One Copper Penny* (*Yi wen qian* 一文錢), a satirical comedy about a wealthy man named Lu Zhi who is so outlandishly parsimonious that he strictly rations his family's food and scavenges the leftovers of beggars.[16] One day he makes a life-changing discovery:

> Lu Zhi, played by the *sheng* 生 (male lead), walks and looks down: Hey, what is this thing on the ground? (*acts out picking it up and looking at it, laughs*) Is this not Heaven sent! A good coin—what happiness, what happiness!
>
> 生走介看地介：呀，前面地上甚麼東西。(拾起看介，笑介) 可不是造化，到是一個好錢。快活快活。[17]

This moment of bliss is quickly displaced by a growing distress over the coin's safekeeping: "I should hide it for the time being. What if I run into the person who dropped it and he recognizes it? That would be no joke" 我且藏過了。倘或掉的人來撞見，被他認去，不是當耍的. Wracked with anxiety over its potential loss, Lu Zhi debates storing the coin in his sleeve or his kerchief or his sock, but his clothes are so threadbare that he worries it will fall out. He finally resolves to clutch it tightly in his hand, a funny bit of stage business that literalizes his general tight-fistedness. But in his paranoia even this is not enough to hide the coin from view:

> *A beggar calls out offstage*. Lu Zhi: You see! You see! Could that be the person who dropped the coin? I'd better go hide somewhere then.
>
> 內做乞兒叫介，生：你看，你看，莫不是掉錢的人。我只是躲過便了。[18]

16. There is a tradition of comic depictions of wealthy misers in earlier *zaju*. In *A Slave to Money* (*Kanqian nu* 看錢奴), an ailing miser tells his son that when he dies his son should not only chop his body in half so he can be cheaply buried in the horse's feeding trough, but that he should do so with a borrowed axe so as not to dull the blade of theirs. Just as Lu Zhi buys one *wen* worth of sesame, in *A Slave to Money* the miser on his deathbed requests one *qian* 錢 (mace) worth of tofu. Zheng Qian, ed., *Jiaoding Yuankan zaju sanshi zhong*, 85–100.

17. Xu Fuzuo, *Yi wen qian*, 4b.

18. Ibid., 5b.

Lu Zhi's hyperfixation on the coin as a material object that is on the verge of dissolving into nothingness and whose departure he anticipates at the very moment of possession is revealed to be an externalization of an existential concern. In the middle of an aria justifying his skinflint ways, he pauses for a citation: "As the ancients said: wealth is life, life is wealth" 古人云財便是命，命便是財.[19] He later reformulates this pronouncement into something decidedly more intimate: "The square hole is my life-source" 孔方是我命根.[20] In place of some vague notion of fortune that exists in a coequal and mutually constitutive relation to life, Lu Zhi asserts a causal relation: money is his root 根; to cut away that root is self-annihilation.

When he is mocked by a group of beggars for his parsimony, Lu Zhi decides to spend his coin so as to dispel this bad reputation. After much deliberation, he buys a penny's worth of sesame, but his object anxiety is merely displaced: like the coin he wanted to add to his cellar hoard, he wants to put the sesame in his stomach, but what if a bird or dog tries to grab it before he has a chance? Lu Zhi decides to retreat to the mountains, safe from all prying eyes and greedy mouths and grasping talons. It is there that he encounters the Buddhist deity Śakra disguised as a poor monk; after conversing with him on the emptiness of all phenomena, Lu Zhi is enlightened and ascends to the Western Paradise.

With this transfiguration the play fulfills the generic conventions of the deliverance play (*dutuo ju* 度脫劇) even as it recalls and undoes the miser's anxious linkage of his life with his money. This ending shows how Lu Zhi's existential fear of dissolving into nothingness is misplaced—his overinvestment in the materiality of the money object and the materiality of the body is the source not of eternal life but of death, of physical and spiritual starvation. It is the twin dispersals at the end of the play, in which Lu Zhi's body is cast off and his hoarded money spread far and wide, that bring into being eternal life and abiding value.

19. Ibid., 4a.
20. Ibid., 8b.

This same terrain is traversed (though in reverse) in another, later *zaju* by the Shandong writer/official/martyr Ye Chengzong 葉承宗 (1601–48, *jinshi* 1646). In the one-act one-man play *Jin Zizhi Changes the Name of Elder Brother Squarehole* (*Jin Zizhi gaihao Kongfang xiong* 金紫芝改號孔方兄), a literatus named Jin Jing contemplates his lifelong poverty: "Although I descend from generations of literati, I am without a penny to my name. As I think back over my life, I have committed no sin other than looking upon wealth as being like excrement and considering misers to be slaves" 俺雖累葉書香，可柰一貧如洗。追憶生平，無甚罪過。只是見了錢財，如同糞土。見個錢虜，如同奴隸。[21]

A reading of Lu Bao's 魯褒 (fl. 300) *Discourse on the Spirit of Money* (*Qianshen lun* 錢神論) inspires Jin Jing to take stock of his contemporaries' precise relation to money. Holding a single coin (a "current circulating issue" 當今通寶, he notes), Jin Jing delivers a disquisition that is at once about and addressed to this coin.

> Jin Jing, played by the *zhengmo* 正末 (male lead in *zaju*): [To the tune "Happiness of All under Heaven"] Circulated over many dynasties since the Jin [when *Discourse on the Spirit of Money* was written], oh Elder Brother, you are advanced in years—this did not happen overnight! The time is right to carefully reconsider your old name.[22] I could call him Teacher Squarehole. No, no, that's not good: I'm afraid he would consider such a relationship too remote. I could call him Ancestor Squarehole. No, that's also not good: I'm afraid he would dislike being so far back in my family register. To call him my father would be best.
>
> 正末：【天下樂】典午傳來歷幾朝，老兄呵年高，非一朝。就着舊稱呼

21. Ye Chengzong, *Luo han*, 10:1b. Ye was the magistrate of Linchuan when Jin Shenghuan 金聲桓 (d. 1649), the regional commander of Jiangxi, rebelled against the Qing. Ye was captured and committed suicide.

22. In *Discourse on the Spirit of Money*, Lu Bao writes that money is "beloved like an elder brother" 親愛如兄. The designation of a coin as an elder brother plays on the character for money 錢, which is formed by the character for gold 金 (*jin*) and two characters for axe 戈 (*ge*, an early form of money). When written out as *Jin gege* 金戈戈, it is a homonym for 金哥哥, that is, Elder Brother Gold; that Jin Jing's surname is also Gold 金 makes the wordplay particularly apt.

仔細再推敲。稱他個孔方老師罷。不好，不好。怕他嫌壇坫踈。稱他個孔方家祖罷。也不好，也不好。怕嫌俺譜牒遥。到不如稱一個家父親纔算好。[23]

Naming the coin "Father Squarehole" 孔方父 elevates money from product to producer, from the more lateral relations of elder and younger brothers to the most venerated and hierarchical of relations between father and son. This provocative filiation of money and man, in which money is not an object man owns but a subject that makes man into its object, is a wry commentary on the role of money in fashioning the self during an age when every signifier of social identity—education, taste, clothes, office, rank—seemed to be for sale. In Ye Chengzong's deeply satirical encomium, a coin is transformed from prop to audience and from excrement to father, while its Confucian interlocutor is transformed into its supplicant. The play ends with Jin Jing singing:

> Father Squarehole, I cling to your knees; to you my most revered father, I piteously beg. With your blessing I can "ride to Yangzhou with ten thousand strings tied around my belt."[24]

孔方父親呵，俺只在膝前倚靠。俺只把你椿庭哀告。是必的保佑俺做兒的揚州萬貫錦纏腰。[25]

23. Here I reproduce the extant text's use of a smaller font to indicate padding words that fall outside of the aria proper. Ye Chengzong, *Luo han*, 10:4a. Such a formulation recalls an observation from a poem that Chu Renhuo 褚人穫 (1635–ca. 1705) attributed to Yuan Hongdao 袁宏道 (1568–1610):

> In my leisure I happened to read *Discourse on the Spirit of Money*;
> Only then did I realize that human feelings today exceed those of the past.
> In ancient times, the square-hole coin was compared to an elder brother;
> Nowadays that "elder brother" surpasses one's own father.

Chu Renhuo, *Jianhu ji*, 6 *ji* 集 1:37b. The opening exposition of Ye's play echoes the first line of this poem, with Jin Jing describing how in his "leisure" he "happened to read" *Discourse on the Spirit of Money*. Qian Zhongshu 錢鍾書 has also noted the link between Ye's play and this poem. See *Guanzhui bian* in *Qian Zhongshu ji*, 4:31.

24. This expression refers to an anecdote that appears in the collection *Minor Accounts* (*Xiaoshuo* 小說) by Yin Yun 殷芸 (471–529), in which a group of men were discussing whether their highest wish was for power, riches, or immortality. One replies that he would like "to ride a crane down to Yangzhou with one hundred thousand strings of coin around his waist," that is, to have all three. Yin, *Yin Yun xiaoshuo*, 131–32.

25. Ye Chengzong, *Luo han*, 10:6b.

At the center of both *Elder Brother Squarehole* and *One Copper Penny* is a single coin so small that even in the most intimate late imperial performance context someone watching would be hard pressed to tell if the actor is holding an actual coin made of copper or a fake coin made of something else or is merely conjuring one through pantomime. The practical indistinguishability of presence and absence—in which it does not matter whether the coin has matter—instantiates the extratheatrical role of the *wen* 文 as an object that treads the boundary between value and valuelessness. The smallest unit of state-minted currency, it is the nominal foundation of late imperial monetary value (nominal because of its supersession by the unminted silver tael (*liang* 兩) as the predominant unit of account and, in many exchanges, the medium of exchange), and yet it is almost worthless as a single unit in the late Ming and early Qing marketplace, where even the smallest of purchases would require a handful of coins.[26]

This smallness and proximity to worthlessness certainly sharpens the satirical lens on these protagonists' overinvestment in a single *wen* coin—in Lu Zhi's case, laden with the weight of his whole life, in Jin Jing's case, with the entirety of human history.[27] This is an investment that, in both cases, leads to a kind of bankruptcy. Lu Zhi abandons all of his possessions—his money, his family, his body; Jin Jing grovels before a dirty coin, begging it for

26. For a list of prices of daily use items from the 1570s through the 1640s, see Chow, *Publishing, Culture, and Power in Early Modern China*, app. 4. Assuming the rate of one tael to one thousand *wen* (a rate that was not stable over this time), a single *wen* could possibly buy a catty of salt or a pair of chopsticks. A catty of beef would be fifteen *wen*; a hundred could buy a cheap book.

27. Late imperial narratives frequently use this denomination to show how the most seemingly insignificant thing is implicated in a much larger system, either as the cause or as the effect. For the former, see "A Small Dispute over a Penny Leads to a Shocking Injustice" 一文錢小隙造奇冤 in Feng Menglong's 1627 vernacular story collection *Constant Words to Awaken the World* (*Xingshi hengyan* 醒世恆言), which features the cascading effects of a single act; for the latter, see "A Chinese Man Changes His Luck in a Chance Encounter with Dongting Tangerines; A Persian Man Reveals the Secrets of a Tortoise Shell" 轉運漢遇巧洞庭紅，波斯胡指破鼉龍殼 in Ling Mengchu's 1628 collection *Slapping the Table in Amazement* (*Pai'an jingqi* 拍案驚奇), in which even the smallest piece of money is controlled by fate.

a future. Both plays conclude in an antisocial dead end in which all previous relations between the self and others are no longer tenable.

It is against this figuration of the deathly power of the money form to cancel out the debts and obligations that make up human society that the plays attributed to the Suzhou circle recast money as something generative. And it is precisely this power of money to make things into commensurable and interchangeable objects that brings into being new subject positions, new kinship relations, and new polities. The circulation of everyday monies—copper coins, paper bills, silver ingots—form the core of a number of Suzhou circle plays like *Fifteen Strings of Cash*, *Cornucopia*, *Between Man and Beast*, and *Three Kinds of Happiness* that are discussed elsewhere in this book. The following discussion focuses instead on two plays, *Dragon and Phoenix Coins* and *Coins of Heavenly Peace*, that are organized not around the ordinary but the extraordinary: the imperial coin treasures of the Tang emperor Xuanzong 玄宗 (685–762, r. 712–56). As the emperor's special issues, these coins are imbued with a history and a meaning legible to cultural and political elites—not unlike a storied jade cup or a resonant peach blossom fan. But in the unexpected circulation of these coins across the stage, both plays show how money resists playing a proper *chuanqi* object.

A Coin with Two Faces

In the opening scene of the *chuanqi Dragon and Phoenix Coins*, attributed to the Suzhou circle playwright Zhu Suchen, Emperor Xuanzong gets a strange impulse.[28] Courtesy of his Daoist magician

28. *Dragon and Phoenix Coins* is attributed to Zhu Suchen in Gao Yi's *New Southern Dramas*, as well as in the early to mid-Qing *Compiled List of Southern Dramas* (*Chuanqi huikao biaomu* 傳奇彙考標目). A summary of the play is preserved in the twenty-eighth *juan* of *Catalogue of Summaries from the Ocean of Song*. Like most of the plays of the Suzhou circle included in the *Ocean of Song*, the authorship is listed as unknown. The only extant edition of the play is an undated manuscript from the

advisor Ye Fashan, he had just taken a trip to the palace of the moon, where he met Chang'e and took in a performance of the legendary rainbow skirt dance. The fantastical details of this trip—which have preoccupied dramatists and poets and composers since the legend first appeared—are of little concern to this play. Rather, it is a whim that Xuanzong gets during his descent back to Earth, a literal throwaway moment, that sets the play in motion. Standing on a magically conjured bridge across the sky, Xuanzong looks down on cities below and decides he wants to toss something down.

But what to throw? In the scene as it appears in the extant edition, the emperor's trusty eunuch Gao Lishi proffers some silver coins, which the emperor tosses down through the clouds in order to "share his enjoyment with the people" 與民同樂 as a good Mencian ruler.[29] He then realizes that he himself happens to have two pieces of gold dragon-and-phoenix money in his sleeve. Before tossing these down he makes a proclamation: "If someone in the city of Chang'an picks up one of these coins that I just threw down, if that person is a man then he will become a Hanlin scholar and if a woman then she will become an imperial concubine" 將來擲下, 如長安城中有人拾得者, 男為翰苑, 女作次妃.[30]

In the next scene, we hear a report about how this was experienced below: "This morning at the time of the fifth watch, all of the people of the city heard the sound of laughing and talking coming from the clouds and then silver coins rained down. Countless people—young and old, men and women—picked them up" 今早五更時分, 滿城百姓都聽得雲中有笑語之聲, 落下銀錢, 無數大小男婦盡皆拾得.[31] The discovery of the gold coins is a much less frenzied affair. As the student Cui Bai and his servant

National Library of China (formerly Beijing Library) collection that is preserved in facsimile in the third series of the *Guben xiqu congkan*. This manuscript prefaces the title with "Newly Composed" (*xinbian* 新編), which could either refer to the newness of the play or indicate that this is a new edition of an existing play. The content of the extant manuscript matches the description in the *Ocean of Song*, with the exception of the ending, which will be discussed further below.

29. Zhu Suchen (attrib.), *Longfeng qian*, 1:3b.

30. Ibid., 1:4a.

31. Ibid., 1:6a.

are wandering the grounds of his residence, his servant spots something shiny on the ground. Cui Bai picks it up and is shocked to discover a gold coin engraved with the image of two dragons playing with a pearl and an inscription on the back: "The divine dragon plays with the pearl, gleaming with a dazzling light. With the phoenix as its mate, longevity and prosperity eternal" 神龍戲珠，燁燁其光。得鳳成匹，萬壽永昌.[32] A similar discovery of a gold coin depicting twin phoenixes is made by the high-born maiden Zhou Qinxin on her morning walk.[33] As per an imperial edict, those who found the silver coins are to report to their county *yamen* where they will be rewarded with a silver ingot. Those who found the gold coins, however, are to report to the palace.[34]

Immediately upon seeing the coin, Cui Bai identifies it as "an imperial plaything" 御戲之物. Indeed, Xuanzong's predilection for creating amusing spectacles with gold coins was well known. According to the *Old Book of Tang* (*Jiu Tang shu* 舊唐書):

> In the *jimao* year, the emperor held a banquet where he had the various nobles and officials gather at Chengtian Gate. He then commanded his attendants to throw gold coins down from the tower above. Those officials at rank five and above in the Secretariat and those at rank three and above in the other various offices were allowed to vie to pick them up, and then gifts were distributed based on rank.

32. Ibid., 1:5b.

33. *Dragon and Phoenix Coins* is in many ways a retread of *Peony Pavilion*, and like that play, it is in the garden that romantic love is made possible. However, *Dragon and Phoenix Coins* is ultimately much less radical than its forebear: whereas *Peony Pavilion* attributes the heroine Du Liniang's self-resurrection to her extraordinary *qing* 情 (sentiment), here it is the *sheng* that summons the *dan*'s soul and who is described (borrowing the language Tang Xianzu uses to describe Liniang) as the most *qing* person in the world.

34. Up until this point, this plot line echoes the seventh story in Ling Mengchu's *Pai'an jingqi*, "Emperor Ming of the Tang is Fond of Daoism and Gathers Eminent Masters; Consort Wu Venerates Chan and Watches a Magic Contest" 唐明皇好道集奇人，武惠妃崇禪鬥異法, in which Fashan takes Xuanzong to the moon and gold coins are tossed as they cross the moon bridge. Reports of these falling coins reach local officials who write memorials to the emperor about the incident.

己卯，宴王公百僚於承天門，令左右於樓下撒金錢，許中書門下五品已上官及諸司三品已上官爭拾之，仍賜物有差。[35]

Stories of Xuanzong and his courtiers and consorts tossing gold coins were recounted in poems and historical records alike, with some claiming that the various coin-tossing amusements of the inner palace made their way into the game playing of urban commoners.[36]

In *Dragon and Phoenix Coins*, the emperor's coin toss is at once a playful and spontaneous act and a symbolic assertion of his power over the production and circulation of value.[37] Xuanzong releases the coins into the city center much as his imperial command to the state mints disburses and disperses his coin across the realm; though in this act the emperor casts himself not as a bureaucrat but as a god, a power on high that wills and in willing brings value into the world.[38] Indeed, what the emperor releases on that bridge are coins but not money per se—neither the silver coins possessed by Gao Lishi nor the emperor's gold coins would have been intended to circulate as currency. Gold and silver coins like the gold and silver Kaiyuan-era coins minted for the historical Xuanzong were intended as gifts, their association with imperial grace and their composition of the most numinous metals making them treasures to be kept as tokens of favor and icons of status, as lucky talismans and objects of divination, not traded for grain or

35. Liu Xu, *Jiu Tang shu*, 1:171.

36. On *jinqian hui* 金錢會 (gold coin feasts), as well as other Kaiyuan-era gold coin-tossing divination and ritual practices, see Dong-fang Qi, "Not an Ordinary Hoard," 54–57.

37. The imperial dispensation of coins undergoes a parodic reversal in the underworld at the midpoint of the play. In the sixteenth scene, the heavenly official who is sent to track down the errant souls of the two female leads is attacked by the Insatiable Great King 無厭大王 and his demon army who wish to kidnap the girls. The God of the Earth devises a plan to scatter silver coins along the road, correctly surmising that "when the ghost army sees the coins, they will vie to snatch them up" 這些鬼兵見了，必來搶奪. As the ghosts abandon their formation in a chaotic frenzy, the God of the Earth ruefully sings that "their greed burns even more intensely than when they were alive" 貪心比生前猶熾. Zhu Suchen, *Longfeng qian*, 1:33a–b.

38. On the cartalist tradition in Chinese thought, see Von Glahn, *Fountain of Fortune*, 15–47.

cloth in the marketplace.[39] That Gao Lishi's silver coins are to be rewarded with silver ingots is perhaps not just a demonstration of imperial largesse—and an implicit assertion that it is the emperor, and not the market, that causes value to multiply, turning silver into more silver—but also a recognition of how different a silver coin and a silver ingot are. The silver coin is a noncirculating treasure, whereas the ingot is the circulating reward and thus a bulwark against the improper circulation of treasure as money.[40]

The emperor's own gold coins are even further removed from the world of circulating currency. Though a numinous and efficacious substance, silver was within the everyday experience of late imperial urbanites; as the de facto currency in which many purchases were denominated, as a common store of value, and as a mode of payment, silver was conceptually and physically available in a way that gold was not. The emperor's coins invoke gold's aura of elemental value: imprinted with the imperial icons of dragon and phoenix on a face of gold, the mythic divinity of the son of heaven commingled with that most efficacious and highly valued metal. Touched by the emperor's body, bearing not merely the sign of imperial power but the transformed image of the son of heaven, the coins are an extension of his physical being into the world—his will given form in these dragon and phoenix avatars. For the emperor's will does not end at the release of these coins into the world; rather, he aims to direct their trajectories back to him—to his harem and to his academy. What he wills into being is a closed circulation that begins and ends with him, an economy in which he is at the center. It is the way the circulation of these coins eludes his control that forms the narrative engine of the play.

This is not the first late imperial play to thematize the unruly circulation of Xuanzong's gold coins. In the *zaju* titled *Li Bai*

39. Xuanzong had Kaiyuan coins minted in gold and silver (identical to copper circulating coins). On the uses of gold and silver Kaiyuan coins, see Dong-fang Qi, "Not an Ordinary Hoard," 49–68.

40. Unminted silver ingots were a primary form of circulating currency during the time the play was written, not during the time the story took place; this kind of monetary ahistoricism was common in late imperial literature.

Arranges a Match Using Gold Coins (*Li Taibai pipei jinqian ji* 李太白匹配金錢記), attributed to the Yuan playwright Qiao Ji 喬吉 and anthologized in Zang Maoxun's 臧懋循 (1550–1620) *Selected Yuan Dynasty Plays* (*Yuanqu xuan* 元曲選, 1615–16), a magistrate receives fifty gold Kaiyuan coins as a gift from Xuanzong.[41] The magistrate gives the coins to his daughter to wear as a talisman, but when she falls in love with a young student, she gives him the coins as a love token. The magistrate eventually discovers the coins in the student's possession and furiously denounces the young lovers for their moral transgressions. It is only through the student's sudden elevation to high office and the intercession of the poet Li Bai that the lovers are married and all are reconciled. To take that which emanates from and stands in symbolic relation to the divine and the imperial and to use it as a private token is a violation that only a hero of the canon can resolve.

In *Dragon and Phoenix Coins*, the path the emperor's coins take is more circuitous and more difficult to untangle. As expected, our *sheng*, the literatus protagonist Cui Bai, discovers the dragon coin and our *dan* 旦 (female lead), Qinxin, finds the phoenix. Even more expected, when they report to the palace, they meet and fall in love, but they are quickly separated as Qinxin is ushered into one of the emperor's palaces as a consort. Using a magical spell and a strand of her hair, Cui Bai summons Qinxin's spirit to his garden and declares his feelings. Upon waking from a trance, Qinxin is consumed by lovesickness. When Cui Bai summons her spirit again the next day, they decide to flee the capital while her lifeless body lies in the palace.

Then, an administrative screwup for the ages: the underworld authorities decide to return Qinxin's roving spirit to her body, but in a moment of confusion, an official accidentally places Qinxin's spirit in the body of Shuxin, a girl who died tragically before her allotted time (and who happens to be the sister of Cui Bai's landlord nemesis), and places Shuxin's spirit inside Qinxin's body.

41. This play is rewritten by the Yangzhou *chuanqi* playwright Xie Kun 謝堃 (1784–1844) as *Twelve Gold Coins* (*Shi'er jinqian* 十二金錢). Xie Kun, *Chuncao tang ji*, j. 15–16.

The remainder of the play finds the two girls attempting to reunite with their loved ones and convince those around them that they are not whom they appear to be. One would think that the dragon and phoenix coins might come in handy in sorting out who is who. But in fact, the coins prove to be largely useless. Shuxin, trapped in Qinxin's body, is kidnapped by a grave robber and sold into concubinage, eventually to be rescued by Cui Bai. Though she is in possession of a phoenix coin, she has no idea why; when Cui Bai goes to talk to Qinxin's father Zhou Yanhui, claiming that he is his son-in-law, he proffers the phoenix coin as proof. But as Yanhui points out, all the coin proves is that Cui Bai is probably the graverobber who kidnapped his daughter.

At this point in the play, both the coins and the bodies to which they are attached can no longer be taken at face value. It is this crisis of personhood—much like that in *Peony Pavilion*, to which *Dragon and Phoenix Coins* is self-consciously indebted—that requires imperial intervention.[42] Unlike the aloof and all-seeing emperor of that earlier play, however, the Xuanzong of *Dragon and Phoenix Coins* is just as baffled as his subjects. He calls forth the girl who claims to be his former consort but looks like someone else; he is struck by her memories of their time together and how much her manner reminds him of Qinxin but is at a loss as to how or why. Unable to adjudicate this jumble of bodies and identities, he sends for Ye Fashan, who explains how the two girls came to inhabit each other's body. This is no mere accident, Ye Fashan argues, but the expression of a predestined marriage bond; the emperor decides that the only course of action is to have both of the girls marry Cui Bai.

In the description of the play that appears in the *Catalogue of Summaries from the Ocean of Song*, the grand reunion scene that concludes the play does not merely reunite the separated husband and wives and parents and children, but also the separated bodies

42. On the treatment of this crisis in *Peony Pavilion*, see Tina Lu, *Persons, Roles, and Minds*, 239–88. Like *Longfeng qian*, Zhu Suchen's *Moon over the Qin Tower*, which is discussed in the next chapter, explicitly references both its indebtedness to and supersession of *Peony Pavilion*.

and souls: using his magical powers, Ye Fashan returns the girls to their original bodies.[43] The extant play text, however, offers no such solution, instead consigning the girls to live out their lives in the other's body.

Little can be known about the extant text except that it is clearly a performance text of some kind—it is (rather sloppily) handwritten with improvised sections omitted but noted—and that it is, as the title page says, newly composed (*xinbian* 新編).[44] It is in the ending that the text seems to deliver on its promise of newness, as up until this point it has closely followed the detailed plot description given in the *Ocean of Song*. This ending is both new relative to putatively earlier versions of this play and seemingly novel within the contemporaneous literary field. The soul separated from its body and the body possessed were common fascinations in late imperial literature, especially in the ghost-obsessed drama of the late Ming and early Qing.[45] The body-swapping plot of *Dragon and Phoenix Coins* shares with those plays certain metatheatrical pleasures, like the actresses' bravura performances of the subtle changes in bearing and voice that mark the *dan* as Qinxin or Shuxin-in-Qinxin and the *xiaodan* 小旦 (secondary female role) as Shuxin or Qinxin-in-Shuxin.[46]

43. Aside from this ending, the plot description in the *Catalogue of Summaries from the Ocean of Song* follows the extant play text, including details like the inscription on the coins. As Guo Yingde has noted, the *Ocean of Song* lists the play as having twenty-eight acts, but the extant play only has twenty-seven. It is not possible that the extant play is missing a final scene, as scene 27 is written as a concluding reunion scene and ends with a coda summing up the play. Guo, *Ming Qing chuanqi zonglu*, 1:649.

44. One such notation appears in scene 26: after the actor playing Ye Fashan enters, he announces to the audience that he has arrived to have an audience with the emperor, which is immediately followed by "(云———)," indicating some spoken section, possibly a summary of the plot as he knows it or some more involved self-introduction. Zhu Suchen, *Longfeng qian*, 2:24b.

45. The urtext being the Tang classical tale "The Story of the Disembodied Soul" 離魂記, anthologized in *Extensive Records from the Taiping Era* (*Taiping guangji* 太平廣記, completed 978) as "Wang Zhou" 王宙. Li Fang, ed., *Taiping guangji*, 358: 2831–32. On the splitting and reconstitution of *Peony Pavilion*'s heroine, see Tina Lu, *Persons, Roles, and Minds*, 28–62.

46. These shifts in voice, register, and modes of speech are frequently remarked on by other characters, further highlighting the bravura performance for the audience.

But body-swapping narratives usually end with the restoration of every body and soul to its rightful place.[47]

The extant *Dragon and Phoenix Coins* ends not only with the two female leads forever entombed in each other's bodies, but also with a scene that foregrounds the emotional and psychological toll of such a fate. In scene 27, titled "Combining the Coins" 合錢, Cui Bai returns home from court to find his new brides bitterly at odds. When they declare that they would rather join a nunnery than persist in this arrangement, Cui Bai calls in their relations to mediate. The patriarch on hand, Qinxin's father Zhou Yanhui, marshals the entire weight of the Confucian tradition, showing the girls how their actions infect each of the cardinal relations and their attendant virtues:

> ZHOU YANHUI, played by the *wai* 外 (older male role type): How can you continue to fight with each other about this and so damage family relations? To not accept the imperial bestowal is disloyal, to not follow your parent's instructions is unfilial. To violate the bond of husband and wife is unfeeling, and to regard each other with jealousy is not virtuous. [To the tune "Even Better"] Jealous after just one night, jealous after just one night. How will you share a thousand years together?
>
> 外: 何得彼此物爭, 有傷和氣。[48] 今日不奉聖恩非忠也。不遵親訓非孝也。伉儷有違非情也。嫉妒相看非賢也。【越恁好】一宵便妒, 一宵便妒, 何以共千年。[49]

On the metatheatricality of these body swaps (a not uncommon trope in early Qing *Peony Pavilion* retreads), see Zeitlin, *Phantom Heroine*, 172–76. As Zeitlin notes, scenes of splitting or swapping "lay bare the most fundamental convention of theater, that of the actor's doubleness—the experience of playing another and bringing this character to life on stage." Ibid., 134.

47. For example, in Ling Mengchu's *huaben* "Elder Sister's Soul Roams to Fulfill a Long-Cherished Wish; Younger Sister Recovers from Illness to Continue a Predestined Bond" 大姊魂遊完宿願, 小姨病起續前緣, a dead woman borrows her sister's life essence to consummate her marriage to her fiancé, but in the end she departs and the living sister marries the fiancé. A similar resolution occurs at the end of Feng Menglong's revision of the *chuanqi* *Snow-Sprinkled Hall* (*Saxue tang* 洒雪堂). Ling, *Pai'an jingqi*; Feng Menglong, ed., *Mohanzhai dingben chuanqi*, vol. 2.

48. Reading 初 as 和.

49. Zhu Suchen, *Longfeng qian*, 2:28a.

Shuxin's mother concurs and offers her own entreaties:

> MRS. LÜ, played by the *laodan* 老旦 (older female role type): What the gentleman said is quite reasonable. My child, you cannot carry on like this. (*singing*) It is difficult to distinguish between self and other; what matters is having the same steadfast heart.
>
> 老旦：老親翁之言，句句在理。孩兒，你決不可如此。(唱) 難分你我，總則是一心堅。[50]

When Shuxin's brother kneels in contrition in her place, a chastened Shuxin-in-Qinxin responds by singing of an envisioned marital conciliation:

> In front of the brocade screen, reading "The Tale of the Jealousy-Quelling Bird"; within the embroidered bed-curtains, a tangle of phoenixes fulfill a vow.
>
> 錦屏前讀一遍倉庚傳，繡幃中混一派鸞凰愿。[51]

Cui Bai thanks his in-laws for restoring the peace, the leads collectively agree that "what was said makes sense" 說得有理, and with that the play ends.

This hurried ending attempts to contain the girls' dissatisfaction and unease within the more legible rubric of female jealousy. Cui Bai and Zhou Yanhui repeatedly diagnose the problem as one of too much *cu* 醋 (lit. vinegar; romantic jealousy), reframing the girls' complaints within the common comic trope of the shrew.[52] The crisis thus becomes one of familial cohesion imperiled by a gendered weakness, and the substance of the girls' grievances is diminished and rendered petty. As Cui Bai sums up the situation

50. Ibid.

51. Ibid. "The Tale of the Jealousy-Quelling Bird" 倉庚傳 by Yang Shen 楊慎 (1488–1559) is a parodic biography of the *canggeng* bird, whose flesh was said to cure jealousy. The story exhorts husbands to maintain strict order within their households to prevent such conflict among their wives. Yang Shen, *Yang Sheng'an congshu*, 3:228–29.

52. On the popularity of this trope in late imperial literature, see Yenna Wu, *A Chinese Virago*.

to his in-laws, "The two ladies are constantly squabbling over trifles" 兩位小姐爭長爭短.[53]

However, what the girls are fighting about is not some trifle, but their own autonomous identities. And any attempt in the second half of the scene to rewrite them as just another pair of women bristling at a bigamist arrangement must contend with the first half of the scene in which their grievances are articulated not in terms of their jealousy over the other's intimacy with Cui Bai but in terms of their jealousy over the other's intimacy with their own dislocated body. As Qinxin-in-Shuxin says, "It is not you, my husband, that I blame; rather I blame the one impersonating me" 奴家也不怪郎君，只怪那冒託奴家的人. Shuxin-in-Qinxin echoes her sister-wife: "It is not you, my husband, that I blame; rather it is that my body should be returned to me and not so lightly borrowed by another" 奴家也不怪郎君，只是我的身子也，要還我個下落也，不是輕易借人的.[54]

The problem is not that there are two of them, as is the case in the typical final act scene in which two wives jockey for position. Their quibble is not with the bigamous arrangement, but rather that they cannot locate themselves within it when their own selves have been fractured and colonized. While the issue of who is where—whose soul is in whose body—is easily grasped, more vexing is the question of who gets to be whom. Should "Qinxin" refer to the body or the consciousness? What is at stake is not just their own sense of coherency but the radiating interpersonal effects, as "Qinxin" and "Shuxin" are not merely names but social and ritual positions. Who will visit Qinxin's father or offer sacrifices to Shuxin's?[55] The intractability of the problem dominates the middle part of the play, as Qinxin's father and Shuxin's mother fight over who gets to claim Qinxin-in-Shuxin as their own. The putative solution of a double marriage fails to reckon with this problem, opting instead to cut the Gordian knot: with

53. Zhu Suchen, *Longfeng qian*, 2:27b.

54. Ibid., 2:27a.

55. Certainly this problem is somewhat (but not entirely) obviated by the subordinated role of unmarried daughters in ritual practices.

her marriage to Cui Bai and incorporation into his lineage, it no longer matters whether Qinxin-in-Shuxin is Zhou or Lü; becoming a wife obviates the need to settle her identity as a daughter.

The unstated but underlying question as to whether the self is more firmly rooted in one's body or one's consciousness reappears throughout the final two scenes of the play. Even the scene in which the girls' identities are supposedly resolved is fraught with inconsistences and slippages. When Ye Fashan explains the body swap to the emperor, he differentiates the girls thus: "Lying prostrate before us is Miss Lü Shuxin; the one staying in Bozhou is Miss Zhou Qinxin" 俯伏的是呂氏書心，亳州暫寓者是周氏琴心. Just a few lines later, however, the emperor describes the girl in Bozhou as Shuxin.

As the final scene opens, a proclamation from the emperor seems poised to settle these questions once and for all:

> Officiant, played by the *jing* 淨 (character actor or painted face): Kneel to receive the emperor's proclamation: "Who was once the daughter of the Zhou family has now become of the Lüs. With sentiment that over a thousand years will not fade, the pair of phoenixes together fly as before."[56] Please present Miss Lü.
>
> Qinxin-in-Shuxin, played by the *xiaodan*, enters singing: Do not consign my powdered face to the underworld; with a laugh I ask if my body can be as before.
>
> Officiant, continuing to read: "Though her lovely form is that of Miss Zhou, her name is Imperial Consort Lü. With ten thousand words I urge you, do not ask who you are."
>
> 淨：伏以，昔是周家女，今為呂氏娘。千秋情不朽，依舊效於飛。奉請呂小姐。
>
> 小旦上：不將紅粉委黃泉，笑問兒身可似前。
>
> 淨又讀：艷質仍周女，芳名是呂姬。叮嚀千萬語，莫問爾為誰。[57]

56. An allusion to the line "the male and female phoenixes fly around" 鳳凰於飛, a common referent to marital bliss, from the *Classic of Poetry* (*Shijing* 詩經), no. 252 ("Juan a" 卷阿).

57. Zhu Suchen, *Longfeng qian*, 2:26a.

The *dan* playing Shuxin-in-Qinxin enters, singing of the rupture (and rivalry) between "form and shadow" 形影. But she will find no answers to their conundrum in the emperor's proclamation, which seems to have given both women the name Lü.

This indeterminacy finds an ironic iteration in the extant text itself, when in the middle of the girls' argument over who is who, the manuscript scribe has failed to note that the speaker has switched from the *xiaodan* to the *dan*, leading to an impossible bit of stage business in which the *xiaodan* points accusatorily at herself.[58] As Cui Bai says, it is simply that "Miss Zhou is Miss Lü, Miss Lü is Miss Zhou" 周小姐就是吕小姐, 吕小姐就是周小姐, and there is no way to separate the two. Neither is Qinxin and neither is Shuxin, but rather both are both. The women are two sides of the same coin, or perhaps more like the two phoenixes on the face of the emperor's coin.

The play lays the foundation for this freighted interchangeability from the beginning: the girls have matching given names like sisters and only have one father and one mother between the two of them. This parallelism that eventually interlocks merely brings to the surface the social reality of many late imperial women, whose "jade bodies" circulated as merchandise, bought and sold as servants, entertainers, courtesans, and concubines. Indeed, not even the *guimen dan* 閨門旦 (female lead of virtue and status)—whose body the emperor attempts to take out of circulation by placing in his harem—is safe from being converted into money, as Shuxin-in-Qinxin is kidnapped and sold into concubinage.[59] By the end of the play, Shuxin and Qinxin appear to be rescued from the fate of the commodity by becoming wives—ritually important, socially rooted, brought into a household and a lineage. But as the play repeatedly tells us, their identities do not matter, only the role they play. As Cui Bai says, his wives "need not be vexed" 不須煩惱 by this situation; if two actresses can play the same role, why should it matter who is playing whom?

58. Ibid., 2:26b.

59. The commodification of bodies is elsewhere thematized in the play by a servant who sells his body to take corporal punishment on Cui Bai's behalf.

In the final scene, both girls lay claim to the phoenix coin—Qinxin-in-Shuxin as the one who first found it and Shuxin-in-Qinxin as the one who gave it to Cui Bai. These competing claims on the coin rehearse the nature of money itself as a thing that is owned by anyone and no one, that multiplies and reproduces, that makes two different things exchangeable such that a low-born girl comes to occupy the same social position as the daughter of a high official and a supporting actress gets to play the lead. In the beginning of the play, the emperor tries to use the coins to fix identities, to declare that this person will be a Hanlin scholar and that person will be a consort. But the coins do the opposite, bringing into being a multiplicity of new identities and desires that even the emperor and his magician and his top scholar cannot sort out. When confronted with the complexity that the coins have generated, all they can do is enlist the old social and affective forms—to render the girls' claims moot through marriage; to disarm their protest with the discourse of female jealousy.

At one point, when nothing is working out the way he intended, the emperor declares, "The dragon and phoenix coins turned out to be so much empty talk" 龍鳳兩錢竟成虛話.[60] But the coins were not the source of the empty talk—the emperor was. By imagining his coins as an extension of his will, Xuanzong stakes his claim on them as his props whose circuit lies entirely within his play. Instead, the emperor's own money gets away from him, has a logic to which he is not privy, and creates new and inexplicable forms of being that will need to wait for other works to unravel.

Coins of Heavenly Peace

The circulation of people and coins into and out of Xuanzong's court also structures the play *Coins of Heavenly Peace*, attributed

60. Zhu Suchen, *Longfeng qian*, 2:22a.

to the Suzhou circle playwright Li Yu.[61] In a departure from the "scholar and beauty" (*caizi jiaren* 才子佳人) pairings embraced by *Peony Pavilion* and its many successors like *Dragon and Phoenix Coins*, this play casts as its hero not a talented young student but an eighty-year-old gardener, Old Man Zhang.[62] As the play opens, Zhang has fallen in love with the sixteen-year-old daughter of his

61. *Coins of Heavenly Peace* is attributed to Li Yu in a number of Qing sources, including Gao Yi's *New Southern Dramas*, *Compiled List of Southern Dramas*, Jiao Xun's *Discourses on Drama*, and Yao Xie's 姚燮 (1805–64) *Textual Criticism of New Music* (*Jinyue kaozheng* 今樂考證). *Catalogue of Summaries from the Ocean of Song* summarizes a version of the play supposedly from the Ming, though no author is given. Dong Kang, ed., *Quhai zongmu tiyao*, 1:696–98. The summary of the play is identical to the three extant editions of the play: an "old" manuscript from the National Library, which was reprinted in facsimile in the third series of the *Guben xiqu congkan*; an "old" manuscript from the collection of the scholar Xu Zhiheng 許之衡 (1877–1935); and a mid-Qing palace edition housed in the Fu Ssu-nien Library at Academia Sinica. Arias from the play appear in *The Great Achievement of the Nine Modes* (*Jiugong dacheng* 九宮大成, 1746) and Ye Tang's 葉堂 *Scores from the Studio of Acquiring Books* (*Nashuying qupu* 納書楹曲譜, 1792), with only minor differences from the National Library and Xu Zhiheng editions. The National Library and Xu Zhiheng editions have mostly minor differences, though the Xu edition includes two rather extraneous scenes that do not appear elsewhere. The Xu Zhiheng edition can be found in *Suizhong Wushi cang chaoben gaoben xiqu congkan*, 10:279–448. Unless otherwise noted, citations are from the National Library edition.

While the National Library and Xu Zhiheng editions are the sorts of scripts utilized by commercial troupes—with lines crossed out, transcription errors corrected, and musical notation written in for select arias—the third extant edition is a carefully copied "four-color" manuscript from the archive of the imperial treasury (see plate 3). This version, which would have perhaps been submitted to imperial censors or members of the imperial household prior to performance, reflects the particular demands of performance within the palace, with various spectacular elements (falling snow, magic tricks) and celebrations of auspicious events (weddings, Spring Festival) added or expanded. Though Li Yu's plays were closely tied to Suzhou-centered commercial entertainment, many found their way into the imperial collection—Ye Xiaoqing recorded twenty-three plays by Li Yu in the palace library catalogue. Ye, *Ascendant Peace in the Four Seas*, 125n150.

62. *Coins of Heavenly Peace* brings together two narratives that first appeared in late Tang classical tale collections and were anthologized in *Extensive Records from the Taiping Era*: "Old Man Zhang" 張老 and "Betrothal Inn" 定婚店, both attributed to Li Fuyan's 李復言 (ca. 775–833) *A Sequel to Records of Mysterious Anomalies* (*Xu xuanguai lu* 續玄怪錄). Li Fang, comp., *Taiping guangji*, 16:112–15, 159:1142–43. Both stories appeared in late Ming anthologies edited by Feng Menglong, and the former was rewritten as the *huaben* "Old Man Zhang Grows Melons and Marries Wennü" 張古老種瓜娶文女 in Feng's 1620 collection *Stories Old and New* (*Gujin xiaoshuo* 古今小說).

neighbor, the official Wei Shu, and is desperate to marry her. Deeply offended at the suggestion of this match, Wei Shu agrees on one very specific condition: "I will marry my daughter to him only if he offers one hundred thousand strings of Taiping coins as the brideprice" 除非有十萬貫太平錢作聘，就把小姐嫁他便了.[63] The next day, Zhang appears at their door with ten carts loaded to the brim.

The large quantity of money that Old Man Zhang offers as a brideprice is unsettling not only as a jest made literal but also for highlighting the "price" of the brideprice. The disruptiveness of the cash is brought into relief by the series of successful gift exchanges that precede it. Before the play begins, the emperor gives Wei Shu a white donkey that was a tribute gift from the western regions.[64] When this donkey wanders onto Zhang's property, Zhang sends it back along with some melons as gifts. Wei Shu and his family then pay Zhang a visit in thanks for the melons. The emperor's gift, which sets the play in motion, both acknowledges and reiterates the particular relationship of emperor and official-subject, in which the bounty of the country is figured as a gift given by the imperial head. This material gift is not intended to beget a material countergift; rather, the display of imperial largesse binds the subject's loyalty to the symbolic object, whose safe-keeping functions as a totem of that loyalty. In the exchange of melons for visit, the material gift moves in the opposite direction, as a humble offering to one's social superior. The countergift of the visit reiterates the particular social relation between peasant and local elite. When Wei Shu, his wife, and his daughter arrive, Zhang is out; in his absence they freely wander his gardens,

63. Li Yu (attrib.), *Taiping qian*, 1:22b.

64. There is no such gift in either the classical tale or the *huaben*. In the classical tale, the missing animal is not a plot point, and the relationship between the Liang emperor and Wei Shu is unknown, as Wei Shu is described simply as a retired official. In Feng Menglong's version, Wei Shu admonishes Emperor Wudi for his support of Buddhism. As punishment he is demoted to the supervisor of the imperial stables. The escaped animal that turns up in Zhang's garden is a white horse also exiled to the imperial stables by the emperor. In the play, Wei Shu's offense remains ambiguous, and rather than being put in charge of the stables, he retires.

examining his melons. When Zhang returns home, he is shocked that they condescended to pay him a visit. Wei Shu thanks him for the melons in a tone befitting a social superior, while Zhang protests that he cannot accept his thanks, as the gift was of such little value, comparing it to presenting a sophisticate with "celery of the rustics" 野人芹.[65]

This early series of exchanges, linking the emperor to Wei Shu and Wei Shu to Old Man Zhang in a clear hierarchy of social relations, is disrupted by Zhang's brideprice for the Wei daughter. Literalizing the unease of the late imperial elite toward the transgressive potential of extreme wealth, *Coins of Heavenly Peace* stages the frightening possibility that anyone with money can insinuate themselves into your family. When Zhang arrives with the cash for the brideprice, Wei Shu balks. Zhang, infuriated that Wei Shu intends to renege on their oral agreement, threatens to kill himself in front of their gate. In its depiction of a gift exchange gone wrong, *Coins of Heavenly Peace* shows a world in which the anxieties, calculations, and tactics of the marketplace have permeated the most ritualized of exchanges, the "supreme gift" of woman.[66]

Certainly the notion of a marriage arrangement located outside of market dynamics or financial considerations has its basis in nostalgic imagination rather than historical experience. Indeed, the advent of marriage-as-transaction was bemoaned long before the late imperial period, and the tremendous imbalance in wedding gifts was not a new phenomenon. The massive brideprice offered by the lower-status suitor for the higher-status daughter seems to reflect the Tang context in which the earliest source text, the classical tale "Old Man Zhang" 張老, was written. According to Patricia Ebrey, betrothal gifts in the Tang were formalized as twice the size of the dowry.[67] The stratospheric demands placed on the

65. Li Yu, *Taiping qian*, 1:13a. Allusion to a story told by Yang Zhu 楊朱 in *Master Lie* (*Liezi* 列子), in which a farmer is mocked for wanting to present his humble crops to the gentry elite. *Liezi*, 95.

66. Lévi-Strauss, *The Elementary Structures of Kinship*, 65.

67. Ebrey, *Women and the Family in Chinese History*, 62–88.

groom and his family became a trope in Tang classical tales. In "The Story of Huo Xiaoyu" 霍小玉傳, the narrator explains that "because the Lus were an aristocratic family, if someone wanted to marry one of the daughters he would have to pay a brideprice of one million; any less and he would be rebuffed" 盧亦甲族也，嫁女於他門，聘財必以百萬為約，不滿此數，義在不行.[68] As in the story of Old Man Zhang, the bestowal of massive brideprices was often associated with supernatural beings. Indeed, who could produce so much money but a fox spirit?[69] In "Wei Mingfu" 韋明府, a fox who insists on marrying a magistrate's daughter is asked to provide a two-thousand-string brideprice.[70] "The Magistrate of Qianyang" 汧陽令, another story of a male fox forcing marriage on an unwilling family, tells of how after the wedding the family did not mind the uxorilocal arrangement, as the wedding gifts given by the fox were quite lavish.[71]

The lavish brideprices demanded by Tang aristocratic families were replaced by an escalation of dowry during the Song. After the Song, dowry sizes diminished—in part, as Bettine Birge notes, as a result of legal changes during the Yuan that made the dowry a nonmoveable part of the husband's family estate.[72] However, dowries remained a centerpiece of competitive marriage strategies; Ann Waltner's study of female infanticide shows continuing pressure to provide lavish dowries at all levels of Ming Jiangnan society.[73]

The demands of a dowry-centered marriage economy can be glimpsed in one of the *huaben* on which *Coins of Heavenly Peace* is based, when Wei Shu laments his family's prospects: "I have a

68. Li Fang, comp., *Taiping guangji*, 487:4008.

69. In addition to having all of the resources of a supernatural being, foxes in classical tales were frequently associated with the vast wealth derived from mercantile modes of accumulation. See Huntington, *Alien Kind*, 151.

70. Li Fang, comp., *Taiping guangji*, 449:3674–75. As in *Coins of Heavenly Peace*, the coins are hidden in the eaves of the supernatural being's house.

71. Ibid, 449:3670–71.

72. Birge, *Women, Property, and Confucian Reaction*, 200–282.

73. Waltner, "Infanticide and Dowry," 193–218.

daughter who is already eighteen *sui*, but since I am an upright official, my family is poor and I don't have the money to marry her off" 有個女兒, 一十八歲。清官家貧, 無錢嫁人.[74] While the appearance of the tremendous brideprice in the *huaben* and drama versions of the Old Man Zhang story echoes this contemporary concern with the financial burden of marriage, a bit of strangeness is generated in depicting the inversion of the late Ming Jiangnan norm. Rather than a lavish dowry procuring a hypergamous union, here an obscene brideprice begets an excessively hypogamous marriage.[75]

The inflation of brideprices in the Tang and of dowries thereafter generate similar anxieties, as the absence of corresponding gifts threatens to upend the symbolic logic of a ritual in which gifts appear to be exchanged for other gifts. However, the dowry and the brideprice are not conceptually equivalent exchanges. The dowry is a gift to the bride—or, more accurately, a gift that adheres to the bride. Before the erosion of women's property rights in the Yuan, the content of the dowry often remained the property of the bride and might return with a widow to her family. But even when legal changes made the dowry a nonmoveable part of the husband's family estate, the symbolism of the dowry as a gift from the bride's family to the bride retains this important distinction from the brideprice, which recompenses the bridal family for the cost of raising their daughter and/or the loss of her labor.[76] There is no monetary value placed on the groom, as he is not being exchanged; the dowry is a gift, the brideprice a payment.

The nature of the brideprice as payment is emphasized in *Coins of Heavenly Peace* by being rendered entirely in specie,

74. Feng Menglong, ed., *Gujin xiaoshuo*, 21:1282. This concern is absent in the classical tale, as the Weis had already begun employing matchmakers.

75. Waltner, "Widows and Remarriage," 129–46.

76. Indeed, while the dowry was no longer legally attached to the bride's body, it remained functionally so, as after the Yuan a widow would likely remain in her husband's home rather than return home or remarry. Birge, *Women, Property, and Confucian Reaction*, 200–282.

rather than in those material objects whose aesthetic value and multifunctionality better mystify their roles as mediums of exchange or stores of value (bolts of silk, embroidery, etc.). The disturbing prospect of the daughter's body as just another thing to be exchanged for other things is made even more explicit when the payment of money is followed almost immediately by the marriage ceremony. In his discussion of the work necessary to obscure the mechanics of the gift exchange, Bourdieu points to the importance of time elapsed, as gift exchange "protracts and so disguises the transaction that a rational contract would telescope into an instant."[77] The play stages such an instant, collapsing the exchange into two scenes: the money arrives in scene 12 and by scene 13 Wei Shu's daughter is whisked away to be wed in a ceremony that the audience never sees.[78] The payment of money has effectively married them, obviating the need for further ritual.

As an index of the power of extreme wealth to sunder long-standing hierarchies of ritual exchange, this "rational contract" of cash for wife evokes the problematic of the newly rich merchant buying his way into prestigious gentry families. However, as their discussion with the matchmaker demonstrates, Wei Shu and his wife are not averse to marrying their daughter into a wealthy merchant family. When the matchmaker announces that she comes bearing a proposal for their daughter, Wei Shu and his wife inquire into the man's background:

> WEI SHU AND WIFE: If we are discussing our daughter's marriage, [Reprise of last tune] (*singing*) then he must be "a prince in tinkling ornaments" reciting "The Cry of the Ospreys," a man of a distinguished lineage.[79]
>
> MATCHMAKER: He is not.

77. Bourdieu, *The Logic of Practice*, 112.

78. In the twelfth scene of the palace edition held by Academia Sinica's Fu Ssu-Nien Library, there is a wedding ceremony sequence, befitting both the pomp of imperial household performance and the auspicious occasions for which such performances were often held.

79. Reference to the first poem of the *Classic of Poetry* about a nobleman looking for a bride.

Wei Shu and wife, singing: Or he can write thousands of poems, each composed in seven steps;[80] his learning fills up the You Mountains, his words astonishing listeners.[81]

Matchmaker: He is not like that either.

Wei Shu and wife, singing: Then he should be like Tao Zhu with gold piled up like hills.[82]

外、老：若論我家姻事，【前腔】定是鳴珂公子咏河洲，共羨蟬聯名胄。

付：不是。

外、老唱：或者文章七步詩千首，驚四座胸藏二酉。

付：也不是。

外、老：想應是陶朱輩黃金似丘。[83]

Wei Shu and his wife enumerate the acceptable matches for their daughter in order of declining desirability: a scion of a distinguished family, a brilliant scholar-poet, and finally a rich merchant. While the first two types of suitors are mentioned without comment, the parents feel compelled to justify their inclusion of the merchant: "If he is from this kind of family, (*singing*) then they can avoid the bitterness and worries of poverty" 若得這樣人家，(唱)也免卻虀鹽苦戾廖愁.[84] But this is also not an accurate description of the suitor; it is when Wei Shu learns that he is but a humble gardener that he mockingly suggests the extravagant brideprice.

Though Zhang produces the money—the magnitude of which is represented on stage in a procession of ten carriages that

80. Reference to Cao Zhi 曹植 (192–232), who supposedly wrote a poem in seven strides as recounted in Liu Yiqing's 劉義慶 (403–44) *A New Account of the Tales of the World* (*Shishuo xinyu* 世說新語), 2:66, in Yu Jiaxi, ed., *Shishuo xinyu jianshu*, 244.

81. On the legend that countless books are stored in the two You mountains, see Li Fang, comp., *Taiping yulan*, 49:3a.

82. Tao Zhu, aka Fan Li 范蠡, is discussed in the next chapter.

83. Li Yu, *Taiping qian*, 1:22a.

84. Ibid. Following the extant text's use of a smaller font to indicate padding words that fall outside of the aria proper.

if piled up would certainly resemble the hills—he is not welcomed as a son-in-law. The problem with Old Man Zhang is not that he does not come from the scholar-official class (or, in the context of the Kaiyuan setting, the aristocracy), as the Weis make clear that a wealthy merchant would be a perfectly acceptable husband for their daughter. Rather, the problem posed by Zhang's brideprice is the failure of money as a sign. The play here undermines any contemporary resonances by making the *nouveau riche* man not *riche* (nor, for that matter, *nouveau*), but rather poor. The rich merchant who offers a stunning brideprice for a gentry daughter is not only recompensing the family for the devaluation of their daughter's status through such a connection, but also demonstrating that what perhaps he lacks in literati bearing he makes up for in providing their daughter with a comfortable life. With the gentry daughter's upbringing and the merchant's deep pockets and literati aspirations, his elevation and her return through the entry of their sons into the bureaucratic system is almost assured.

Here, however, the massive brideprice of one hundred thousand rare coins is not shorthand for great wealth; it is not the promise of material comfort for the daughter and status for their sons. Quite the contrary, this tremendous wealth is used to buy the daughter into, not out of, poverty. The appearance of the money neither marks nor heralds a change in Old Man Zhang's economic situation. Both immediately before and after the exchange of money, Old Man Zhang remains, by all appearances, a poor gardener. There are no more riches hiding in Old Man Zhang's eaves; when Wei Shu sends a servant to look in on his daughter, he is shocked to find her shoddily dressed and farming melons with her husband.

The disgust felt toward those who eke out a living on the margins is echoed in the play's other main plotline, which offers a mirror image of this match of the impoverished gardener and the official's daughter: the official's son and the poor orphan girl. Wei Shu's son Wei Gu, who prides himself on his strict "Three Kinds I Won't Marry" 三不娶 policy, had gone to the capital hoping to secure a match to the daughter of a high official. When the Old Man in the Moon 月下老人 tells him in a dream that he is instead fated to marry a starving, shivering child, he is livid. Though the play's source materials frame the delay in marrying age as the primary objection to the prophesy, *Coins of Heavenly Peace*'s Wei Gu is more furious that his intended is his social inferior.[85]

The young orphan, Hui'e, first appears onstage with her elderly nursemaid as part of "a mass of starving people young and old raising a din" 老幼饑民喧嚷 in the street.[86] A *yamen* official, drawing on the rolls of registered households, distributes food rations to the hungry villagers. The nursemaid's name is called, and she implores the official to give rations to Hui'e as well, even though she is merely an infant and not properly registered. The official relents and the nursemaid shuffles away with their food. When Wei Gu happens upon "the poor hag in beggar's clothes and the little wretch covered in dirt" 老貧婆乞丐裝, 小孽種腌臢相, his disgust is so visceral that he attempts to murder Hui'e with his own hands.[87]

To one on the precipice of officialdom and marriage and entry into their attendant networks of institutional and affinal

85. Li Fuyan's classical tale emphasizes Wei Gu's anger over this age difference; the Feng Menglong *huaben* version depicts the age difference as the primary objection of the Weis.

86. Li Yu, *Taiping qian*, 1:14b. Here the play diverges from the source material by making Wei Gu's future wife a beggar. In the classical tale, when Wei Gu asks about his intended's family background, the Old Man in the Moon replies that she is "the daughter of the old woman who sells vegetables north of the inn" 店北賣菜家嫗女. In the Song edition of *A Sequel to Records of Mysterious Anomalies*, Wei Gu seems bothered more by her appearance than her social status: "I am from an eminent official family; I should marry a woman of equal standing. If such a marriage is not possible, then I should at least elevate a talented courtesan to the position of wife. Why should I marry the ugly daughter of this blind hag?" 吾士大夫之家, 娶婦必敵。苟不能娶, 即聲伎之美者, 或援立之。奈何婚眇嫗之陋女. This line does not appear in the *Taiping guangji* or *Qingshi leilüe* editions. See Wang Bijiang, ed., *Tangren xiaoshuo*, 224.

87. Li Yu, *Taiping qian*, 1:14b. While Li Fuyan's Wei Gu promises his servant ten thousand cash if he kills the infant, this Wei Gu dismounts his horse to stab the girl himself as his trusty strongman acts as lookout.

obligations, the spectral beggar is the uncanny negation.[88] Like the hermit gardener, Hui'e sits outside of human commerce—the buying and selling of the marketplace, the reciprocity of social obligations. She takes but does not give, subsisting on surplus and largesse; she is the dead end of circulation, a disturbing prospect in a story (and genre) that centers around a series of exchanges, around social ties formed through the circulation of favors and objects and people.

The revulsion and upheaval that these two unions provoke in the first third of the play is undone by twin revelations: in the second third of the play, that Zhang is a Daoist immortal and in the final third, that Hui'e is the daughter of a scholar-official and the adopted daughter of the prime minister.[89] These shocking reversals conjure the hairpin turns in fortune experienced in times of rapid commercialization and political disruption. That the Wei men misrecognize their (social, cosmic) betters as their inferiors dramatizes an anxiety about the ability to "see" social station and cultural identity during such a period. The discovery that a powerful deity could disguise himself as a penurious old man functions as the inverse corollary of the anxiety surrounding the increasing ease with which a merchant could cloak himself in the accoutrements and affectations of the literatus.[90] That people are somehow illegible, that their outward indications of identity are misleading, points to a rupture in which social meaning is no longer adequately conveyed through the available forms.

88. A similar anxiety pervades the early Qing play *The Ingot Go-between* (*Yuanbao mei* 元寶媒, preface dated 1681), in which a nameless and placeless beggar is brought from the fringes into the center and given a name through the circulation of imperial money.

89. This rewriting makes both of these transformations more dramatic. Old Man Zhang appears to have received a promotion from the *huaben*, where he describes himself as the heavenly immortal Zhang Gulao of the Eternal Happiness Palace 上仙長興張古老. In *Coins of Heavenly Peace*, he is conferred the title of the Eastern Floriate Celestial Emperor 東華大帝 and given the fief of Mount Wangwu. Hui'e is similarly elevated: In "Betrothal Inn," the orphaned girl is the daughter of the unnamed magistrate of Songcheng and is later adopted by his younger brother Wang Tai, the prefect of Xiangzhou. The play makes Wang Tai (here the magistrate of Pingyao) her father and gives her the more illustrious Han Xiu as her adopted father.

90. Clunas, *Superfluous Things*, 141–65.

The extreme reversals through which *Coins of Heavenly Peace* facilitates these unions heightens the impact of the final revelation that there are invisible economies in which even those on the margins who seem to be completely outside of systems of exchange—the beggars, the orphans, the hermits—are actually enmeshed. Zhang's abstention from human commerce masks his centrality in a cosmological economy through which infinite wealth and power circulates, while the orphan girl is incorporated into a larger economy of obligations between her dead father and his classmate. That these various economies are ultimately brought into interrelation through the repeated exchange of the same coins points to an imagination of a social whole constructed out of the circulation of money—a circulation that pointedly excludes the emperor.

By merging the "Old Man Zhang" narrative with "Betrothal Inn," *Coins of Heavenly Peace* creates a chain of perfect exchanges radiating outward: Zhang gives one hundred thousand strings to the Weis as a brideprice for their daughter; Wei Gu then pays the one hundred thousand strings to Chancellor Han Xiu as the brideprice for his daughter.[91] This money that is constantly in circulation is not only the constitutive force in generating families through the buying of women but also delimits the social whole. In his first self-introduction, Zhang describes himself as "having neither wife nor child, a lonely man by himself; being neither merchant nor trader, my abode a desolate four walls" 無妻無子，孑爾一身。不賈不商，蕭然四壁.[92] Just as the absence of wife and son is literally parallel with abstinence from buying and selling, Zhang's entrance into a money economy is his entrance into human society. The transfer of money from Zhang to Wei to Han traverses the register of status, from farmer to scholar to high official, and in so doing reverses the dynamic of the earlier series

91. This is another of the play's narrative innovations. In "Betrothal Inn," no request for engagement gifts is ever made.

92. Li Yu, *Taiping qian*, 1:1b. A similar formulation appears in *The Joy of Fisherfolk* (*Yujia le* 漁家樂), attributed to Zhu Zuochao: "I, Zhao Tu, my whole life had no trade and no profession, no wife and no children" 我趙圖一生一世，無行無業，無家無室. Zhu Zuochao (attrib.), *Yujia le*, 54a.

of exchanges in which gifts circulated from the emperor on down. The cash that passes from Old Man Zhang to Han Xiu links the margins and the center, the supernatural and the mundane, the immortal and the historical.

But this cash is not just any cash. In the vernacular story from which the play draws, what makes this money distinctive is its extreme amount, its functionality as currency, and its metallic purity: "one hundred thousand strings of ready cash . . . all copper coins with no gold coins mixed in" 十萬貫見錢 . . . 並要一色小錢, 不要金錢准折.[93] In the play, the brideprice demand hinges instead on a specific issue, the titular Taiping coins, and the impossibility of this request rests precisely on their unreadiness as cash: "Taiping coins are the treasures of the treasury; not even high officials have one hundred thousand strings of them, let alone this old man!" 太平錢乃是鎮庫之寶, 就是官家也沒有這十萬貫, 料這老兒呵.[94] Though the origins or metallic composition of the Taiping coins are not addressed in the play, they appear to be of a piece with the gold coins of *Dragon and Phoenix Coins*: treasures bestowed and not currency circulated. To circulate such coins is not only logistically puzzling but potentially treasonous. No one in the play asks where these coins came from: Were they magically conjured out of nothing by the immortal? Or were they removed from the Tang treasury?

These questions of authorization and ownership become increasingly pressing in the final scenes of the play, in which Emperor Xuanzong invites Old Man Zhang to court to perform magic for him and Yang Guifei.[95] After several impressive transformations, Zhang jumps inside a gourd and vanishes; he is later seen riding a crane out of the city gate. In the final scene of the play, Wei Gu, his father-in-law Han Xiu, and his wife Hui'e encounter the eunuch Gao Lishi in the mountains. The eunuch recounts how he was charged with bringing Zhang back to court, but even when

93. Feng Menglong, ed., *Gujin xiaoshuo*, 21:1283.

94. Li Yu, *Taiping qian*, 1:23a.

95. While the classical tale and *huaben* are set in the early sixth century, the play moves the story to the Kaiyuan period (713–41) of Xuanzong's reign.

faced with an imperial edict commanding his return, Zhang "resolutely refused" 決意不從允 to go back.[96] While the earlier scene figures Zhang as a court jester, amusing his royal hosts with marvelous tricks, his abrupt departure and refusal to return reveal a power beyond the emperor's control.

The inability of the emperor to keep Old Man Zhang in his court is not unlike his inability to keep his treasure coins in the imperial treasury. Both slip the net of imperial regulation, an ending not without resonance for an audience in early Qing Suzhou. While the imperial state sought to hold things in place as objects of administration, by the late Ming, the mobility of money and men increasingly compromised such a logic of governance, and previously marginal positions gained a new autonomy that was deeply unsettling to the center.

The Xuanzong of both *Dragon and Phoenix Coins* and *Coins of Heavenly Peace* is ultimately shown to be the minter but not the author of the value that circulates within his realm. This money is granted its own logic, governed by the oft-invisible hand of "heaven" or "fate." As the cast sings in the final coda, "The Taiping coins have fittingly settled the accounts of heaven and earth" 太平錢作合氤氳賬, though "heaven and earth" fails to capture the complexity of the concept of *yinyun*, a vaporous and harmonious intermingling of *yin* and *yang*, or, as Giles puts it, "the generative influences of heaven and earth by which all things in nature are constantly reproduced."[97] The coins, then, have themselves brought the conjugal forces of the cosmos—metaphysical and matrimonial—back into balance. This line is of course a classic bit of final coda grandiosity; *Dragon and Phoenix Coins* similarly ends with the promise that "even when the oceans run dry and become mulberry fields, no one will forget the dragon and phoenix coins [i.e., the play *Dragon and Phoenix Coins*]" 滄桑莫忘卻龍鳳錢. But there as here, the audience is left with an image of the titular coins as something beyond the force of political will, with the circulation of coins akin to the primordial

96. Li Yu, *Taiping qian*, 2:32b.
97. Ibid., 2:33b; Giles, *A Chinese-English Dictionary*, 2:1636.

dynamism of the cosmos. Whereas plays like *Palace of Eternal Life* posit money as that which corrupts an object, *Dragon and Phoenix Coins* and *Coins of Heavenly Peace* recast money as that which generates all subjects.

Coda: A Coin from the Former Dynasty

In the early Qing, a coin was a particularly loaded prop both on stage and off. Around the same time that these plays were first circulating in Jiangnan, another story was also being passed around that cast money in a starring role. That story centered around Lin Gudu 林古度 (1580–1666), a poet active in late Ming literary circles and the son of a prominent (though persecuted) Ming official.[98] After the fall of the Ming, Lin Gudu lived out his remaining years in poverty and encroaching blindness.[99] It was in this quiet coda of life that Lin came to occupy a new symbolic role. Championed by younger luminaries such as Wang Shizhen 王士禎 (1634–1711), who published a collection of his poetry, Lin became known among early Qing literati not only for his literary output but also for his performance of a particular kind of loyalist theater.[100]

This performance was staged at—or was retroactively imagined to have been staged at—the second of Wang Shizhen's famed gatherings at Red Bridge 紅橋 in Yangzhou, held in the spring of 1664. The presence of the octogenarian Lin Gudu at this gathering was freighted with symbolic weight and itself became a topic of poetic composition. One of the members of Wang's literary circle at the gathering, Wang Ji 汪楫 (1626–89), presented Lin with a

98. Lin was particularly close with fellow Fujian-native scholar-official Cao Xuequan 曹學佺 (1574–1646), as well as the playwright Tu Long 屠隆 (1542–1605). On Lin's participation in late Ming literary circles, see Xu Jiankun, "Wanli guimao nian Fuzhou shitan shengshi kao," 87–116; Xu Jiankun, *Cao Xuequan yu Wan Ming wenxue shi*, 99–102.

99. Wang Zhonghan, *Qingshi liezhuan*, 17:5697–98.

100. On Lin's participation in Wang Shizhen's Red Bridge gathering in Yangzhou, see Meyer-Fong, *Building Culture in Early Qing Yangzhou*, 66–67. Lin Gudu was previously acquainted with Wang Shizhen's grandfather.

poem written in seven-character regulated verse titled "Mr. Lin Maozhi came again to Guangling and I was moved to write this poem for him" 林茂之先生重來廣陵感贈.[101] In this poem, Wang imagined the eighty-five *sui* Lin, who "has not been to Yangzhou in fifty years" 不到揚州五十年, navigating a new world in which "no one uses Wanli coins to buy wine" 沽酒都非萬曆錢. The disorienting terrain of this new order is captured in the final line, "Over and over he asks about the Fifth Spring west of the city" 數問城西第五泉. In a world of disappeared people and places, Lin is anxious to see if the Fifth Spring has "turned into mulberry fields" 桑田改. The poem ends on this note of uncertainty—does the Fifth Spring flow as before and will Lin find his way back there? Located on the grounds of the Daming Temple 大明寺, whose name (with its inadvertent recall of the past dynasty) was changed in the early Qing, the spring remains but still perhaps cannot be found.[102]

This poem begets another. In the preface to his seven-character ancient-verse poem "Ballad of a Coin" 一錢行, Wang Ji writes:

> In spring of the Jiachen year [1664], Lin Maozhi came to Guangling and I presented him with a poem. At the line "no one uses Wanli coins to buy wine," his eyes widened and he loudly exclaimed, "How strange! Did you know that I have a Wanli coin on me?" He stretched out his left arm to show me, and his flesh warm and tender hid a surprising gleam. How deep is his sentiment! Thus I composed "Ballad of a Coin."
>
> 甲辰春，林茂之先生來廣陵，余贈以詩，有沽酒都非萬曆錢之句，先生瞠目大叫曰：異哉。子知我有一萬曆錢在乎。舒左臂相示，肉好溫潤，含光懾人。蓋先生之感深矣。更為賦《一錢行》。[103]

The poem that follows, like the previous one, sees the eighty-five-*sui* Lin Gudu returning to Yangzhou. But here the focus shifts

101. Wang Ji, *Huizhai ji*, 675.

102. This temple, which was named for the Xiaowu emperor of the Liu Song but would invariably conjure the "Great Ming," was renamed Xiling Temple 棲靈寺 in the Qing.

103. Wang Ji, *Huizhai ji*, 662.

from Lin's interior life to his effect on those around him when halfway through the poem the titular coin appears. This Wanli coin, tied to his left arm for twenty years, is, like Lin Gudu, "an old thing out of joint with his time" 舊物不逢時. Though children in the marketplace pay it no mind and passersby snigger, "his guests pass it around, overcome with sadness" 座客傳看盡黯然. The gloom dissipates in the final line: "Then, smiling, they drain the wine bottle; no need to let tears fall recalling that bygone time" 且共開顏傾濁釀, 不須滴淚憶當年.[104]

Wang Ji here restages the seemingly private, intimate moment he describes in his preface as a more public scene of recognition and catharsis. A similarly theatrical moment is staged in Wu Jiaji's 吳嘉紀 (1618–84) ancient-style poem, also titled "Ballad of a Coin" 一錢行. Like Wang Ji, Wu imagines the disorienting experience of Lin Gudu returning to Yangzhou for the first time in fifty years and realizing that "the rivers and mountains are as before but the generations are different" 江山宛然人代改. Then, as in Wang's poem, there is a shift from the mutability of life to the unchanging coin:

滿地幹戈杜老貧	The earth is filled with shields and pikes, old Du Fu is poor;[105]
囊底徒餘一錢在	at the bottom of his moneybag, a single coin remains.
桃花李花三月天	In the third month with the peach and plum blossoms in bloom,
同君扶杖上漁船	With you leaning on a staff, we board a fishing boat.
杯深顏熱城市遠	Deep in our cups, faces flushed, the city far away,
卻展空囊碧水前	you slowly unroll your moneybag above the emerald ripples.

104. Ibid.
105. Reference to Du Fu 杜甫, "Kuizhou Songs: Ten Quatrains" 夔州歌十絕句: "Though shields and pikes fill the earth, the wanderer's grief dissipated; the sun in the clouds was like a fire, but there the blazing heavens were cool" 干戈滿地客愁破, 雲日如火炎天涼. *Quan Tang shi*, vol. 4, 229:2508; Owen, *The Poetry of Du Fu*, 4:169.

酒人一見皆垂淚	Your drinking companions take one look and all shed tears:
乃是先朝萬歷錢	it is a Wanli coin from the former dynasty.[106]

The Wanli coin functions as Yang Guifei's stocking will twenty years later in *Palace of Eternal Life*, as a prop that focalizes both personal nostalgia and collective trauma, situating individual experience within historical time. But while Li Mo alone sobs over the stocking as it is fondled by strangers, these poems foreground the community formed by the coin's circulation. Wang Ji writes of Lin Gudu's companions "passing [it] around to have a look" 傳看; the phrase also appears in a variant version of Wu Jiaji's poem:

誰家酒壚可賒飲	Whose wine shop would sell him wine on credit?
一錢先與人傳看	The single coin is first passed around to give people a look.[107]

The coin moves from hand to hand, paying for wine and jogging memories, an index of the many small transactions that make up a society. Here we see the formal similarities between the circulation of a coin and the circulation of a poem—especially as the circulation of this poem about the circulation of this coin generates social capital for the younger, lesser-known poets. However, the circulation of poem and coin is here not simply a commercial or social act, but a political one. The minted coin does not make claims to an enduring, transhistorical value but to a value that is situated in dynastic time. As the coin itself tells us, it was given form and value during the Wanli reign, a period evocative of late Ming Jiangnan high culture while remaining sufficiently distant from the chaotic final years of Chongzhen.

106. Wu Jiaji, *Wu Jiaji shijian jiao*, 41. Translation adapted from Chaves, "Moral Action in the Poetry of Wu Chia-chi (1618–84)," 431.

107. Shen Deqian, ed., *Qing shi biecai ji*, 6:38.

The Wanli coin functions as an apt symbol of a particular mode of Ming loyalism. Unlike the paths of self-extermination chosen by loyalists like Lin Gudu's close friend and fellow Fujian native, the scholar-official Cao Xuequan 曹學佺 (1574–1646), Lin's persistent survival as a Ming remnant becomes its own kind of embodied rebuke. In these sociable exchanges of poetry and wine, these two near-worthless Wanli relics—the single coin of negligible value, the old and impoverished man—become invested with new symbolic value.[108] The small coin, whose surface is lovingly examined by a series of hands, and the elderly man, whose emotional depths are plumbed by the next generation of poets, become invaluable totems of a world lost and catalysts for the living. In a reversal of the *zaju* plays *One Copper Penny* and *Elder Brother Squarehole* discussed above that anxiously pathologize the overvaluing of the single copper coin, here the act of overvaluing is a balm and a generative force.

Lin Gudu's tiny coin, like the smallest of capital investments, begets a growing body of poems and anecdotes. By staying in circulation—even if its currency is more literary and social than monetary—the coin generates a community of sentiment that functions outside of the Qing's attempt to mint authority, outside of the Qing's schema of valuation, outside of Qing imperial time. While the twinning of Lin's body and coin formally echoes the disquieting late imperial motif that transforms money into man and man into money, here the imbrication of man and money—the warm, soft flesh that unfolds to reveal the cold, sharp glint of metal—redeems rather than impoverishes human society.[109] Against the anxious possibility of commodification, in which coins turn people and things into objects that can be bought and sold, here a coin turns people into subjects, trauma into poetry, and money into a politics.

108. On the devaluation of Wanli coins in the early Qing, see Vogel, "Chinese Central Monetary Policy."

109. On this motif, see Fox, "Precious Bodies."

TWO

Every Man a Merchant

The traveling merchant is a figure of much anxiety and mistrust in the late imperial imaginary, his movements across both spatial and social boundaries a frequent source of unease. Such mobility is not unique to the merchant; the path from student to official can be measured both in rungs on the "ladder of success" and in *li* 里 traversed. But the movements of the merchant and the aspiring official are freighted with very different meanings. The aspiring official moves within set circuits, from home to exam site and from exam site to home or to the imperial academy or to an official post. His circulation around the empire serves to mark the administrative terrain: his journey to the (prefectural, provincial, imperial) capital links the almost bewildering multitudes of people and places to the center(s); on his departure from the capital as a newly minted agent of the bureaucracy, he traces the very enclosure of the realm.

The traveling merchant, however, is drawn from place to place by an amorphous and invisible web of surpluses and needs that reaches across administrative borders. Such sojourns, in exposing the porousness and vulnerability of these borders, create problems both ontological and diplomatic for the imperial court. In crossing the boundaries between elite and common, Chinese and other, inside and outside, the merchant gives the lie to the unity and stability of the symbolic order by which the realm assumes conceptual coherence.[1]

1. During the mid- to late Ming, this theoretical violence to the court's claims to sovereignty was made real in the increasing confusion of trade and piracy (with

The dynastic empire—a radiating network of hierarchical relations coterminous with a bounded territory—is thus placed in tension with an empire of silver, in which all relations are horizontal, transactional, and geographically unbounded. It is the merchant's loyalty to the latter at the expense of the former that underlies much of the anxiety about the traveling merchant in elite discourse. Like his precious silver, the merchant is fluid and leveling, his circulation drawing those around him into differently ordered social relations. The merchant accomplishes this by trafficking not so much in goods as in abstractions—multiplying his capital through speculative hoarding and strategic pricing and compounded interest. The suspicion in orthodox Confucian thinking toward the generation of value out of movement and abstraction is enshrined in the oft-cited division of human activity into an occupational hierarchy of *shi* 士 (scholars), *nong* 農 (farmers), *gong* 工 (artisans), and *shang* 商 (merchants), at the top of which sit the productive cultivators of earth and mind while the "secondary" occupation of parasitic merchants is relegated to the bottom.

This particular imagination of "merchants" and "scholars" as distinct social and moral categories is nowhere more evident than in the *chuanqi* that were crowding the studies and the stages of late imperial Jiangnan. Though the merchant is not a frequent presence in *chuanqi* texts, when he does appear he is often found lurking in the narrative margins, his circulation of literati objects as commodities in the marketplace functioning as a sign of social dysfunction and cultural decay. His parasitic commodification of literati value is expressed not only as a theme but also as a structure—these merchants only appear on stage by leeching onto the stories of the scholar- and statesmen-heroes.

Such a distinction between scholar and merchant is one that *chuanqi* as a genre is uniquely positioned to stage: the imbrication

maritime restrictions turning many Chinese merchants into "Japanese pirates") and the intrusion of merchants acting as extrabureaucratic diplomats into the affairs of foreign regimes. Li, *The Ming Maritime Trade Policy in Transition*, 17, 123–27; Brook, *The Confusions of Pleasure*, 120, 278n87.

of occupation and character finds its analogue in *chuanqi*'s role types, in which the "work" of the drama is divided among the *dan* 旦 (female lead), *sheng* 生 (male lead), *jing* 淨 (character actor or painted face), *mo* 末 (older secondary male), and *chou* 丑 (clown). These categories simultaneously encompass narrative, musical, and moral roles, with social position, moral character, and narrative possibility braided into gesture, costume, and register. A particular role type will identify himself in certain ways and behave in certain ways and move and sing in certain ways—his character and his place in the world inseparable from his body and its movements through the space of the stage.

At the same time, this division of the world into discrete social and dramatic categories was increasingly in tension with the everyday experiences of those living in and around the urban centers of late imperial Jiangnan. Late Ming and early Qing writers frequently observe the fluidity with which those around them move into, out of, and across a range of social positions; their accounts tell us of men from scholar-official families engaging in trade, sons of merchant families attaining positions in the bureaucracy, literati from poor families marrying the daughters of wealthy merchants, and wealthy merchants devoting themselves to literary pursuits, adopting scholarly affectations, and performing the ritual and charitable roles associated with the landed gentry.[2]

Though this lived experience of occupational fluidity and social hybridity is largely effaced from the late imperial stage, a number of the Suzhou playwrights began experimenting with the formal and narrative possibilities of *chuanqi* for decoupling occupation and character. Many of these playwrights drew on contemporaneous vernacular stories—frequently written by acquaintances and collaborators also living around Suzhou—that took the marketplace as their locus and the merchant as their

2. Yü Ying-shih, *Rujia lunli yu shangren jingshen*, 155–212; Xu Min, "Shangye yu shehui bianqian," 135–42; Elman, *A Cultural History of Civil Examinations in Late Imperial China*, 152–53, 246–47, 376; Clunas, *Superfluous Things*, 141–65; Guo, *Ritual Opera and Mercantile Lineage*, 50–36.

hero.[3] In plays that center around the denizens of the marketplace, the Suzhou circle brings to the fore those who were often pointedly excluded from the roles of romantic lead or Confucian exemplar.

This chapter explores the commercial inscription of subjecthood by looking at plays that introduce characters who slip the net of their role type, upending expectations of how a merchant can look or speak or act. The recasting of the merchant as a sympathetic subject appears across late Ming philosophical and literary discourses, but more than just a genre-specific iteration, the plays discussed in this chapter make use of the generic conventions of *chuanqi* drama to deconstruct and open up the nature and meaning of merchanthood. Here the merchant is recuperated not only as a moral subject but as a universal one.[4] At a moment of unprecedented commercial penetration, the merchant becomes a nexus of meaning through which the early modern subject grapples with his own self-conception.

The Same Heart

Though the rhetoric of the four hierarchically ordered occupations continues to hold sway in Neo-Confucian writings throughout the late imperial period, starting in the mid-Ming, the failure of these categories to map onto the complexity of social forms in flux became impossible to ignore. Contemporary observers such as Gui Youguang 歸有光 (1506–51) began taking stock of a new kind of social fluidity: "The four categories of people of ancient times had

3. A number of Suzhou circle plays—such as *Winning the Prize Courtesan*, *Between Man and Beast*, and *The Sound of Reading*—are based on *huaben* from the collections of the Suzhou native Feng Menglong. Other sources for Suzhou plays include the collections of Ling Mengchu, from which *Three Kinds of Happiness* draws both of its narrative strands, and of Li Liweng, as in the Chen Erbai 陳二白 play *The Double Crowning* (*Shuang guan gao* 雙冠誥).

4. Cf. "Every man thus lives by exchanging, or becomes in some measure a merchant, and the society itself grows to be what is properly a commercial society." Smith, *The Wealth of Nations*, 24.

different occupations; when we get to later generations, the literati have become mixed up with the farmers and merchants" 古者四民異業，至於後世而士與農商常相混。[5] Certainly many saw in this mixing the seeds of social disintegration and reacted by jealously guarding status boundaries.[6] Others, however, subjected the occupational category itself to a reconceptualization.

For some thinkers, this took the form of challenging the hierarchies that assign moral and social value to certain kinds of work, as in He Xinyin's 何心隱 (1517–79) provocative assertion that "merchants and traders are superior to farmers and artisans" 商賈大於農工。[7] Others attempted to dismantle this hierarchy entirely by decoupling occupation and character, as in Li Mengyang's 李夢陽 (1473–1529) declaration that "merchants and literati have different expertise but the same heart" 夫商與士，異術而同心。[8] This sentiment is expanded upon in a 1525 epitaph written by the Neo-Confucian philosopher Wang Yangming 王陽明 (1472–1529) for a man who had abandoned scholarly pursuits for a career in trade:

> The four types of people in ancient times had different occupations but traveled the same path of exerting themselves to the utmost. The scholar uses this utmost exertion to cultivate his virtue and bring order to the realm, the farmer uses it to grow crops, the artisan uses it to fashion tools, and the merchant uses it to circulate goods. Each does his occupation according to his own capability, to the best of his power, seeking to exert himself to the utmost.
>
> 古者四民異業而同道，其盡心焉一也。士以修治，農以具養，工以利器，商以通貨，各就其資之所近，力之所及者而業焉，以求盡其心。[9]

5. Xu Min, "Shangye yu shehui bianqian," 138.
6. See Clunas, *Superfluous Things*, 141–65.
7. Xu Min, "Shangye yu shehui bianqian," 138.
8. Li Mengyang, "Minggu Wang Wenxian muzhiming" 明故王文顯墓志銘, quoted in Yü Ying-shih, *Rujia lunli yu shangren jingshen*, 156–57. Wang Xian 王現 (Wenxian 文顯), the subject of this epitaph, was a merchant.
9. Wang Yangming, "Jie'an Fang gong mubiao" 節庵方公墓表, in *Wang Yangming xiansheng quanji*, 10:21b.

This shift in elite discourse is matched in the literature written for merchant consumption; as Richard Lufrano notes in his study on handbooks used by mid-level merchants, traders adapted notions of Confucian self-cultivation in the reconceptualization of their social roles.[10] In the emergence of categories such as *shishang* 士商 (gentry merchant) or *rushang* 儒商 (Confucian merchant) we can see an attempt to name the complexity occurring both within and across occupational categories.[11]

Elite literary production in the late Ming frequently brought to the surface anxieties about this new social terrain, often by casting a class-crossing merchant as a threat to literati-encoded social roles, moral values, and aesthetic signifiers. The *ne plus ultra* of this type is Ximen Qing, the antihero of *Plum in the Golden Vase* (*Jin Ping Mei* 金瓶梅), the sprawling late sixteenth-century epic of the decadence and depravity of the merchant *nouveau riche*. Over its hundred chapters, the novel tracks an economy of extreme accumulation and expenditure, as Ximen Qing's rapacious acquisition of women and goods and political influence—in contravention of social norms, moral qualms, and legal restrictions—leads inexorably to the breakdown of hierarchical relations, the bankrupting of the family coffers, and the extinction of the familial line.

Plum in the Golden Vase's imagination of the merchant as corrupted and corrupting, depleted and depleting—spending his silver and spilling his semen to the point of bankruptcy and death—is iterated across the late Ming and early Qing literary field. The merchant's insatiable consumption across class lines as both a cause of and a proxy for the breakdown of the social order was a familiar formulation in late Ming literature, and from the vantage of the early Qing, the fall of the Ming dynasty seemed to confirm that such chaotic consumption could only end in cultural annihilation.

10. Lufrano, *Honorable Merchants*, 51–67.

11. On the conceptualization of *gudao* 賈道 (the way of the merchant), see Yu, *Rujia lunli yu shangren jingshen*, 155–212, 234–357; Guo, *Ritual Opera and Mercantile Lineage*, 56–74; and Lufrano, *Honorable Merchants*, 51–67.

Against the apocalyptic possibilities proffered by *Plum in the Golden Vase*, a countertradition emerged out of the vernacular story collections that appeared across the seventeenth century. In the collections of late Ming writers and editors such as Feng Menglong and Ling Mengchu 凌濛初 (1580–1644) and in the early Qing innovations of Li Liweng and Aina Jushi 艾衲居士 (ca. 1660s), a diversity of merchant characters appeared. Some of these characters are cast in the same mold as Ximen Qing: governed by self-interest and greed, they use their money to buy other men's wives;[12] trapped in compulsive cycles of accumulation and expenditure, they take too much and spend too much (or, in the case of the profligate's mirror opposite, the miser, too little).[13] Other stories portray the social destabilization wrought by the merchant's long sojourns away from home.[14]

More significant, however, were the many stories in which the merchant functions not as an antagonist but as a protagonist: an everyman whose experience of extraordinary coincidences and improbable fortunes stood in for the wild vicissitudes of late imperial life;[15] a moral exemplar who acted against his immediate financial interest, generously sending the dowry of his unfaithful wife to her new husband or returning a pouch of silver to its rightful owner or buying a dead benefactor's daughter out of bondage.[16]

12. For examples, see "Du Shiniang Sinks Her Jewel Box in Anger" 杜十娘怒沉百寶箱 and "Qiao Yanjie's Concubine Ruins the Family" 喬彥傑一妾破家, both in Feng Menglong, ed., *Jingshi tongyan*, and "Jiang Xingge Reencounters His Pearl-Sewn Shirt" 蔣興哥重會珍珠衫, in Feng Menglong, ed., *Gujin xiaoshuo*.

13. For example, "Du Zichun Thrice Enters Chang'an" 杜子春三入長安, in Feng Menglong, ed., *Xingshi hengyan*.

14. See "Jiang Xingge Reencounters His Pearl-Sewn Shirt," in Feng Menglong, ed., *Gujin xiaoshuo*; and "A Young Wife Gifts Money to a Young Lad" 小婦人金錢贈年少 and "Qiao Yanjie's Concubine Ruins the Family," in Feng Menglong, ed., *Jingshi tongyan*.

15. See "Yang Balao's Extraordinary Encounter in the Kingdom of Yue" 楊八老越國奇逢 in Feng Menglong, ed., *Gujin xiaoshuo*, and "A Chinese Man Changes His Luck in a Chance Encounter with Dongting Tangerines; A Persian Man Reveals the Secrets of a Tortoise Shell" in Ling Mengchu, *Pai'an jingqi*.

16. "Jiang Xingge Reencounters His Pearl-Sewn Shirt"; "Lü Dalang Returns the Money and Recovers His Flesh and Blood" 呂大郎還金完骨肉 and "Magistrate Su's

But even while the merchant is recuperated as the hero of his story, the most radical possibilities of this recuperation remain out of reach: the social slippage between the merchant and the scholar is almost entirely absent. While the reader might be told at the end of a story that the moral and successful merchant protagonist will go on to have sons who pass the exams and ascend the bureaucracy, the merchant himself remains just that. Underlying this skittishness toward the potential merchant-scholar is the sense that merchant hearts are not, after all, the same. Instead, these portrayals often betray an ambivalence toward their subjects, whether by depicting the merchant's crises in conscience or lapses in courage or by countering descriptions of the merchant's high-minded behavior with the narrator's vulgar attention to his body and its baser functions.[17]

These depictions of merchants—be it the anxiety of extinction that pervades *Plum in the Golden Vase* or the assertion of

Gauze Shirt Brings about a Reunion" 蘇知縣羅衫再合, both in Feng Menglong, ed., *Jingshi tongyan*; "Two Magistrates Vie to Arrange the Marriage of an Orphaned Girl" 兩縣令竟義婚孤女, in Feng Menglong, ed., *Xingshi hengyan*. Even the seemingly upstanding merchant often ends up being a bringer of chaos, with long-distance trading appearing as part of larger critiques of the erosion of cultural values that seemed to accompany the merchants' social ascendancy. The threat that a commercial economy—reliant on the frequent travels of many men—poses to the Confucian social order was famously thematized in "Jiang Xingge Reencounters His Pearl-Sewn Shirt," in which a young husband's long-distance trading trip leaves his wife vulnerable to corruption. This conceit was staged not only in the several adaptations of this story, such as Yuan Yuling's 袁于令 (1592–1674) *chuanqi Pearl-Sewn Shirt* (*Zhenzhu shan* 珍珠衫) and Ye Xianzu's 葉憲祖 (1566–1641) *zaju Encountering the Fragrant Shirt* (*Hui xiangshan* 會香衫), but also in more loosely inspired plays such as *The Auspicious Painting* (*Jiqing tu* 吉慶圖), attributed to Zhu Zuochao, in which the merchant paterfamilias's departure sets in motion a ghastly series of events (an affair, a murder, a false accusation, an unjust ruling), creating a social rupture that can be healed only by an upright official putting his only son to death.

17. The moment of moral behavior, both for Merchant Tao in "Magistrate Su's Gauze Shirt Brings about a Reunion" and Lü Yu in "Lü Dalang Returns the Money and Recovers His Flesh and Blood," occurs while urinating. The virtuous merchant girl in "Li Xiuqing Honorably Marries the Chaste Miss Huang" 李秀卿義結黃貞女 (in Feng Menglong, ed., *Gujin xiaoshuo*) proves her lifetime of filial and chaste behavior through a graphic virginity test. That the baser functions and urges of the merchant's body express the impulses and excesses of the market is a central motif in *Plum in the Golden Vase*.

fundamental difference in Feng Menglong's collections—were embodied on the late imperial stage in ways already familiar to readers of late Ming vernacular fiction: as in Feng Menglong's stories, merchant characters inhabited a different moral and narrative space than the scholar- and statesmen-heroes, and in keeping with the polemics of *Plum in the Golden Vase,* their circulation of literati objects as commodities in the marketplace functions as a sign of social dysfunction and cultural decay. For example, the antiques dealer in Kong Shangren's *Little Thunderclap* (*Xiao Hulei* 小忽雷) is portrayed as a duplicitous cheat taking advantage of literati appreciation of antiquities; that a precious lute falls into his hands is a kind of desecration that must be remedied.[18] A similar unease adheres to the character of Innkeeper Wang in Hong Sheng's *Palace of Eternal Life*, whose profit from Yang Guifei's stocking is portrayed as not only parasitic but perverse and socially troubling.

But while the elite stage was frequently the place where the merchant's insidious commodification of literati value could be rehearsed and condemned, it also contained the possibility of a different imagination of identity-in-commerce, one that made use of the grammar of role playing and the conventions of role types to suggest another moral and narrative path. Just as space was being created at the margins of philosophical discourse for a differently ordered relation between labor and the moral self, so were characters on the edges of elite drama given form that treated the slippage between merchant and literatus as a source of moral exemplarity, of humane generosity, of a just and civilizing politics, of enlightenment and transcendence. Rather than a site of loss and parasitic depletion, the merchant is recuperated as fundamentally productive, generating not only profit but also families, communities, and empires.

18. Zeitlin, "The Cultural Biography of a Musical Instrument," 412–13.

The Merchant Recluse

The Suzhou circle was not the first to move a merchant-hero to center stage. Late imperial audiences would have also been familiar with another tradition, emerging out of the stories about the Warring States strategist Fan Li 范蠡, which romanticized rather than demonized the life of the wealthy and itinerant merchant.

Fan Li's exploits are recounted in two chapters in Sima Qian's 司馬遷 *Record of the Historian* (*Shiji* 史記). In "The Hereditary House of King Goujian of Yue" 越王勾踐世家, Sima tells of how Fan Li enlisted the great beauty Xi Shi to help the king of Yue defeat the state of Wu. When the king of Yue began to turn against his former advisors, Fan Li moved to Tao, where he was henceforth known as Lord Zhu of Tao (Tao Zhugong 陶朱公).[19] In "Biographies of the Money Makers" 貨殖列傳, Sima Qian elaborates on what happened to Fan Li after he withdrew from his political career:

> Fan Li then boarded a small skiff and floated around the rivers and lakes of the Yangzi delta. Changing both his surname and his given name, he traveled to Qi and took the name Master Winesack, and then on to Tao, where he was known as Lord Zhu. He noticed that Tao was positioned in the center of the realm, where feudal lords passed through from every direction and all manner of goods were traded. So Fan Li went into the business of stockpiling goods, selling them when the time was right and without making demands on others. Therefore, one who is good at making a living knows how to choose the right men and act at the right time. Over nineteen years, Fan Li accumulated a thousand catties of gold three times and twice gave it all away to poor friends and distant relatives. This is what is known as a rich man who enjoys acting virtuously. In later years when he was old and in declining health, he let his sons and grandsons take over. These sons and grandsons improved and expanded the business, eventually reaching a profit in the tens of thousands. Therefore, when people speak of rich men, they always speak highly of Lord Zhu of Tao.

19. Sima Qian, *Shiji*, j. 41, 5:1740–55.

乃乘扁舟浮於江湖，變名易姓，適齊為鴟夷子皮，之陶為朱公。朱公以為陶天下之中，諸侯四通，貨物所交易也。乃治產積居。與時逐而不責於人。故善治生者，能擇人而任時。十九年之中三致千金，再分散與貧交疏昆弟。此所謂富好行其德者也。後年衰老而聽子孫，子孫修業而息之，遂至巨萬。故言富者皆稱陶朱公。[20]

Here the life of the merchant functions as an alternative reclusion narrative. Like a hermit withdrawing to the mountains, Fan Li floats along the rivers and lakes, mapping his retreat from political affairs with the ever-increasing distance. Commercial activity is rewritten in the hermetic language of self-sufficiency and selfless abnegation (e.g., "not making demands on others" 不責於人) and comes across as a vaguely Daoist practice—like Zhuangzi's Butcher Ding, striking in exactly the right spot, Fan Li sells "at the right time" 與時逐, accumulating (and giving away) vast sums of money with ease.

The story of Fan Li and Xi Shi was frequently mined in late imperial literature, though often in ways that divorced the romance of reclusion from mercantile activities.[21] Indeed, with the rising social prominence (and perceived cultural encroachment) of people engaged in commerce in the late Ming and early Qing, trade was not a way out of the world of politics but increasingly a way in. Arguably the most influential adaptation during this period was Liang Chenyu's 梁辰魚 (ca. 1521–ca. 1594) *Washing Silk* (*Huansha ji* 浣紗記). This play, considered one of the earliest written for *kunqu* performance, recasts the political gambit as a romance, with Fan Li and Xi Shi as the central pair buffeted by circumstance and history. The play ends with Fan Li adopting the name Master Winesack and setting sail with Xi Shi in a fishing boat. With Fan Li and Xi Shi singing of escape and reclusion, the final scene frames the departure of the two lovers as a retreat from the vicissitudes of political life. No mention is made in this scene or elsewhere of Fan Li's second career as Lord Zhu of Tao. Rather, Fan Li's final lines serve as a repudiation of the pursuit of profit:

20. Ibid., j. 129, 10:3257.

21. On the antecedents of the late imperial versions of the Xi Shi legend, see Milburn, "The Silent Beauty."

> [To the northern tune "Clear River Prelude"] The life of man is meeting and parting, to say nothing of flourishing and declining. Wealth and rank are like the passing clouds; the affairs of the world are like child's play. I only wish that the husbands and wives of the world could be like you and me.
>
> 【北清江引】人生聚散皆如此，莫論興和廢。富貴似浮雲，世事如兒戲。唯願普天下做夫妻都是咱共你。[22]

Other late imperial authors write against this romantic tradition. Shan Ben's 單本 (1562–1636) *chuanqi The Banana-Leaf Kerchief* (*Jiaopa ji* 蕉帕記) depicts Xi Shi as a fox spirit who impersonates a young girl in order to procure the semen of her unsuspecting suitor. Another parodic take on the popular love story can be found in "Fan Shaobo Gives Xi Shi a Water Burial" 范少伯水葬西施, the second story in *Idle Talk under the Bean Arbor* (*Doupeng xianhua* 豆棚閒話) by the pseudonymous Aina Jushi. In this retelling, one of the frame narrators launches an attack on the romanticized and heroic story of Fan Li and Xi Shi as told in plays like *Washing Silk*.[23] Citing various nonextant (and possibly fabricated) sources, the old man recounts an alternative narrative, in which the vaunted beauty Xi Shi was just a gussied-up village girl and both Fan Li and Xi Shi are derided for their disloyalty. Most shockingly, this revisionist narrative ends not with the pair sailing off into the misty rivers and lakes, but with Fan Li drowning Xi Shi.[24] While Sima Qian attributes the wealth of Lord

22. *Huansha ji*, 2:80a–b.

23. A young man in the frame narration tells the storyteller, "The other day plays were put on in the village; I saw a performance from *Washing Silk*" 昨日前村中做戲，我看了一本《浣紗記》. Aina Jushi, *Doupeng xianhua*, 2:6b, in *Guben xiaoshuo jicheng*, 102:42.

24. The story of Xi Shi's murder at the hands of Fan Li predates this account. For example, a nonextant "Yuan *chuanqi*" called *Fan Li Drowns Xi Shi* (*Fan Li chen Xi Shi ji* 范蠡沉西施記) is recorded in the Suzhou circle playwright Zhang Dafu's aria manual, and a nonextant *zaju* called *Lord Zhu of Tao Drowns Xi Shi in the Five Lakes* (*Tao Zhugong wuhu chen Xi Shi* 陶朱公五湖沉西施) is attributed to Wu Changling 吳昌齡 (fl. before 1330) in the *Compiled List of Southern Dramas*. Zhang Dafu, *Hanshan tang Xinding jiugong shisan diao nanqupu*, 646; *Chuanqi huikao biaomu, bieben* 別本, j. 21, in *Zhongguo gudian xiqu lunzhu jicheng*, 7:253.

Zhu to his trading acumen, the old man asserts that Fan Li's wealth was in fact stolen from the state of Yue—while Fan Li was an official, he embezzled tremendous riches that remained hidden until he left the country. Only Xi Shi knew the real source of his wealth; worried that the king of Yue would learn the truth and track him down, Fan Li pushes Xi Shi into a watery grave.[25]

While *Idle Talk under the Bean Arbor* deploys Fan Li's greed to deflate the romantic narrative of *Washing Silk*, both of these retellings excise or elide Fan Li's merchant persona. *Washing Silk* ends with a voyage into the mist, with any future mercantile activities remaining unmentioned; *Idle Talk under the Bean Arbor* depicts not a successful merchant who gives away his considerable fortune, but a thieving hoarder. One of the few late imperial depictions of Fan Li as a merchant can be found in Wang Daokun's 汪道昆 (1525–93) one-act *zaju Roaming over Five Lakes* (*Wuhu you* 五湖遊). The play opens after Fan Li, played by the *sheng*, has resigned and he and Xi Shi have begun their new life on the water. While anchored in the middle of the lake, they encounter a fisherman and his wife in a rowboat, with whom they trade wine for fish and folksongs. After they part ways, Fan Li and Xi Shi sing of their departure from worldly affairs and continue their aimless voyage. While the lyrical mysticism of the scene echoes the romanticism of *Washing Silk*—and indeed seems to follow naturally from that play's concluding scene—*Roaming over Five Lakes* almost immediately acknowledges that the man at the center of this scene is a wealthy merchant. The play opens with Fan Li's self-introduction, which includes a brief mention of his newfound riches in language that directly recalls Sima Qian's: "I am Master Winesack . . . In the past I was called Fan Li. I have accumulated a thousand catties of gold three times; now I have taken the name

25. Around the same time as *Idle Talk under the Bean Arbor*, Xu Shiqi 徐石麒 (1578–1645) wrote a *zaju*, *Drowning Xi Shi* (*Fu Xi Shi* 浮西施), that similarly ended with Fan Li "ordering the boatman to throw her into the Yangzi" 教水手抛下江去. Xu Shiqi, *Tan'an Fu Xi Shi zaju*, 5b. In this version, however, Fan Li is not trying to protect his riches, but is concerned that Xi Shi might continue to wreak political havoc if left alive (a similar motivation for leaving with Xi Shi is also mentioned by Fan Li in *Washing Silk*).

Zhu of Tao" 自家鴟夷子是也 . . . 昔稱范蠡，千金三致，今號陶朱.[26] Though Fan Li's mercantile activities warrant no further comment in the scene, the scene itself is structured around a series of trades of clothing and songs for wine—a fantasy enactment of a prelapsarian world of barter-centered sociality.

In *Roaming over Five Lakes,* both of Fan Li's personas are treated as interchangeable. The character is named in the stage directions as Master Winesack, and this is the name he first uses to introduce himself to the audience.[27] At the same time, he tells the audience that he has taken the *hao* of Lord Zhu of Tao, which appears in the full title for the play, *Lord Zhu of Tao Sets His Boat Adrift on the Five Lakes* (*Tao Zhugong wuhu fanzhou* 陶朱公五湖泛舟). Unlike in the *Record of the Historian* version, the name Master Winesack is not temporally separate from Lord Zhu; rather these identities coexist in a quiet acknowledgment of the complexity of late Ming social roles. That Wang Daokun finds Lord Zhu's mercantile success reconcilable with the contemplative, Daoist-inflected persona of Master Winesack is not surprising, as Wang was himself a descendant of Huizhou salt merchants and, in various biographies of local merchants, a defender of their moral possibilities.

It is this imagination of Fan Li to which a number of Suzhou circle plays are indebted—not the least of which the play *Fifteen Strings of Cash*, which names its heroic merchant Tao Fuzhu 陶復朱 (lit. another Zhu of Tao).[28] Unlike his namesake, however, this latter-day Fan Li's exemplarity comes not from reclusion but engagement with the world, and it is to this play we now turn.

26. Wang Daokun, *Wuhu you*, 2:1b.

27. Ibid.

28. The surname Tao was commonly used for merchant characters as a gesture to Fan Li. See, for example, the Feng Menglong story "Magistrate Su's Gauze Shirt Brings about a Reunion," as well as another play attributed to Zhu Suchen, *Moon over the Qin Tower*.

The Merchant Plays the Hero

The eighth scene of *Fifteen Strings of Cash*,[29] attributed to the Suzhou playwright Zhu Suchen, is set on a merchant ship docked near Maple Bridge 楓橋 outside of Suzhou.[30] Before setting off, a group of merchants assemble on the deck of the boat and extol the virtues of Suzhou as a trading center:

> ALL: As we go back and forth to trade our merchandise, we are fortunate to meet in Suzhou. We are truly like flesh and blood kinsmen on the road.
>
> MERCHANT 1, played by the *jing*: That's very true. Our ship is loaded with merchandise from Suzhou; when we go to Henan to sell, we are sure to make at least a 50 percent profit.
>
> MERCHANT 2, played by the *mo*: On that we can rely! Around here the boatmen are all honest folks; as we go forth, we can be at ease.

29. Alternatively titled *Dream of Two Bears* (*Shuang xiong meng* 雙熊夢) after a prophetic dream that plays on the surname of the two brothers at the center of the story. Among the earliest and most complete extant editions is a carefully copied manuscript dated the second month of the seventh year of Shunzhi 順治 (1650). Though this date might be a later emendation, there is evidence that this edition was written prior to the Qianlong era. Lu and Fu, eds., *Shiwu guan xiqu ziliao huibian*, 24. I will be quoting primarily from this edition, which was reproduced in facsimile in the third series of the *Guben xiqu congkan*. Other editions consulted include a complete manuscript from Zhang Yusen's 張玉森 (d. 1929) collection currently held in the National Library of China, a complete manuscript from the Zhang Zidong 張紫東 (1881–1951) family collection held in the China Kunqu Museum, a fourteen-scene fragment collected by Nagasawa Kikuya 長澤規矩也 (1902–80) held in the Sokodo Collection at Tokyo University, and a fourteen-scene fragment and a thirteen-scene fragment collected by Fu Xihua 傅惜華 (1907–70) held in the Traditional Drama Research Institute at the Chinese National Academy of Arts.

30. *Fifteen Strings of Cash* is one of the *chuanqi* attributed to Zhu Suchen in Gao Yi's *New Southern Dramas*; however, as the earliest extant editions of the play are manuscripts on which Zhu's name does not appear, the attribution of particular texts to Zhu should remain tentative. The *Catalogue of Summaries from the Ocean of Song* states that "some have said it was written by You Tong" 或云亦尤侗筆也, though this possibility is generally rejected by scholars. Gao, *Xin chuanqi pin*, *xu* 續 3b. Dong Kang, ed., *Quhai zongmu tiyao*, 2:1530. The play draws primarily on two *huaben*: "A Joke about Fifteen Strings of Cash Leads to Tragedy" 十五貫戲言成巧禍, which appears in Feng Menglong's *Constant Words to Awaken the World*, and Li Liweng's "A Handsome Man Tries to Avoid Doubts and Instead Attracts Suspicion" 美男子避惑反生疑 from his 1656 collection *Silent Operas* (*Wusheng xi* 無聲戲).

眾: 我每往來商販貨物, 僥倖在蘇州相遇, 就是旅邸骨肉了。

淨: 老客長說得是。舟中貨物, 多是蘇州土產。我每載往河南發賣, 少也有五分利息哩。

末: 仰賴仰賴。此間船板主人, 甚是忠厚。我每一路前去, 可也放心。[31]

The poetic romance of the Suzhou waterways is transfigured into a commercial frenzy as they sing of "ten thousand people shrouding Chang Gate like mist, myriad merchant boats ringing Maple River like stars" 金閶, 萬人家煙籠, 楓江, 眾客艖星拱.[32] After celebrating the bounty of Suzhou, the merchants turn to a description of the bounty of an itinerant life:

> MERCHANT 3, played by the *wai*: Scholars, farmers, artisans, and merchants, each carries out a line of work. Although our occupation is the lowest of the four, we freely travel the rivers and lakes, while the others pitifully toil for half of their lives. How can they lead happy lives like we do?
>
> MERCHANT 1: Indeed. To be an artisan means to work for hire from dawn to dusk. To be a farmer means to plow in the spring and till in the summer. Pitifully toiling for half of their lives, how can they lead happy lives like we do?
>
> MERCHANT 3: Forget the mean occupations of the farmers and artisans; even those who are scholars are truly not carefree and unrestrained like we are. Instead, they are often frustrated and only rarely strike it rich.
>
> 外: 列位士農工商, 各執一業。我等雖居四民之末, 每常放浪江湖, 可憐他每半世辛勤, 那得似我每快活。
>
> 淨: 正是。爲工的朝傭暮作, 爲農的春耕夏耘, 可憐半世辛勤, 那得似我每快活。
>
> 外: 不要說農工微業, 就是爲士的, 到底不似我每灑落, 偃蹇的多, 發達的少。[33]

31. Zhu Suchen (attrib.), *Shiwu guan*, 1:31b.
32. Ibid., 1:32a. Jinchang 金閶, translated above as Chang Gate, was used to refer to both the gate itself and the commercial area on either side of it.
33. Ibid., 1:32a–b.

While held in low regard, these men agree that the merchant actually has a much better lot than his social superiors. In a figuration indebted to literary depictions of Fan Li, the merchant here is recast as a Zhuangzian "free and easy wanderer," whose traffic in worldly goods unexpectedly removes him from the worldly cares and constraints that plague scholars, artisans, and farmers. As an example of how the more exalted classes have worse lives, one of the merchants shares a story he just heard on shore of a young student who met with misfortune.

Unbeknownst to them, that student's brother, Xiong Youlan, is working on the ship as a helmsman; upon hearing that his brother is accused of adultery, theft, and murder, Youlan faints.[34] While the other merchants chastise the helmsman for not being careful, the merchant played by the *mo* has the sailors anchor the boat so they can talk with him. Youlan tells them how a student like him ended up on that boat—how poverty forced him to sacrifice his aspirations to support his brother's. But, he sings despairingly, "in vain I threw down the brush to travel to the edges of the earth to learn to steer the helm" 枉了我投筆天涯學舵工.[35] It is all for nothing, he cries, as he tries to throw himself into the water.[36] The *mo* is particularly touched and suggests they take action to help Youlan repay the fifteen strings his brother supposedly stole:

> Friends, to save a man's life brings greater merit than building a seven-story stupa. Although his brother's execution warrant is already drawn up, this wrong can still be made right. If these fifteen strings are not produced in time, the punishment will be hard to endure.

34. A similarly disorienting scene in which a character learns of his family's private matters through its public dramatization appears in the scene "Storytelling at the Temple" 廟書 in *Coins of Heavenly Peace*, which is attributed to Li Yu and was discussed in the previous chapter.

35. Zhu Suchen, *Shiwu guan*, 1:34b.

36. By alluding to the story of the Eastern Han general Ban Chao 班超 (32–102) "throwing down his brush to join the army" 投筆從戎, Youlan equates his decision to work on the merchant boat with the need to take action when the state is in crisis. Here, it is a crisis in the family (often figured as a microcosm of the state) that requires decisive action.

There are a number of us working together on this boat, so if everyone gave one or two strings—however much you wish to donate—we will be able to raise the fifteen strings. Then Youlan can deliver the money to the authorities and perhaps save his brother's life. If he were to petition the court, how could we be sure that there won't come a day when his case is retried? Friends, how about it?

列位, 從來救人一命, 勝造七級浮屠。他令弟大辟雖已擬定, 將來還可申雪。只這寶鈔十五貫, 立限追比, 實難禁受。我每同舟合伙, 卻有數人在此, 每人一貫的、兩貫的, 隨意捐助, 湊足十五貫, 前往交納, 便可留他性命, 此去再行告理, 焉知沒有開招之日。列位, 可使得麼。[37]

While the merchant played by the *wai* applauds this plan ("This is a good thing to do; who wouldn't go along with this?" 這是好事, 誰敢不從),[38] a fourth merchant turns the terms of the conversation from the language of charity to that of commerce:

MERCHANT 4, played by the *chou*: Hold on, we still need to do some calculations. The profit we earn from our capital—these copper coins and pieces of silver—was hard to come by. His brother committed the crime, so why must we be the ones to suffer a loss?

MERCHANT 1: Quite right! Those one or two strings could buy enough oil to last for a year or two.

丑: 且住, 還要算計算計, 我們將本求利, 銅錢銀子, 好不難撰, 他家兄弟犯了事, 我們衆人倒要破起財來。

淨: 不差不差, 有這一貫兩貫, 買些脂油, 吃他一年兩年。[39]

The merchant played by the *mo* is exasperated by the imposition of such a calculus:

Alas, to hear you talk like this, it seems like there isn't a single compassionate feeling left in the world. From ancient times it has

37. Zhu Suchen, *Shiwu guan*, 1:35a–b.
38. Ibid., 1:35b.
39. Ibid.

been said that to see the righteous path but not act is cowardice.[40] I am Tao Fuzhu, originally from Wuxi. At the age of eighteen I left home to become a merchant; now I am fifty-nine. I have been plying my trade on these rivers and lakes for over forty years. Where have I docked and not spent a few taels of silver? Since all of you fellow merchants are unwilling to help, forget it! Elder brother Xiong, I will help you by myself!

咳，如此說，難道天地間再沒有個慈悲之念了。自古見義不爲，是無勇也。在下叫做陶復朱，原是無錫人氏。十八歲出外爲商，今年五十九歲，在江湖上走過四十多年。那一處馬頭上，不費幾兩銀子。既衆客商不願協助，罷。熊大哥，我就獨力捐助你去。[41]

Unlike those main characters who introduce themselves at the beginning of their first scene, often with a reflective aria and a prose monologue that signal their narrative import, Tao Fuzhu only introduces himself here, toward the end of the scene. Fuzhu's disclosure of identity—of both his moral character and his narrative importance—is unexpected, almost contingent, a figure on the margins momentarily drawn into the center. Before this moment, he was but one of a group of merchants (who themselves remain nameless); it is by acting in a noble, morally righteous way that he differentiates himself from the group and "earns" a name.

This righteous act begets a far braver one. After Fuzhu gives him the fifteen strings, Youlan sets off to try to free his brother, but Fuzhu later learns that his gift was used to implicate Youlan in an unrelated crime. At once Fuzhu decides that he will tell the prefect, singing, "If his poor bones are unjustly buried, then in vain is the boldness of my chivalrous heart" 若將他窮骨冤埋，枉卻我俠腸雄壯.[42] Such an intervention into a murder investigation is not without risks, especially for an uneducated merchant who could easily become a scapegoat. Fuzhu, however, has no patience

40. A reference to the *Analects* (*Lunyu* 論語) 2.24: "To see the righteous path but to not act is cowardice" 見義不為，無勇也. *Shisan jing zhushu*, 23:29.

41. Zhu Suchen, *Shiwu guan*, 1:35b–36a.

42. Ibid., 2:28a.

for caution: "How could I abandon my good heart? When jumping into a well to save someone, what does it matter that you might also drown?" 我怎肯良心喪，拚做救人從井，同溺何妨.[43]

The prefect is impressed with Fuzhu's sense of justice in coming forward and remarks with astonishment on his gift of the fifteen strings: "Can it really be that you were this generous for the sake of righteousness?" 難道你這樣疏財仗義. The irony that the one who gives away his money so freely is a career merchant is not lost on any of the characters. As Fuzhu's fellow merchants note, "For an old merchant to have this sense of righteousness is rare indeed" 老客長這般仗義，也是難得的哩.[44]

As with the late Ming valorization of sentiment (*qing* 情), the righteousness (*yi* 義) that is celebrated here is spontaneous and intuitive, embodied most fully by those who have been excluded from elite intellectual life.[45] In this way Fuzhu recalls the other figures on the social and narrative margins valorized throughout the early Qing plays of the Suzhou circle who demonstrate moral exemplarity in moments of crisis: servants who are willing to sacrifice their lives for their masters; commoners who die valiantly for the imperial house.[46]

However, Fuzhu acts not out of personal loyalty but out of a broader commitment to a concept of justice like the knights-errant (*xia* 俠) with whom he identifies. For a merchant to take on the role of a self-abnegating knight-errant presents a seeming contradiction, as the latter's complete disregard of personal interest appears at odds with the merchant's desire to multiply his

43. Ibid., 2:28b. A reference to *Mencius* (*Mengzi* 孟子) 2A6, in which the distress one would feel upon seeing a child falling into a well is evidence of the fundamental goodness of human nature. *Shisan jing zhushu*, 25:112.

44. Zhu Suchen, *Shiwu guan*, 1:37a.

45. This way of imagining the socially marginal as a site of moral and aesthetic possibility has roots in the teachings of Wang Yangming and his followers, notably Wang Gen 王艮 (1483–1541) and He Xinyin 何心隱 (1517–79).

46. For a discussion of this topos in Suzhou plays, see Li Mei, *Ming Qing zhiji Suzhou zuojia qun yanjiu*, 142–94. On the moral elevation of marginal characters in early Qing drama (especially in the work of Suzhou circle playwrights), see Goldman, *Opera and the City*, 145–74; Sibau, "Maids, Fishermen, and Storytellers"; and Liu Chiung-yun, "Huanguan, xiaji, he nüyi."

capital. But in the late imperial imagination the knight-errant and the merchant are fellow travelers of the *jianghu* 江湖 (rivers and lakes) on which Fan Li famously set sail. The *jianghu* conjures not a specific space but a liminal world, inhabited by an ever-shifting community of rebels, dropouts, vigilantes, and hucksters, that operates outside of both state institutions and the normative moral order.[47]

Several Suzhou circle plays make explicit reference to a kind of fellowship between knights-errant and merchants. Both *The Amber Lute* (*Hupo chi* 琥珀匙), attributed to Ye Shizhang, and *The Diamond Phoenix* (*Jingang feng* 金剛鳳), attributed to Zhang Dafu, feature outlaw heroes who champion chivalric codes of honor that forbid the robbing of merchants.[48] In *Returning in Brocade* (*Jinyi gui* 錦衣歸), attributed to Zhu Suchen, a brigandess who commands a Liangshan-like mountain stronghold articulates a reason for this prohibition:

> To be a merchant you must ford rivers and climb mountains, suffering great hardship; many risk their lives for silver. How could they be considered the same as corrupt officials? From now on, when you encounter a merchant you may only inspect his goods and levy a tax, and you may not seize his goods by force.
>
> 那為商的，涉水扳山，擔辛受苦，多將性命換銀，豈是貪污一例。今後遇有此等商人，只許驗貨抽分，不得恃強過取。[49]

In a reversal of the discourse of the merchant as parasitic, the merchant is here placed on the side of the suffering righteous against the extractive greed of those officials who are the targets of

47. From its earliest mention, the *jianghu* is a place of coming and going, of anonymous roaming: "When the springs dry up and the fish are left stranded on the ground, they spew each other with moisture and wet each other down with spit—but it would be much better if they could forget each other in the rivers and lakes" 泉涸，魚相與處於陸，相呴以濕，相濡以沫，不如相忘於江湖. Watson, *Chuang Tzu*, 76; *Zhuangzi jishi*, 1:242.

48. These examples are cited in Li Mei, *Ming Qing zhiji Suzhou zuojia qun yanjiu*, 97.

49. Zhu Suchen (attrib.), *Jinyi gui*, 1:11a. Reading 艮 as 銀.

the brigandess's activities.[50] But beyond the paternalism that directs the knight-errant's protection of weaker, marginal others, here the knight-errant and the merchant are brought into a symbiotic economy: the merchant's "tax" contribution to the knight-errant supports the latter's struggle against the corrupt and exploitative officials who imperil them both.

In these depictions, the knight-errant and the merchant remain distinct figures whose social positions and interests happen to coincide. Indeed, while the knight-errant, as historical phenomenon and literary trope, came from and circulated among a range of social backgrounds, and the merchant shared his itinerancy and disengagement from (or potentially antagonistic relationship with) the political realm, nevertheless, stories of knights-errant who were also merchants are rare.[51] Within the medieval classical tale tradition from which the late imperial archetype emerges, knights-errant from explicitly merchant backgrounds are generally women, like the eponymous heroines of "Jing the Thirteenth" 荊十三娘, "The Story of Xie Xiao'e" 謝小娥傳, and "The Merchant's Wife" 賈人妻.[52] In these stories, the protagonist's adjacency to the market at once anticipates and authorizes her potentially transgressive movement into and out of spaces and roles an elite woman would not dare occupy. At the same time, neither Xie Xiao'e nor the merchant's wife (who is herself a merchant) are engaged in any sort of commercial activity once they come to inhabit the role of knight-errant, and while Jing the Thirteenth is introduced as a "female merchant" 女商, the nature of her occupation remains obscure.

As for male knights-errant, their association with the market often remains implicit; though not merchants themselves, they can often be found in and around the marketplace, like the hero

50. This dynamic, in which the merchant is figured as productive against the parasitic official class, will be discussed further in relation to another play attributed to Zhu Suchen, *Cornucopia*, in chapter 4.

51. On the varied social origins of historical knights-errant, see Wang Yonghao, *Zhongguo youxia shilun*, 18–28. On literary depictions of female knights-errant, see Altenburger, *The Sword or the Needle*.

52. Li Fang, comp., *Taiping guangji*, 196:1472, 491:4030–32, 196:1471–72.

of "The Curly-Bearded Stranger" 虯髯客傳.[53] The story "The Kunlun Slave" 昆侖奴 offers a reversal of the stories in which a female merchant abandons her occupation to become a wandering avenger—here a knight-errant is found, years later, selling medicine in the marketplace.[54] The slave's mysterious career turn iterates the trope of reclusion in the marketplace that can be traced to stories about Fan Li and frequently appears in late medieval literature: for example, in "Zhao Xu" 趙旭, a man falls in love with a female immortal who leaves him with texts and tools to help him attain immortality. Years later he is spotted selling goods in the marketplace, his body smaller than before but his visage just as handsome; none of his contemporaries recognize him.[55] The contradictory appearance of the powerful immortal or *neidan* 内丹 (inner alchemy) adept, in need of neither money nor goods yet exchanging both in the marketplace, evokes the medieval imagination of the Chang'an markets as the nexus of separate worlds: the Chinese and the foreign, the human and the nonhuman.

The knight-errant who is not just a merchant but whose knight-errantness and merchantness are interrelated and mutually constituting are largely absent from the medieval and late imperial page, but appear in several guises in two other plays attributed to Suzhou circle playwrights. In *The Auspicious Painting* (*Jiqing tu* 吉慶圖), traditionally associated with Zhu Suchen's brother Zhu Zuochao,[56] the character Li Zhen, played by the *jing*, is described

53. Ibid., 193:1445–48.

54. Ibid., 194:1452–54.

55. Ibid, 65:404–6.

56. While a play by this title is attributed to Zhu Zuochao in *New Southern Dramas*, it is unclear if the thirty-two-act performance-oriented script (with *gongche* 工尺 musical notation) that appears in the third series of the *Guben xiqu congkan* has any relation to Zhu's play. Another play with this title but an entirely different plot is summarized in the *Ocean of Song*. This version (which is not attributed to Zhu but is located in the same volume as other Suzhou circle plays) survives in two scenes anthologized in *Coat of Patched Fur*. Which version should be associated with Zhu Zuochao has been subject to debate. In some respects, the subject matter of the *Guben xiqu congkan* version echoes other plays attributed to Zhu Zuochao, such as the attention to historical personages at the moment of dynastic crisis or transition.

However, the play's more conservative ethos, especially its deeply critical treat-as a *haojie* 豪傑 (heroic man of outstanding talent) with a strong *yiqi* 義氣 (sense of righteousness) and introduces himself thus: "The brawniest of all, my skills with spear and dagger outstanding. It is only because the world is disordered at present that I didn't want to seek an official position. Instead I live in this village and work as a martial arts instructor" 膂力超群，鎗刀出眾，只因世事紛紛，不願求官，寄身於此，做個拳棒教師。[57] But what is supporting Li Zhen's rather large household—which includes his wife, his concubine, his daughter, a number of servants, a large compound, and a pumpkin patch perfect for burying a dead body—is not a *gongfu* academy but a long-distance trading operation.

Li Yu's *Register of the Pure and Loyal*, meanwhile, features a motley crew of laborers, tradesmen, and merchants who swear allegiance to one another and the cause of justice. In this retelling of the 1626 citywide uprising against the eunuch Wei Zhongxian 魏忠賢 (1568–1627) and his proxy agents, the five soon-to-be martyrs describe themselves as "knights-errant from Suzhou, heroes of the Wu marketplace" 姑蘇任俠，吳市英豪，[58] at once

ment of the villain's *fengliu* 風流 (romantic) nature, diverges from other Suzhou circle plays; though the Suzhou circle is often positioned as the conservative counterpart to the radical ethics of *qing* embraced by Tang Xianzu and his successors, their plays usually treat the *qing*-addled romantic as hapless (like the protagonist of *Three Kinds of Happiness*) and not as an unredeemable danger to the social fabric as here. As the extant script is dated 1819, such a divergence need not point to a different original author but could be attributed to a later rewriting during the Neo-Confucian retrenchment of the high Qing. The many scenes of fighting could also reflect a rewriting to accommodate high Qing tastes. Though this play has received very little attention, scholars tentatively treat the *Guben xiqu congkan* version as the one with potential links to Zhu Zuochao's authorship. See Kang Baocheng, "Zhu Zuochao, Ye Shizhang pingzhuan," 88; Li Mei, *Ming Qing zhiji Suzhou zuojia qun yanjiu*, 246; Guo Yingde, *Ming Qing chuanqi zonglu*, 1:684.

57. Zhu Zuochao (attrib.), *Jiqing tu*, 1:5a. Cf. Robert Hegel on the distinction between knights-errant and *haojie* in *Forgotten Tales of the Sui* (*Sui shi yiwen* 隋史遺文). Hegel, *The Novel in Seventeenth-Century China*, 130.

58. Li Yu, *Qingzhong pu*, 2:50a. The earliest extant edition of *Register of the Pure and Loyal* was published as *The Southern Drama "Register of the Pure and Loyal" Compiled by the Master of the Hut of the Bamboo Hat* 一笠菴彙編清忠譜傳奇, with Bi Wei, Ye Shizhang, and Zhu Suchen listed as coeditors 同編, and Wu Weiye contributing the preface. This edition, which is reproduced in the third series of the *Guben xiqu congkan*, was published during the Shunzhi period; Guo Yingde argues based on Wu Weiye's records of his travels to Suzhou that the play was written before 1659. Guo Yingde, *Ming Qing chuanqi zonglu*, 1:547.

subsuming their various occupational identities of sedan puller, wholesaler, and shopkeeper into the shared identity of "the people of Suzhou" 蘇州人.[59] Here the imagination of the city 城市 of Suzhou is centered not around the walls 城 but the market 市. The Suzhou marketplace becomes the *jianghu*, a space outside of orthodox values or elite culture, a place of gambling, of rowdy performances, of fights and sworn brotherhoods and riots.

The merchant-knight's distance from literati identity is made physical on stage by role types like the *jing* or *mo*, whose dress, vocal timbre, carriage, and use of dialectal language immediately codes them as not-*sheng*.[60] Often the merchant-knight himself brings this distance to the surface, explaining to the audience how his own self-conception is formed in contradistinction to (and often in repudiation of) orthodox values and elite culture; for example, "I, Yan Peiwei, have been unconventional my whole life and brash and bold for half my life. I do not read poetry or the classics in order to guard my innate genuine nature. I only know the broad outlines of ritual propriety and detest the elite learning of the pedant" 俺顏佩韋。一生落拓，半世粗豪。不讀詩書，自守著孩提真性。略知禮義，偏厭那學究斯文.[61]

But within these *chuanqi*, the heroism of the merchant-knight is contingent on his alignment with, and self-subordination to, the elite. Li Zhen of *The Auspicious Painting* is neighbors with the early Ming general Lan Yu 藍玉 (d. 1393), with whom he has "a shared sense of justice" 義氣相投.[62] Though friends, they

59. Ibid., 1:49a, 67b. Elsewhere characters self-identify as "the common people of Suzhou" 蘇州百姓 1:80a, 2:60a. Throughout the play there appear varying modes of articulating a new identity that was coming into focus: by place ("people of Wu" 吳民), number ("ten thousand people" 萬民, "masses of people" 黎民), non-elite status ("the [common] people" 人民, "little people" 小民), and shared emotional state ("people outraged over a public injustice" 公憤民).

60. This role is usually played by the *jing* (*The Auspicious Painting*'s Li Zhen, *Register of the Pure and Loyal*'s Yan Peiwei) or *mo* (*Fifteen Strings of Cash*'s Tao Fuzhu, *Register of the Pure and Loyal*'s Yang Nianru).

61. Li Yu, *Qingzhong pu*, 1:64a. This distance is given a comedic treatment in the introduction of the *xia*-like Fisherman Wu of *The Joy of Fisherfolk*, who is so outside Confucian learning that he hears "collected explications of the Six Classics" 六經講集 as "six catties of river anchovies" 六斤江鰣. Zhu Zuochao (attrib.), *Yujia le*, 8b.

62. Zhu Zuochao, *Jiqing tu*, 1:4b.

are not social equals; by the end of the play, Li Zhen marries his virtuous and heroic daughter to Lan Yu as a concubine. The five heroes of *Register of the Pure and Loyal* rise up against the persecution of the official Zhou Shunchang 周順昌 (1584–1626), who remains outside of their circle of sworn brotherhood—their social distance instantiated in the play by their physical remoteness on stage, with the five only twice sharing the same scene with the man for whom they give up their lives.[63] When they all meet as ghosts, the five immediately recognize Zhou Shunchang (who fails to recognize them), surrounding him and bowing down on the ground; Zhou returns this obeisance with a more slight bow with his hands clasped and then helps the men up.

Tao Fuzhu of *Fifteen Strings of Cash* similarly recognizes and defers to the student Youlan as his social better, calling the much younger man in his employ *dage* 大哥 (elder brother). He tells Youlan that the fifteen strings he gives him are not merely buying Youlan's brother out of torture, but buying Youlan back into his proper class: "Please take these strings, go to the county seat, and turn them in. You need no longer be vexed with this lowly occupation of helmsman" 你可收下，前往縣中交納。這當梢賤業，也不好再煩了.[64] In these moments, the social threat posed by the merchant-knight is defused; their distance from (and in some cases, hostility to) elite culture does not imperil normative hierarchies but rather renders them the ultimate guardians of the social order—the self-appointed protectors of the few "good" elites who are not themselves compromised by the aesthetic indulgences, moral laxity, and careerist maneuvering that had perverted late imperial literati culture and threatened effective governance and social harmony. The end of these merchant-knights' self-sacrifice is a purification of the elite that restores all to their proper place.

Like Tao Fuzhu, the knightliness of the five merchant-knights of *Register of the Pure and Loyal* is expressed by their willingness

63. The five meet Zhou Shunchang in scene 11 during the uprising and then again as ghosts in scene 20.

64. Zhu Suchen, *Shiwu guan*, 1:36a.

to give everything away, from their livelihood to their lives: "Unconventional and uninhibited, we put little value on our lives and love righteousness" 落拓不羈，輕生好義.[65] It is this radical giving away that allows for the merchant-knight to shed any resemblance to the miserly, hoarding merchant and join the ranks of those whose heroism comes from a rejection of their economic interests that verges on the self-destructive: the fisherfolk of *The Joy of Fisherfolk* (*Yujia le* 漁家樂), who give away the earnings on their fish, the beggar of *The Ingot Go-Between* (*Yuanbao mei* 元寶媒), who gives away all of his handouts.[66]

But rather than washing away the stink of merchanthood, these acts of self-abnegating sacrifice are shown to be not in conflict with the merchant ethos but emerging from it. In *Register of the Pure and Loyal*, the market is a locus of camaraderie, a site of politics, and ultimately a self-referential venue of performance—simultaneously the setting for the uprising and a potential site for the staging of the play itself.[67] *Fifteen Strings of Cash* similarly recuperates the market as a site of sociality and generosity, resolving the seeming contradiction of the heroic merchant by showing how Fuzhu's exceptional righteousness actually springs from his identity as a merchant.[68]

As demonstrated by Fuzhu's attempt to rally his fellow merchants to Youlan's aid, the late imperial imagination of justice was itself a form of economic thinking. In his speech, Fuzhu cites the common formulation that equates the meritorious acts of

65. Li Yu, *Qingzhong pu*, 2:50a.

66. In *The Joy of Fisherfolk*, a family selling their fish in the marketplace meet a poor student who has been forced by poverty to sell his books; they give him all they have earned and later risk their lives for him. *The Ingot Go-Between* (preface 1681), by the Songjiang playwright Zhou Zhilian 周稚廉 (1662–1701) and which is based on the Li Liweng *huaben* "A Beggar Does Charitable Deeds; An Emperor Acts as Go-Between" 乞兒行好事，皇帝做媒人, features a famous beggar who refuses to beg from the same person twice and uses his earnings to help those in need.

67. The second scene depicts a storytelling performance in front of King Li Temple 李王廟 and describes similar performances in front of Xuanmiao Temple 玄妙觀. Both would have been sites of worship, performance, and commerce.

68. Cf. *Analects* 4.16: "The gentleman understands what is right; the petty man understands what is profitable" 君子喻於義，小人喻於利. *Shisan jing zhushu*, 23:56.

saving a life and building a stupa, gesturing toward the kind of calculative and transactional logic that underpinned popular understandings of cosmic justice or karma. The karmic economy operates abstractly, almost mechanistically, through the balancing of surplus and debt; the merit that one saves through good acts in order to buy one's way out of bad ones functions as a form of currency—the accumulation and spending of which were often recorded in ledgers of merit and demerit (*gongguo ge* 功過格) whose formal resemblance to merchant account books is not coincidental.[69]

Just as late imperial conceptions of justice are internal, not external, to the logic of the marketplace, the kind of generosity and fellowship that Fuzhu offers is not conceptually foreign to the merchant ethos, but rather is fundamental to it. That merchants are capable of such spontaneous and intuitive moral behavior is anticipated in the eighth scene by the *wai*, who describes the life of the merchant as "unrestrained and carefree" 灑落. And while the gift of the strings functions as an extraordinary rupture that sets Fuzhu apart from the other, nameless merchants, the foundations of an economy rooted in sentiment were also established in that earlier scene. The merchants describe their contingent and ad hoc community as a brotherhood, "flesh and bone kinsmen on the road" 旅邸骨肉, and make clear that their very ability to profit hinges on their creation of "trustworthy" 忠厚 networks.[70]

The intimacy and sociability that emerges out of the merchant community is contrasted throughout the play with the increasingly toxic households in which the four leads are trapped, in which every family relation is monetized and instrumentalized, in which every family member is a potential commodity to be sold: in addition to Youlan selling his labor to support the education of

69. See Brokaw, *Ledgers of Merit and Demerit*. In the late imperial period, karma was the fabric of both moral and narrative universes. Karma provides the structure of the *huaben* on which this play is based—the debt that must be repaid, the action that has a reaction. The role of karma in structuring early vernacular short fiction has been much discussed. See, for example, Kao, "Bao and Baoying," 115–38.

70. Zhu Suchen, *Shiwu guan*, 1:31b.

his brother Youhui, Youhui's future love interest, played by the *xiaodan*, is bought as a child bride, and Youlan's future love interest, played by the *dan*, runs away when her stepfather threatens to sell her off. As the domicile becomes the site of ever more insidious commercialization, the commercial realm and the relationships forged therein become familiar and familial—the place where the possibilities of a noneconomic calculus are kept alive.

Prior to Tao Fuzhu's entrance, both money and men are stuck: younger brother Youhui is languishing in jail, accused of stealing a neighbor's fifteen strings of cash that a rat had dragged into its nest, while elder brother Youlan is grinding away on the merchant ship, his hopes for an official career moribund. Tao Fuzhu's gift of fifteen strings undoes these blockages, freeing up cash, people, and the plot to flow. Fuzhu, an invention of the play, here functions as a structural device that links the narrative threads of the two different stories that serve as source material, allowing one story to intersect with another: Youlan, on his journey home to repay his brother's supposed theft, encounters the *dan*, and they are likewise swept up in false accusations of robbery and murder. With all four leads stuck in jail, Fuzhu intervenes a second time, vouching for Youlan's innocence and leading to their exoneration (and, consequently, their marriages and careers). By introducing the joy of circulation, allowing for the creation of new stories and, by the end of the play, new families, the traveling merchant is positioned as the generative force at the very center of social relations.

The Hero Plays the Merchant

The character of Tao Fuzhu does not appear in the two *huaben* on which *Fifteen Strings of Cash* is based, though Zhu Suchen might have been drawing from another *huaben* from Feng Menglong's collection *Comprehensive Words to Warn the World* (*Jingshi tongyan* 警世通言). In "Magistrate Su's Gauze Shirt

Brings about a Reunion" 蘇知縣羅衫再合, a Merchant Tao 客人陶公 fishes a wronged magistrate out of the water and offers him safe haven in his home village. This Merchant Tao, however, demonstrates none of Tao Fuzhu's unwavering moral certitude. While the Tao of *Fifteen Strings of Cash* seeks out the prefect without a second thought, this Tao frets over the magistrate's powerful enemies and urges the magistrate not to pursue justice. As discussed above, this sort of twinned occupational and moral segregation is typical of the vernacular stories in Feng's collections, in which any sympathetic treatment of the merchant character invariably runs into its limits. The Tao Fuzhu of *Fifteen Strings of Cash*, conversely, is characterized by his boundlessness—as a source of escalating gifts that can never be repaid, as an example of bravery that can be exhausted only by death, and as an embodiment of the porousness and multiplicity of late imperial identity.

The crossing that the play enables—in which a merchant can also be a knight-errant—is not confined to the merchant on the margins. Rather, in a departure from the source material, *Fifteen Strings of Cash* writes these slippages into every major character: by the end of the play, the two brothers have passed the civil service examinations, and the one-time boatman Youlan is married to an orphan from a formerly illustrious family whose stepfather peddles meat, while his younger brother weds the former live-in daughter-in-law of a traveling merchant turned shop owner. Tao Fuzhu might be the only career merchant, but the trajectories of these four leads reveal that there is neither person nor place untouched by commerce.

The new universality of commercial experience is thematized across the plays of the Suzhou circle in what appears as the mirror image of the merchant who reveals himself to be a hero: a hero who reveals himself to be a merchant. In a number of these plays, what had been a career merchant in the *huaben* source material is transformed into someone with a more complex and class-crossing occupational history. A young man of limited means with a string of business ventures under his belt becomes in *Three Kinds of*

Happiness an examination failure with no prior business experience; a beggar who has sought a living on a merchant ship becomes in *The Sound of Reading* a student on his way to the civil service examinations. Other plays give the merchant-hero a redeeming pedigree, as in *Cornucopia*, in which a legendary businessman turns out to be the scion of a literati-loyalist household. These transformations are largely required by generic convention—if a lead is to be played by the *sheng*, then something in his past must account for his fine diction and noble mien. But this limitation of the conventional *chuanqi* form also opens up new possibilities for imagining merchanthood not as a static identity but as a state of being that one invariably passes into and out of. Nowhere is this clearer than in Li Yu's late Ming play *Winning the Prize Courtesan*.[71]

This play is based on the *huaben* "The Oil Peddler Wins the Prize Courtesan" 賣油郎獨占花魁 from Feng Menglong's 1627 collection *Constant Words to Awaken the World* (*Xingshi hengyan* 醒世恆言), and the contours of the narrative remain unchanged: Qin Zhong and Shen Yaoqin are both refugees from Kaifeng who flee south after the Jin defeat of the Northern Song. Qin Zhong takes up oil peddling and falls in love with Yaoqin, who was sold to a brothel by her villainous neighbor Bu Qiao and quickly becomes the most sought-after courtesan in Hangzhou. After Qin Zhong rescues Yaoqin from a particularly cruel patron, Yaoqin buys herself out of bondage and marries Zhong. The happy ending is complete when the young couple is reunited with family members from whom they had become separated in the chaos of war.

In the *huaben*, the two romantic leads are both commoners. Qin Zhong's father Qin Liang sells him to the proprietor of an oil shop and then joins a monastery; Yaoqin's parents owned a grain shop and eventually come to work in Qin Zhong's oil shop. The play, however, gives the erstwhile peddler and courtesan far more

71. The earliest extant edition of *Winning the Prize Courtesan* is an illustrated edition published as *The Southern Drama "Winning the Prize Courtesan" Newly Composed by the Master of the Hut of the Bamboo Hat* 一笠菴新編占花魁傳奇 during the Chongzhen period (1627–44); this version is reproduced in the third series of the *Guben xiqu congkan*.

elevated lineages. Qin Liang is made a high-ranking Song military official, a commander general 統制官 charged with defending the Jingmen Garrison 荊門鎮. At the end of the first scene, Qin Liang rushes off to help defend the throne from the Jin attack on the capital. When he appears in Hangzhou at the end of the play, he has been given the highest military commission by the emperor.[72] Yaoqin's deceased father was also a high-ranking official, and her uncle/guardian is a eunuch in the imperial household.[73]

In the *huaben*, Qin Zhong is raised as an apprentice in the oil shop; when other shop workers conspire against him, he decides to take up oil peddling. Eventually Qin Zhong returns to the shop, restoring the business to profitability and taking over when his adoptive father dies. The play, however, casts Qin Zhong's entry into the oil business as necessity, rather than vocation, after he flees Kaifeng alone. While staying at the inn in Hangzhou in order to seek out information about his missing father, Qin Zhong finds himself quickly running out of money. With only three taels left, his options for an occupation are limited; as the innkeeper says, "With a large capital investment, you can undertake a large venture, and with a small investment you can undertake a small venture" 大本大做, 小本小做. It turns out that the innkeeper used to work as an oil peddler and offers to tutor Qin Zhong on the particulars of that appropriately small trade.

Qin Zhong is not the only character in *Winning the Prize Courtesan* who must negotiate an unfamiliar commercial landscape. Shen Yaoqin is sold into a West Lake brothel, whose economics—the costs to buy a girl, train a girl, rent a girl, and sell a girl—dominate much of the play. Though Yaoqin is at first resistant to playing the part of compliant courtesan, she soon settles on a long-term business plan of sorts to sock away money until an

72. As Guo Yingde has pointed out, Qin Liang's long sojourn over the course of the play—kidnapped by enemy forces, a daring escape, and an unexpected attack—borrows from the heroic exploits of Hong Hao 洪皓 (1088–1155) as recounted in *juan* 373 of the *History of the Song* (*Song shi* 宋史).

73. That the play rewrites Yaoqin's uncle as a palace eunuch 太監 who is not a villain is an interesting choice considering the politics of the late Ming (and anti-eunuch Suzhou circle plays such as *Register of the Pure and Loyal*).

opportunity to marry out of the profession presents itself. Surrounding these two leads is an entire city of people trying to make a buck—madams and gazetteer vendors and tea sellers.

In the eleventh scene we see how all these individual hustlers are interwoven into larger regional economies that constitute the new commercial landscape. Earlier in the play, Shen Yangqiao, a servant of Yaoqin's family who is married to Yaoqin's maid Su Cui'er, becomes separated from his wife and the young mistress in his charge as they flee south after the invasion of Kaifeng. He decides to make his way from Yangzhou to Hangzhou in order to seek out news about their whereabouts. En route he passes through Shengzezhen 盛澤鎮, a market town south of Suzhou that was a center of silk production—or rather, it would be in the mid- to late Ming; its appearance here is anachronistic for the twelfth-century setting.[74] There we meet a silk broker whose brokerage sells the finished product from all of the hundreds of local weaving households (*jihu* 機戶). Recently, traveling merchants from all over have come to pick up the merchandise and their arrival has brought into being lively ad hoc economies of leisure, with itinerant performers (including a trafficked Cui'er) and a charm-selling Daoist master competing for the merchants' silver.[75]

In this scene we get a sense of what is fueling the smaller economies at play in the story—how the silver from the textile trade is used to pay entertainers like Yaoqin and Cui'er, which is then used to pay small vendors like Qin Zhong. The silk economy reappears in the seventeenth scene, in which the recently tonsured Bu Qiao plots to have an affair with Cui'er. To get her husband out of the way, Bu Qiao ropes him into a business venture in which silk is

74. Household textile production was not introduced to this region until the Hongxi and Xuande reigns, and Shengzezhen did not become a center of production until the mid-sixteenth century. Shih, *Chinese Rural Society in Transition*, 113. Shengzezhen was well known for silk manufacturing in the late Ming and is described at length in the *huaben* "Shi Runze Encounters a Friend at Tanque" 施潤澤灘闕遇友 in Feng Menglong, ed., *Xingshi hengyan*. For the town's location, see map 1.

75. During the late Ming, the merchants would lodge at the brokerages; this changed with the establishment of *huiguan* 會館 (native-place lodges) in the early Qing.

purchased in Huzhou 湖州 and then sold for a multifold profit in Suzhou. If the earlier scene portrayed the silk industry as a formal system of *jihu* and established brokerages and long-distance traders and hundreds if not thousands of taels exchanging hands, here it is a small-time affair undertaken by a monk and a tea shop proprietor operating on the margins with only a few dozen taels of capital at a time.

If, as Tina Lu has pointed out in her discussion of a later Li Yu play, *chuanqi* provide a map of the empire, here we have a map of an alternative empire structured not by political boundaries but by commercial networks that traces the local (Qin Zhong's daily route from shop to shop within Hangzhou), the regional (Yangqiao's several-day journey of one hundred miles from his tea shop in the scenic Jiulisong 九里松 area by West Lake to Huzhou to Suzhou), and the transregional (the long-distance traders who "travel ten thousand *li* entrusted with their master's thousand taels" 主因信實千金托, 客為公平萬里來).[76] Set during a moment of literal dislocation between the fall of the Northern Song capital of Kaifeng and the establishment of the Southern Song capital in Hangzhou, when the actual site of political power cannot be located and claims to the throne are multiple and multiplying, the play suggests a new emplacement and a new directionality: against the bodies fleeing south, we have silk moving from the south outward. Whereas a map of a polity delimits firm boundaries, this map of a commercial empire has no such limits; instead it radiates endlessly outward from the new center of Suzhou and its environs.[77]

As in *Fifteen Strings of Cash*, all commercial exchanges in *Winning the Prize Courtesan* are ultimately governed by karma, and it is through this moral economy that a broken society is reconstituted. When Yangqiao discovers that his wife Cui'er had been sold as a singing girl, he indignantly demands her return; but her buyers are not eager to part with their hundred-tael

76. Tina Lu, *Accidental Incest, Filial Cannibalism, and Other Peculiar Encounters*, 1–21; Li Yu, *Zhan huakui*, 1:40a.

77. There is no mention of Suzhou and its environs and industry in the source material. It is not unexpected that Li Yu would shift the center of gravity away from Hangzhou and back to Suzhou and its industries.

investment. Appropriately, it is the silk broker who deftly negotiates between these competing claims on Cui'er as a person and as a commodity: "As she is your legal wife, it is only right that she should return with you. But she said that they were not the ones to abduct her, so it is only right for you to give them some money for their trouble" 既是令政，自然歸於足下。但令政原說不是他拐的，自然要處些財禮與他.[78] But Yangqiao has run through his travel funds and has no money with which to pay them. So like Tao Fuzhu, the broker quickly offers a gift: "I'll help you out with these few taels of silver" 些少銀兩，老夫助些便了.[79] As in *Fifteen Strings of Cash*, when the world of officials and their mismanagement tears families apart, it is the merchant who with his money redeems the social whole, repurchasing families back into being.

The broker brokers a solution that preserves commercial and communal integrity, making sure that everyone is made whole. In so doing he echoes the major drama of the play, in which the romantic courtship of Qin Zhong and Yaoqin is accomplished through the mechanisms of commercial transaction. When the poor peddler learns that a night with the celebrated courtesan costs ten taels, he does some calculations: "If starting now I save three *fen* [0.03 taels] from each day's profits, I will only need one year to reach my goal" 我自明日為始，逐日將本錢扣出，積趲三分，只消一年，事便成了.[80] While this seems like an extravagant expenditure for one living hand to mouth—the brothel maid tells him that his total payment of twelve taels (ten for the courtesan fee plus two for the madam) is enough to buy her out of servitude—it turns out to be a wise investment.

On the night of Qin Zhong's scheduled visit, Yaoqin returns late from another appointment. Highly inebriated, she collapses on her bed. Qin Zhong attentively waits on her, offering her his sleeve when she needs to vomit, serving her tea, and watching over her

78. Li Yu, *Zhan huakui*, 1:42a.

79. Ibid.

80. Ibid., 1:51a. This language is taken almost verbatim from the *huaben* source materials.

while she sleeps. The next morning, Yaoqin recalls his kindness and is deeply moved. Realizing that he spent all of his savings and did not even get what he paid for, Yaoqin is aghast: "You operate a business; why not use your savings to support your family?" 你做經紀的人, 積些銀兩, 何不留下養家.[81] Qin Zhong explains that he is single, but Yaoqin insists on giving him twenty taels of silver "as capital [for your business]" 為資本.[82] Against the transactional payment of silver for sex, in which the act of exchanging money dissolves the bonds between buyer and seller, love is figured as a capital investment that intertwines the two in increasing bonds of attachment and obligation, with the payment of twelve 十二 taels mirrored and enlarged by the twenty 二十.

In the *huaben*, these twenty taels do indeed serve as capital—Qin Zhong returns to his adopted father's shop and invests Yaoqin's money into the enterprise, turning a failing business into a profitable one. This success allows him to hire an employee, who ends up being Yaoqin's father. After Yaoqin buys herself out of the brothel, she brings with her three thousand taels worth of valuables, which they use "to slowly buy up property and enlarge the family's holdings" 慢慢的買房置產, 整頓家當. They put her father in charge of the oil shop, and "in less than a year, their business earnings were such that they were living in luxury" 不上一年, 把家業掙得花錦般相似.[83] Thanks to these savvy investments, a peddler of limited means becomes the proprietor of a profitable shop and finally the wealthy owner of a thriving family enterprise. The happy ending here is not so much a transformation as an elaboration: the principal characters go from struggling merchants to rich merchants.

The play *Winning the Prize Courtesan*, however, not only gives our heroes more elevated beginnings but also ends with their complete liberation from the cycle of buying and selling. As in the *huaben*, Yaoqin redeems her indenture, bringing to her new marital home trunks filled with "a Lord Zhu of Tao hoard from

81. Ibid., 2:26b. As above, the language here is mostly taken from the *huaben*.
82. Ibid., 2:27a.
83. Feng Menglong, ed., *Xingshi hengyan*, 24:185.

the boudoir" 閫內陶朱蓄 (plate 4).[84] But this money is not reinvested anywhere. The play ends not with the grand family reunion, which occurs in the penultimate act. Rather, in that last scene, Qin Zhong and Yaoqin are reunited with their proper stations, as the emperor enfeoffs them back into the elite:[85] Zhong is given the position of supervisor of the Dongxiao Temple 洞霄宮提舉 and Yaoqin is made commandery mistress of Lin'an [Hangzhou] 臨安郡君.[86] In his comfortable sinecure at the Daoist temple—historically given to retired officials of great stature—Qin Zhong is thus removed not only from the toil of commerce, but all toil.

With the enfeoffment of Qin Zhong and Yaoqin, the emperor formalizes a transformation that has been taking place over the course of the story, in which a group of refugees from Kaifeng become residents of Hangzhou. In their trading of oil and tea

84. Li Yu, *Zhan huakui*, 2:47a.

85. Once their titles are conferred, Qin Zhong and his wife change their clothes to reflect their elevation in station. This return to their roles as the children proper to their parents and the subjects proper to their emperor is demanded by the *chuanqi* convention that conjoins moral and social possibility and arcs toward reunion and return. However, in the performance tradition, where complete productions of entire plays were very rare, this return almost never happens. The *Coat of Patched Fur* anthologizes six scenes: "Advising the Courtesan" 勸粧, in which Yaoqin learns about her new profession; "The Tavern" 酒樓, in which Qin Zhong spies on Yaoqin from the upper floor of a tavern; and a grouping of four scenes ("Seeds of Love" 種情, "Performing Plays" 串戲, "Snowy Embankment" 雪塘, "Winning the Courtesan" 獨占) that depict Qin Zhong's first brothel visit, Yaoqin's distressing excursion with an abusive client on West Lake, her subsequent rescue by Qin Zhong, and their return to the brothel where they spend the night together (what appears as one scene in the full play is broken up into two scenes here: "Performing Plays" and "Snowy Embankment" are both from scene 23). The first two scenes are of the comic kind with ample clowning frequently found in the *Coat of Patched Fur* anthology. The four-scene group, meanwhile, works as a unified minicycle—with unrequited devotion in the first scene recompensed in the last, with violent disruption resolved in a romantic union. These scenes continue to be the most popular ones to this day, with "The Tavern" and "Seeds of Love" (frequently titled "Receiving the Vomit" 受吐) remaining in the repertoires of *kunqu* companies. Though the scene "Winning the Courtesan" preserves descriptions of their elite parentage, it is primarily as buyers and sellers of bodies and oil that Qin Zhong and Yaoqin occupy a place in the *kunqu* canon. Qian Decang, *Huibian jiaozhu Zhuibai qiu* , 2:282–87, 5:2144–64, 2484–90.

86. Dongxiao is located to the southwest of Hangzhou. Lowell Skar, "Dongxiao gong," in Pregadio, *The Encyclopedia of Taoism*, 374–75. On these ranks, see Hucker, *A Dictionary of Official Titles in Imperial China*, 494, 201.

and songs and sex, Qin Zhong, Yaoqin, Cui'er, and Yangqiao have re-formed fractured bonds of kinship and become woven into the fabric of the city. The emperor, in attaching the name of Hangzhou and its environs forever to their given names, has made Qin Zhong and Yaoqin properly "of" Hangzhou. At the same time, the emperor effectively blunts the most radical possibility of an identity constructed around the city, preventing them from becoming townspeople by making them aristocrats. What had appeared to be a commercial space is reinscribed by the emperor as an imperial one; Hangzhou becomes the site of a temple for imperial rites, a commandery needing defending, a new capital.

But this imperator ex machina presents a fantasy of exiting commerce that is predicated on the entrance into it: it is through buying and selling that Qin Zhong and Yaoqin go from strangers to lovers, from outsiders to insiders, from refugees of Kaifeng to protectors of Hangzhou. They are only able to escape from a life of buying and selling because they are so good at it—unlike Bu Qiao, who squanders his windfall early in the play, Qin Zhong and Yaoqin both prove to be savvy merchants of love, saving and spending at exactly the right time: Qin Zhong scrimping to invest all his savings on a night of intimacy, Yaoqin socking money away to buy herself into a marriage of her choosing. It is by inhabiting the role of merchant—with all of its social and geographic and moral fluidities—that they are able to become something else.

Reading the Riot Act

After the fall of the Ming, Li Yu would return to the transformative possibilities of the subject positions formed in the marketplace, though this time he would no longer be compelled to repudiate the merchantness of the hero or the marketness of the city by folding them back into the hierarchies and bureaucratic structures of the state.

In the early Qing, Li Yu and his collaborators turned away from the *huaben* sources on which his late Ming plays like *Winning the Prize Courtesan* were often based, instead mining recent local histories of unrest, upheaval, and dislocation. These urgent and often violent plays, such as *Reunion over Ten-Thousand Li* (*Wanli yuan* 萬里圓), *Slaughter of the Thousand Loyalists* (*Qianzhong lu* 千忠戮), and *Two of Beard and Brow* (*Liang xumei* 兩鬚眉), depicted both the terrifying destruction and the liberatory potential of a new order. With the collapse of certain self-defining modes of being in the world (e.g., "Ming subject"), other ways of envisioning the self became a matter of existential import, and in plays like *Register of the Pure and Loyal*, Li Yu repeatedly returns to the city of Suzhou as the locus of a differently oriented identity. But it is in a nonextant play attributed to Li Yu that the political possibilities of such an identity would have been fully realized.

Though no copies of *Peace for the Ten Thousand People* (*Wan min an* 萬民安) survive, an extensive summary is preserved in the *Catalogue of Summaries from the Ocean of Song*.[87] According to this summary, the play recounts the lead up to and aftermath of the riots that embroiled Suzhou early in the summer of 1601.[88] In

87. According to the *Catalogue of Summaries from the Ocean of Song*, *Peace for the Ten Thousand People* was "written by someone from late Ming Suzhou, but his identity is unknown" 明季蘇州人作，不知誰筆. Dong Kang, ed., *Quhai zongmu tiyao*, 1:603; *Chuanqi huikao*, 2:35b. This is not unusual, as *Ocean of Song* fails to identify Li Yu, Zhu Suchen, Zhang Dafu, and other Suzhou circle playwrights as the authors of many of the plays commonly attributed to them in seventeenth- and eighteenth-century sources. Deng Changfeng argues that this proves that the authors of the early to mid-Qing source texts for *Ocean of Song* had not read *New Southern Dramas* and were not from the Suzhou area. See Deng Changfeng, "*Chuanqi huikao* tanwei," 237, 240. On the various editions of the *Chuanqi huikao*, see Jiang Jurong and Urabe Yoriko, "*Chuanqi huikao* jiqi xiangguan xiqu kaoshi shumu." According to Jiang and Urabe, this summary of *Peace for the Ten Thousand People* was also included in the newly discovered editions of the *Chuanqi huikao* held in Japanese collections.

88. Version of this event were retold in a variety of seventeenth-century sources, including the Chongzhen-era *Wu County Gazetteer* (*Wuxian zhi* 吳縣志), the accounts of local literati like Wen Bing 文秉 (1609–1669), and Sun Pei's 孫珮 (fl. ca. 1686) records of the imperial factories in Suzhou. Niu and Wang, *Wuxian zhi*, j. 11; Wen, *Dingling zhulüe*, j. 5; Sun, *Suzhou zhizaoju zhi*, j. 12.

this telling, the official Huang Jianjie is sent by the court to Suzhou to oversee taxation.[89] Huang Jianjie, along with his retinue and hangers-on, sets up checkpoints at each of the city gates and levies taxes on all goods: peddlers are assessed a tax rate of 10 percent, shopkeepers a rate of 20 percent, and workshops a rate of 30 percent. Unable to maintain profitability, the textile firms that dotted the eastern side of the city are forced to shut down production.[90] Meanwhile, the fees extracted on the myriad goods coming into and going out of the city's gates cause the price of goods within the city to skyrocket.[91] Unable to make a living, a mass of weavers and spinners, whose industry is generally concentrated on the east side of the city, and peddlers and shopkeepers, who generally do commerce around the western gates, meet in Xuanmiao Temple 玄妙觀 in the heart of Suzhou to plan a citywide strike. Among them is Ge Cheng 葛成, a silk worker employed by a textile firm who figures prominently in most firsthand accounts of the events of 1601.

The effect of these taxes is great—thousands of taels of silver seized, thousands of Suzhou residents left without any source of income. But it is not fury at the massive scale of this injustice that turns the strike into a riot. Rather, it is something very small and human-sized that causes the eruption of violence. Man Lali, a young peddler who is mentioned in other sources but is here alone given a name, is transporting melons into the city when a group of Huang's lackeys confiscate his wares. The smallness of this haul (according to an account attributed to Chen Jiru 陳繼儒 [1558–1639], the peddler boy is taxed a few melons and a liter of rice) makes the boy's reaction all the more pitiful: he bursts into tears.[92] And the city erupts. Ge Cheng leads the crowd to the taxation office, where they find one of Huang Jianjie's henchman; while Ge Cheng wishes to make an example of the henchman by

89. The central role of palace eunuch Sun Long 孫隆 is omitted in this telling.

90. According to the *Veritable Records of the Ming* (*Ming shilu* 明實錄), "a levy of three mace on every loom" 每機一張稅銀三錢 provoked the factory strike. *Da Ming Shenzong Xian huangdi shilu*, 361:5b, in *Ming shilu*, 112:6742.

91. Niu and Wang, *Wuxian zhi*, 11:40a; Shen Shixing, *Cixian tang ji*, 40:11a–b.

92. Suzhou lishi bowuguan et al., *Ming-Qing Suzhou gongshangye beike ji*, 383.

sending him to Huang in a cangue, the crowd strips the man and throws him in the river. Then they set Huang's office on fire, beat Huang to death, and throw him into the fire.[93]

Despite this shocking violence, the plot summary makes clear that the play does not treat the uprising as a chaotic free-for-all but as an organized, quasi-militaristic attack: "Ge Cheng brandished his banana leaf fan and the ten thousand people all assembled together" 成以蕉扇一揮，萬衆俱集.[94] We are told that the people of the city will later refer to him as General Ge. Like a good general, Ge Cheng repeatedly discourages wanton theft and murder, even if he is unable to fully contain the fury of the crowd when confronted with the corrupt tax officials. The rioters are thus figured as a kind of army, but unlike their nearest referents—imperial troops and bandits—they serve neither the court nor their own id. In their refusal to reclaim the funds expropriated by the tax officials, they distance themselves from marauding bandits and poorly behaved soldiers alike. This refusal to pillage speaks to their larger purpose: unlike bandits, it is not money they seek but the restoration of their livelihoods; unlike imperial troops, they are defending not a polity but an economy.

Like *Register of the Pure and Loyal*, *Peace for the Ten Thousand People* depicts a confederation of Suzhou residents, and when all of those who make their living in the markets of Suzhou rise up against the agents of the state, the mass that they form incarnates the interconnectedness and interdependence of an urban ecosystem of traders and brokers and shopkeepers and peddlers and money changers and innkeepers and day laborers and factory workers and healers and entertainers. The subsumption of individual interests in the sublime will of the crowd as it riots against vicious eunuchs and corrupt tax collectors produces something more—an identity of, not just within, the market.

93. The townspeople converge on the houses of the tax collectors, who were dragged into the city streets and beaten to death as their houses were burned to the ground. According to accounts, the eunuch Sun Long escaped to Hangzhou. Sun Pei, *Suzhou zhizaoju zhi*, 12:1a–2b.

94. Dong Kang, ed., *Quhai zongmu tiyao*, 1:605.

This identity of the market excludes the elite—much as *Register of the Pure and Loyal* puts much narrative and stage space between the heroes of the marketplace and the wronged literatus with whom they are allied, in *Peace for the Ten Thousand People* none of the local magistrates or celebrated literati who are sympathetic to the rioters and later come to Ge Cheng's defense are themselves swept up in the seething violence.[95] Rather they participate in ways proper to their station: through the writing of reports and affidavits and memorials and commemorations. In both of these plays, the depiction of local elite participation undermines any reading of the uprisings (a reading that in modern scholarship is often extended to the Suzhou circle plays themselves) as generating a new category of "urbanite" that seamlessly subsumes elite and commoner interests.[96] Indeed, that the local elites of *Peace for the Ten Thousand People* use the moniker Ge the Worthy 葛賢 and not Ge the General speaks to this continuing cleavage. The rioters see Ge Cheng as leading them into battle in defense of the market, and it is as a general that they commemorate him a decade later with a living shrine on the Xuanmiao Temple market grounds. For the local elites, however, Ge Cheng is celebrated not for leading people into battle but for resolving it—for attempting to constrain the fury of the crowd and for later claiming responsibility on their behalf. Through the language of Confucian ethics, Ge Cheng is made into an object of slightly removed respect rather than a subject of authority.

But in one key sense the relationship of the elite to the demands of those in and of the market is reversed in these two plays. *Register of the Pure and Loyal*'s portrayal of the 1626 upris-

95. A military commander is sent in to pacify the eastern part of the city and ferret out the party responsible for inciting the riot. Ge Cheng claims responsibility for the incident, earning the admiration of local officials and scholars. Although the county and prefectural magistrates along with the celebrated literatus Zhang Xianyi 張獻翼 and various students and licentiates plead for leniency, the military defense commissioner sentences Ge to death; this sentence is later commuted to imprisonment.

96. For a critique of the common formulation that pits urbanites against the autocratic state, see Von Glahn, "Municipal Reform and Urban Social Conflict in Late Ming Jiangnan," 300.

ing effaces the way in which those rioting shopkeepers and workers may have been acting in defense of their own interests by overthrowing the oppressive tax regime implemented by Wei Zhongxian.[97] Instead, these individual concerns are subsumed by a shared moral outrage at the persecution of the Donglin faction. While *Register of the Pure and Loyal* depicts the townspeople rioting in support of the political interests of the local elite, *Peace for the Ten Thousand People* shows the local elite rallying behind the economic interests of the townspeople. In *Peace for the Ten Thousand People*, the market is no longer the *jianghu*, the margin that delimits and ultimately protects the center; rather, it becomes the center that needs to hold. The denizens of the marketplace become the subjects through which injustice is focalized, as it is the brutality enacted on the small-time peddler and the laborer—not the renowned literatus—that elicits identification and empathy and action from the audience stand-ins.

It is in this focalization, by which figures of the market are repeatedly positioned as sites of self-identification for those on stage and off, that *Peace for the Ten Thousand People* points toward a more expansive urban culture in which these various interests might productively align. Like many Suzhou circle plays, *Peace for the Ten Thousand People* thematizes the affective power of spectatorship, as when the sight of the peddler boy "wailing on the road" 號哭於路 enrages the people of the marketplace, causing them to take to the streets. The audience's double identification, with the suffering of the boy and with the anger of the crowd that identifies with the suffering of the boy, is part of the larger metatheatrical architecture of the play. Much like the city of Suzhou itself, the play is centered around Xuanmiao Temple, where the various merchants and shopkeepers and wage laborers gathered and

97. Santangelo, "Urban Society in Late Imperial Suzhou," 104. Li Mei criticizes the participants of the 1601 uprising as "not going beyond the scope of protecting their own interests" 沒有超出維護自身利益的範圍 and praises the "feeling of social responsibility" 社會責任感 of the townspeople involved in the 1626 uprising who are motivated by a "sense of integrity" 正直態度 (even though she notes that obviously they had a personal interest in eradicating Wei Zhongxian). Li Mei, *Ming Qing zhiji Suzhou zuojia qun yanjiu*, 107–9.

emerged as an army of *min* 民, a mass of common people with intersecting economic interests. According to the summary in the *Catalogue of Summaries from the Ocean of Song*, "Since they could no longer support themselves, all of the common people of the city agreed to stop the market [by going on strike]. They assembled in Yuanmiao Temple;[98] the sound of their cries shook the heavens" 俱不聊生，滿城百姓，相約罷市，齊集元妙觀中，呼聲震天。[99] One imagines it was not just heaven that their cries shook. While no performance of the play was recorded, if the attribution to Li Yu is correct, it can be assumed that the play was intended for performance.[100] For an audience in Suzhou to feel the vibration of those cries—perhaps in the very same place where those cries were originally cried, since theatrical entertainments were held on Xuanmiao Temple grounds—is an instantiation of the immediacy of theater, in which the past is experienced as the present.[101] But unlike those plays (including many by Li Yu himself) that depict the heroics of Yue Fei or the perfidy of Zhu Di in present tense and with an eye toward current events, in this play the characters on stage would be telling the story of the audience itself.

An audience in Suzhou would have been primed to have such a moment of self-recognition. Seventeenth-century drama made frequent use of the metatheatrical, and the Suzhou circle's plays are particularly rife with plays (and storytelling) within plays.[102]

98. During the Kangxi era in which the base text for this summary (and, possibly, the play itself) was written, Xuanmiao was renamed Yuanmiao to avoid the taboo word *xuan*, which was part of the Kangxi emperor's given name.

99. Dong Kang, ed., *Quhai zongmu tiyao*, 1:605.

100. As noted in the introduction, many of the extant scripts attributed to the Suzhou circle bear markers of performance, and contemporaries discussed attending their plays and the popularity of these performances. Based on the scenes anthologized in *Coat of Patched Fur*, some of the most popular scenes on the eighteenth-century stage depicted the kind of violence and mass uprising that might have been found in *Peace for the Ten Thousand People*, like the "Storytelling Ruckus" 書鬧 scene from *Register of the Pure and Loyal*.

101. Dramatic performances were frequently held in the Xuanmiao Temple. Xu, *The Chinese City in Space and Time*, 183–90, 299n82. On temples as sites of performance more generally, see Liao Ben, *Zhongguo gudai juchang shi*, 111–30.

102. For a discussion of this trope in the plays of the Suzhou circle, see Li Mei, *Ming Qing zhiji Suzhou zuojia qun yanjiu*, 216–32.

Just as Youlan in *Fifteen Strings of Cash*, hearing the narration of his brother's fate, is struck with the sudden realization that the story being told is his own—that he is not just audience but also actor—the Suzhou spectators watch a performance of their own civic identity coming into being whose very watching restages the production of such an identity: both on stage and off, a cacophony of interests are momentarily subsumed into a single subject position (rioter, spectator) centered in the Suzhou market.[103] Any boundary between (historical) actor and audience dissolves in this moment of empathetic self-recognition in which the audience becomes the riot, "crying out and stamping their feet in an outpouring that threatened to literally bring down the house" 嘄呼跳蹴, 洶洶崩屋, and the actors playing spectators-turned-rioters themselves become spectators of the audience's riotousness.[104]

If *Fifteen Strings of Cash* shows mercantile identities to be a moral subject position, able to buy back into existence the world as it should be, and *Winning the Prize Courtesan* casts mercantile identities as a universal subject position that all will come to occupy and through which all will intersect, then *Peace for the Ten Thousand People* suggests that the mercantile is not only moral and universal but also potentially sublime, overcoming existing subjectivities in the production of a new identity—"the [common] people of Suzhou" 蘇州人民—that reaches across memory and history, diegetic and extratheatrical spaces, to lay claim to the entire city.

103. A similar moment occurs in *Coins of Heavenly Peace*. Wei Gu, who has returned to the human world after visiting his sister in the immortal realm, finds that many years have passed; it is through the performance of a storyteller that he learns about what happened to his family.

104. From Zhang Dai's 張岱 (1597–1684?) description of a performance of his *Record of Ice Mountain* (*Bingshan ji* 冰山記), which narrates the same events as *Register of the Pure and Loyal*. Zhang Dai, *Tao'an mengyi*, 124. This passage is further discussed in Keulemans, "Onstage Rumor, Offstage Voices," 186.

Coda: Playing Peddlers and Peddling Plays

A contemporary of the Suzhou circle playwrights, the scholar-poet Bao Bingde 包秉德 (1607–52), took stock of late Ming Jiangnan and, in a pithy line that segues abruptly from Smithian economic philosophy to Shakespearean metatheater, declared: "All of human nature is that of merchants; affairs of the world are like a play" 人情皆商賈，世事如戲劇.[105] Or to put it another way, all the world's a stage and all the men and women merely merchants.

The notion that the self is mercantile and its experiences theatrical is intended by Bao as an indictment and is followed by an illustrative reference to the Warring States negotiator Su Qin 蘇秦. When Su Qin returns from a failed mission, impoverished and in his threadbare cloak, his family refuses to even look at him. As recounted in the *Strategies of the Warring States* (*Zhanguo ce* 戰國策), he laments, "My wife does not regard me as her husband, my elder sister-in-law does not regard me as her brother-in-law, my parents do not regard me as their son" 妻不以我為夫，嫂不以我為叔，父母不以我為子.[106] Later Su Qin attains a position of prestige and notices that these same relatives now treat him with respect, which his sister-in-law tells him is thanks to his newly acquired riches. "Alas!" Su Qin sighs, "If one is poor, one's parents do not regard one as a son" 貧窮則父母不子. When read alongside Bao Bingde's earlier pronouncement, this story not only exposes the self-serving impulse that treats kinship as profit-seeking enterprises but also shows how one's socially emplotted identity is an interconnected series of roles that can be donned or shed like a tattered cloak.

Playwrights associated with the Suzhou circle such as Zhu Suchen and Li Yu share Bao Bingde's attention to the ways in which mercantile and theatrical modes mutually constitute the

105. Bao Qizhen, "Ni da" 擬答, *Bao Yinhe shiji*, j. 1, in *Taiwan zhencang shanben congkan, Gu chaoben mingdai shiwen ji*, 5:261–62. Bao had another given name, Qizhen 啓禎; his courtesy name was Yinhe 飲和.

106. *Zhanguo ce zhushi*, 1:75.

human experience, but without the moral baggage that freights Bao's provocation. To imagine the self as a merchant on stage is not to imply, as Bao does, that there is a better mode of being in the world, purged of self-interest and pretense and reconstituted around the recognition of something more real and true. Rather, the convergence of the mercantile and the theatrical opens up new possibilities for the self in the world.

The work of these playwrights frequently foregrounds the deep structural links between the theater and the market by thematizing the economics of entertainment and the theatricality of commerce. This double movement, where the theatrical world is shown to be a market and the market a kind of theater, reoccurs throughout the play *The Appearance of the Star of Literature* (*Wenxing xian* 文星現), attributed to Zhu Suchen.[107] In the seventh act, a blind *chantefable* 說唱 performer sets up in front of Suzhou's North Temple 北寺.[108] He tells a few jokes while collecting money from the gathering crowd and then launches into the main attraction: a rich description of the history of the temple, the various structures and treasures to be encountered inside, and the bustling marketplace that assembles on its grounds. Among the well-known copyists and fortune tellers and concocters of medicinal prescriptions that he names is one "Liu Longquan peddling play scripts" 劉龍泉販賣這商詞戲文.[109]

If here theatrical experience—as both performance and text—is shown in situ as a commercial transaction, a few scenes later, a

107. This play, which draws on stories about the celebrated Suzhou literary and artistic circle of Zhu Yunming 祝允明 (1461–1527), Tang Yin 唐寅 (1470–1524), Wen Zhengming 文徵明 (1470–1559), and Shen Zhou 沈周 (1427–1509), survives in a Qing-era manuscript preserved in the fifth series of the *Guben xiqu congkan*. While the manuscript cannot be precisely dated, it contains an added foreword dated to 1871. Attribution based on Gao Yi, *Xin chuanqi pin*, 273.

108. North Temple, also called Bao'en Temple 報恩寺, is located in the northern part of the walled city between the Qi and Chang Gates (see map 2). A storytelling performance in a temple marketplace is also central to the play *Register of the Pure and Loyal*: in the scene "Storytelling Ruckus," a performance of the story of Yue Fei riles up and unites the five heroes

109. Zhu Suchen (attrib.), *Wenxing xian*, on the verso of the seventeenth page of the unpaginated manuscript.

commercial transaction unfolds as a multivalent theatrical experience. In the tenth scene, the secondary lead, the famous mid-Ming literatus Zhu Yunming 祝允明 (1461–1527), disguises himself as a hawthorn peddler in order to approach a young woman with whom he has fallen in love. The framing of this scene is explicitly metatheatrical, with Zhu Yunming talking of "renting the peddler's costume" 與他賃下這付行頭 and "learning some hawthorn jingles" 習熱了這幾句查梨賦 in order to "play this role" 扮此脚色.[110] It is also built around a theatrical in-joke, with the entire scene an intertextual reference to the Yuan *zaju The Hundred Flowers Pavilion* (*Baihua ting* 百花亭); not only does the scene borrow its overall conceit from the earlier play (in which a character impersonates a hawthorn peddler to get close to the object of his affection), but also the various jingles Zhu Yunming recites that comically oversell the properties of his wares are taken largely verbatim.

In *The Appearance of the Star of Literature* as in *The Hundred Flowers Pavilion*, the shtick turns on the similarities of vendor and actor, who both use well-turned phrases and catchy tunes to convince the buyer-audience that what is not so is actually so. Of course, these similarities are less a coincidence than a surfacing of the historical interpenetration of peddling and playing. As Stephen West has pointed out for earlier *zaju*, the sonic traces of food vending can be found in the names of *qupai* 曲牌 (tune titles) like "Fresh Hawthorn" 生查子, "Foreign Grapes" 番葡萄, "Steamed Bun Song" 包子令, and, as in the eighth scene of *The Appearance of the Star of Literature*, "Selling Good Wine" 沽美酒.[111]

Through this performance of vending as pretending, formal resonances between merchant and actor become legible.[112] Both

110. The play is structured around a series of disguises: Zhu Yunming and Tang Yin had earlier disguised themselves as beggars; Tang Yin for much of the play pretends to be a servant; a conman tries to pass himself off as first a Daoist priest and then Tang Yin; Zhu Yunming will later himself impersonate a Daoist priest. This scene, however, is the only one that highlights its similarity to theatrical role play with its explicit references to costuming and memorizing lines.

111. West, "Playing with Food," 90–91.

112. On the function of vendor calls in nineteenth-century performance texts

temporarily play a role not written by them, a role that can and will be played by others. There is something fundamentally generic about making a sale or selling a line, in which the particularities of one's life and history are momentarily submerged in the generic constraints of the interaction—in which the rules of performance and commercial exchange allow for only some limited improvisation. It is this similarity that Marx points to in his likening of commerce to the donning of a character mask, in which inhabiting an economic role ("buyer," "seller") is a mode of self-alienation analogous to that experienced by the actor playing his part.[113] What exactly the performer is performing does not constitute himself in a concrete way—a buyer today plays the role of the seller tomorrow, just as an actor may play an official and a farmer in different scenes. Rather it is the act of performing "on the economic stage" within and across a shared set of scripts and the kind of community formed thereof that becomes constitutive of subjectivity.

If the fluidity of social roles comes into being through commercial society, it comes into self-awareness through drama. Unlike a market exchange, drama allows the audience to experience their commercial embeddedness simultaneously as contemplation (of the character-actors who articulate their social condition back to themselves) and immediacy (through the commercial transactions that constitute theatergoing). Indeed, the heightened metatheatricality of these onstage performances of selling, in which an actor

---

"both to evoke and to discipline the attractions of the marketplace," see Keulemans, *Sounds Rising from the Paper*, 124–44.

113. "As we proceed to develop our investigation, we shall find, in general, that the characters who appear on the economic stage are merely personifications of economic relations; it is as the bearers of these economic relations that they come into contact with each other." Marx, *Capital*, 1:179.

"As the conscious bearer [Träger] of this movement, the possessor of money becomes a capitalist. His person, or rather his pocket, is the point from which the money starts, and to which it returns. The objective content of the circulation we have been discussing—the valorization of value—is his subjective purpose, and it is only in so far as the appropriation of ever more wealth in the abstract is the sole driving force behind his operations that he functions as a capitalist, i.e. as capital personified and endowed with consciousness and a will." Ibid., 1:254.

acts as if he were acting, explicitly extends Bao Bingde's dictum to all participants in the theatrical experience. From the characters who take up buying and selling to the actors who sell their performance of buying and selling to the audience-customers who purchase the experience of imaginatively inhabiting the world as focalized through the eyes of someone buying and selling, in this world generated around the stage, all relate to one another as merchants.

Such a moment is produced in another play by Zhu Suchen in which the commercial situatedness of its own performance is brought to the surface. The early Qing drama *Moon over the Qin Tower* is a fictionalized retelling of a recent courtesan romance, possibly commissioned by the literatus paramour.[114] The *chou* plays the comic supporting role of the friend of the literatus hero, a benignly dissolute hustler whose name "Old Tao" 老陶 conjures Fan Li's *nom de commerce*. In the eighteenth scene, Old Tao excitedly tells the audience about a new venture:

> Recently I've been short on cash. But luckily in Suzhou there are a few gentlemen who write new plays, and they said to me, "Old Tao, you don't seem to have much work these days. We each have here two new plays, and we heard that all across Zhejiang people are emulating Suzhou in their love for new plays. Take them and sell them for some silver that you can use. On your way back just pick up for each of us a bolt of plain weave silk fabric and a catty of silk floss. Think of this as our way of helping to support you."
>
> 我老陶近日手中乾癟，虧了蘇州有幾位編新戲的相公說道：老陶，你近日無聊。我每各人有兩本簇新好戲在此，聞得浙江一路，也學蘇

114. As discussed in the introduction, this is one of the few Suzhou circle plays that survive in a contemporaneous print edition with the full complement of paratext. This print edition, which is reproduced in the third series of the *Guben xiqu congkan*, was prepared in the late 1670s, probably ca. 1677, when a poetry gathering that involved most of the contributors to the publication took place in Suzhou. Guo Yingde notes that the love affair on which the story is based probably started after 1676 but prior to 1678. See Guo and Ling, "Fresh Faces for Those Full of Emotions," 82n41. The play was completed at the very latest by 1680, which is when Li Liweng, who contributed both commentary and additional scenes, died.

州，甚興新戲，拿去賣些銀子用用。歸來每位送匹綿綢，送斤絲綿便罷，只算扶持你。[115]

As if the connection were not already clear, the line about the new plays written by Suzhou gentlemen is marked with emphatic punctuation in the woodblock edition, prompting the reader to note that the play in which Old Tao speaks is itself one of the plays he describes: a new play about recent events that was printed up by a commercial publisher in Suzhou and sold in the surrounding region.

As in *The Appearance of the Star of Literature*, what this moment of metatheater does is make explicit the ways in which everyone—the characters in the play and the actors portraying them, the audience watching the performance and the literatus reading a copy in his study—has a particular relation to the play as a commercial object. The playwrights offstage (both within and behind the play) are similarly implicated in this economy. While not acting the role of merchants per se—this they leave to the professional Tao—and half-shielding their commercial enmeshment with talk of favors and silk, Tao's playwright friends have nevertheless identified a demand in the marketplace and in so doing frame their plays not as (or not exclusively as) incommensurable vessels of literary expression but as exchangeable commodities that can fetch enough silver to buy some lower grade silk and still have a decent amount to spare. Such an attitude toward writing for profit would certainly not be foreign to the playwrights of the Suzhou circle such as Zhu Suchen, who churned out plays at a rate double or triple that of his contemporaries—plays that were widely available for purchase and whose release was known to cause a buying frenzy among performers and aficionados.[116]

115. Zhu Suchen, *Qinlou yue*, 2:15a. The self-consciousness of this moment has been pointed out by Wang Yongkuan and Guo Yingde. See Wang Yongkuan, "Mingmo Qingchu Suzhou diqu xiqu chuangzuo fanrong de shehui yuanyin," 180; Guo Yingde, "Xinxi shengcheng, nüxing yuedu yu yimin yishi," 37. A discussion and translation of this moment also appears in Guo and Ling, "Fresh Faces for Those Full of Emotions," 67–68.

116. See, as discussed in the introduction, Feng Menglong's description of people rushing out to buy new editions of Li Yu's dramas (which no doubt informed Feng's

The winking reference to the "number of gentlemen"—*xianggong* 相公 not implying high birth per se but rather a sense of classed respect for literary men and perhaps a sense of urbanity[117]—evokes not merely Zhu Suchen but his entire circle; Old Tao is approached not by a single playwright but several who here speak in one voice. The intimation of some sort of group engaged in similar or perhaps shared theatrical projects maps onto the writing practices of the Suzhou circle, who cowrote plays and often served as each other's editors.[118] By assigning the role of playwright to not one but many, Zhu (and his collaborators) cast both these plays and this play as communal products of the marketplace, the work of many hands and voices.

That these "gentlemen" remain nameless and unseen in the play is not unlike the fate of the Suzhou circle playwrights more generally, who remain shadowy figures to modern scholars, leaving behind only the thinnest of biographical scraps. Such a fate is in part because, while the plays and formularies compiled by these playwrights reflect a high level of specialized literary knowledge, to a man they lacked the pedigrees of their peers. Unlike a Tang Xianzu or a Feng Menglong, the playwrights associated with the Suzhou circle did not come from families of note, and there is no evidence that any of them served in the bureaucracy in any capacity. Rather, with their social itinerancy, literary facility, and well-connected friends, they occupied a liminal space between literatus and merchant as scholars of the marketplace and merchants of culture.

In their metatheatrical instantiation of characters, actors, authors, audience members, and readers as economic subjects,

---

decision to publish his own versions of these plays). Feng Menglong, ed., *Mohanzhai chongding Yong tuanyuan chuanqi*, *xu* 2a–b.

117. On the use of *xianggong* as a mark of urban identity in the south, see Goldman, *Opera and the City*, 32, 279n48.

118. Zhu Suchen was frequently associated with such projects as the multiauthored *Four Grand Celebrations* and *Four Spectacular Sights*, as well as the nonextant *Passing the Examinations*; he is listed as co-editor of Li Yu's *Register of the Pure and Loyal* along with his fellow Suzhou playwrights Bi Wei and Ye Shizhang, and as proofreader of Li Yu's *Expanded and Standardized Formulary of Northern-Style Lyrics*.

these playwrights point toward not an antisocial and atomized individual but a subject enfolded into a differently oriented community. That community is the city, though not one enclosed by its walls or carved into administrative districts; instead, the playwrights recenter the city with which they identify and frequently invoke (in their self-given names and in the settings, historical events, and personages that fill their work) around sites of performance and commerce: Xuanmiao Temple, Maple Bridge, North Temple, Tiger Hill.[119] All of this city is a stage and all of its inhabitants merchants.

It is through the transformation of the merchant into the universal everyman—a role that everyone from fisherman to literatus would at some point play—that makes possible an identity that is properly early modern: the Jiangnan urbanite who is socially emplaced in the market and whose self-conception is forged through the lateral relations of commerce. Not unlike the *chōnin* 町人 of Osaka or the freemen of London, this was an identity in which the performance of certain commercial relations makes one properly "of" a city.

But the merchant is, after all, a traveler. Mapping the city through the commercial performances of its inhabitants at the moment of its full entrance into global trade networks generates a space not bound by Chang Gate or the Ikoma Mountains or the Thames or the Leidsegracht. Rather, this was an imagination of the city as radiating out into local, regional, and transregional networks, like the commercial empire mapped in *Winning the Prize Courtesan*, traced by the pathways of small-time peddlers and large-scale traders winding their way from teashop to brothel to tavern to silk factory to merchant ship to the world beyond.

119. The playwrights associated with the Suzhou circle made the city central to their literary identities, taking Suzhou-centric pen names, adapting materials from other Suzhou writers, and dramatizing Suzhou history and famous personages (as in *The Appearance of the Star of Literature*, in which an earlier Suzhou circle—Shen Zhou, Wen Zhengming, Tang Yin, and Zhu Yunming—perhaps stands in for the present one).

THREE

Ventures over, under, and beyond the Seas

Ever since Fan Li "boarded a small skiff and floated around the rivers and lakes" 乃乘扁舟浮於江湖, the imagination of the mercantile has been tied to waterways that constitute not so much a place as an unplace: a moveable and amorphous society of marginal and mobile people on the periphery of the administrable state, a marketplace that is constituted and dissolved with each exchange.

Alongside the unlocatable and ungovernable flux of the *jianghu* imaginary was the growing body of specialized, technical knowledge that rendered these waterways mappable, navigable, and manageable. By the mid-Ming, the rivers and lakes of Jiangnan were part of an increasingly integrated transportation system that connected the canals of Suzhou to the Grand Canal, the Yangzi, and the seas beyond. In route books and maps aimed at both merchants and officials,[1] the world of the waterways is conceptualized not as an obscure maze, appearing and vanishing like bubbles on the water, but as a totality, a single "unified system" (*yitong* 一統) of land and water routes that can be comprehended in its entirety.[2]

1. On the dual audience for these texts, see Chow, "The Merging of *Shi* and *Shang* in Travel."

2. For example, Huang Bian 黃汴, *Illustrated Comprehensive Route Guide* (*Yitong lucheng tuji* 一統路程圖記), published in Suzhou in 1570 and repeatedly edited and combined with other texts. For a discussion of these texts, see Du, *The Order of Places*.

This unified system is often described as encompassing "all under heaven" (*tianxia* 天下), whose boundaries are coterminous with the ruling purview of the imperial state.[3] The waterways can thus be folded into a larger imagination of the empire; the single system to which these waterways belong is the imperial state. At the same time, the increasingly expansive God's eye view of interconnected rivers and distant seas suggests a differently unified system. If you zoom out far enough, the distinction between all of these named and demarcated waters falls away and it is as Hong Mai 洪邁 (1123–1202) said: "There is one sea and that is all" 海一而已.[4] Here the singular, unified thing is not the empire but its negation, as the center shifts from the Middle Kingdom bounded by the four seas to a mass of water—the Middle Sea, perhaps—that pushes landed polities to the margins.[5]

The tensions latent in the early modern waters—these sites of immutability and impermanence, of public knowledge and cliquish secrecy, of imperial centering and global decentering—appear repeatedly on the stages of Suzhou, a city of canals, where life happens on and via the water. In plays set on merchant boats and deserted islands, strange harbors and underwater kingdoms, water functions as both a historical site of and a heuristic for conceptualizing new social relations that remake the limits of community and humanity.

3. Other titles for later *Illustrated Comprehensive Route Guide* editions and expansions include *Water and Land Routes of the Realm* (*Tianxia shuilu lucheng* 天下水陸路程) and *A Comprehensive Guide for the Lost Traveling Merchant to the Water and Land Routes of the Realm* (*Keshang yilan xingmi tianxia shuilu lucheng* 客商一覽醒迷天下水陸路程). See Du, *The Order of Places*; Brook, *Geographical Sources of Ming-Qing History*; Wilkinson, "Chinese Merchant Manuals and Route Books."

4. Hong Mai, "Sihai yi ye" 四海一也, in *Rongzhai suibi*, 1:33.

5. As Gu Yanwu points out, the sea had long been used as a metaphorical demarcation of the empire. Discussing the use of this term in the *Rites of Zhou* (*Zhouli* 周禮), Gu argues that "the word 'sea' [in 'the four seas'] is not the name of a real body of water" 海非真水之名, rather it functions as the boundary between habitable territory and barren darkness. Gu Yanwu, *Rizhi lu jishi* 4:1256.

Vessels and Vassals

Halfway through the play *Three Kinds of Happiness*, attributed to the Suzhou circle playwright Zhang Dafu, our hero Jiang Chi finds himself on a merchant ship bound for Japan.[6] That Jiang Chi should be on board this boat is rather unexpected, as he is not a merchant by trade. Jiang Chi, in fact, has no trade to speak of—a dissolute *fengliu* 風流 (his self-given name Chi 癡 "The Infatuated" a testament to his tendency toward obsession and aesthetic pleasure), he is goaded into finding some sort of occupation by his increasingly troubled wife, Ying'er. After arguing that he is unsuited for, or lacks the resources to pursue, the work of a scholar, artisan, or farmer, his wife points out that this leaves the fourth occupation: "Then you may as well do a little trading" 做一些商賈也好. Jiang Chi decides that this is a feasible profession for him, declaring a bit arrogantly, "I think trading will not be too difficult" 我想生意原是不難的. But, he continues, "the only problem is (*singing*) I don't know where to buy and where to sell" 只是一件 (唱) 不知買於何處, 賣於哪裡.[7]

Ying'er sends Jiang Chi out into the streets of Ningbo to learn how to be a successful merchant, where he encounters his old friend Wang Qifeng, who has graduated from his regional trade in firewood to more lucrative overseas ventures. Wang Qifeng encourages

6. *Three Kinds of Happiness* survives in a manuscript housed in the Traditional Drama Research Institute at the Chinese National Academy of Arts that bears the inscription "copied by Bian Duanfu of Suzhou in the *yihai* year of Chongzhen [1635]" 崇禎乙亥姑蘇卞端甫錄, though this inscription should be considered with some skepticism. This edition contains many transcription errors; the musical notations and stage directions indicate that it was a performance script. There is also an "old" manuscript from Wu Mei's collection that was included in the third series of the *Guben xiqu congkan*; this edition is carefully copied and contains no musical notation or punctuation. Neither of these editions lists an author; the attribution comes from *New Southern Dramas*. See Gao Yi, *Xin chuanqi pin*, 274. According to Guo Yingde, there is also a Republican-era edition housed in the National Library of China and an undated manuscript in the Peking University Library. On these editions, see Guo Yingde, *Ming Qing chuanqi zonglu*, 1:556; Zhou Gongping, "Zhang Dafu xiqu zuopin kao ban," 122. All quotes are from the *Guben xiqu congkan* edition.

7. Zhang Dafu (attrib.), *Kuaihuo san*, 1:39b.

Jiang Chi to join him on his upcoming trip to Japan, where merchandise purchased in Ningbo would fetch a tenfold profit. While Jiang Chi is initially excited by this opportunity, he is aghast to learn that overseas commerce is not, in fact, "not difficult" 不難 and requires many months away from home. As Wang Qifeng explains, this sort of occupation is not compatible with family life: "The merchants I mentioned who are going on this trip don't have wives. They are only involved in trade to make money" 說起來方纔個星客人，纔是無家婆個，做生意只要賺銀子.[8] Jiang Chi ruefully bemoans this new world of risky ventures far from home: "From ancient times, money was made by the south of the bridge, not in the southern seas. If fortune is meant to be mine, then naturally it will be mine. Why must I endure such hardship going [overseas] to seek it?" 自古道錢在橋南，不在海南。該是我的，自然是我的。為什麽苦苦要出去求他.[9]

No sooner have they parted ways than Ningbo is beset by vicious pirates. As the city is enveloped in the chaos of looting and raping and killing, Jiang Chi makes his way home, but his wife is nowhere to be found. Distraught and unmoored—already an orphan and now presumably a widower—Jiang Chi makes a last-minute decision to join the merchant expedition. There is only one problem: he does not have any capital or merchandise and the boat is departing soon. Fortuitously, he comes across a sealed barrel on the street that was abandoned during the pirate raid and brings it with him, hoping that whatever is inside can be sold in Japan.

But they never land in Japan. Once out at sea, a massive storm sweeps all of the merchants and their merchandise overboard, leaving only Jiang Chi, the head helmsman, and the still-sealed barrel on an island country call Qiuci 邱慈. They open the barrel to discover it is filled with olives, which they agree suits their "sour situation" 酸態. Suddenly they are approached by a group of curious locals; in a goodwill gesture, Jiang Chi offers them some olives. After the locals throw some silver their way, Jiang

8. Ibid., 1:47a.
9. Ibid.

Chi and the helmsman realize that they can sell the remaining olives for the incredible rate of one silver coin per olive.[10]

The general contours of these events—the lifelong failure of a protagonist who becomes an accidental success by selling fruit for a great profit overseas—would be familiar to late imperial readers from the *huaben* "A Chinese Man Changes His Luck in a Chance Encounter with Dongting Tangerines; A Persian Man Reveals the Secrets of a Tortoise Shell" 轉運漢遇巧洞庭紅, 波斯胡指破鼉龍殼, the first story of Ling Mengchu's popular 1628 collection *Slapping the Table in Amazement* (*Pai'an jingqi* 拍案驚奇).[11] In that telling, a hapless and broke Suzhou merchant named Wen Ruoxu brings a basket of the titular tangerines on an overseas trip as a snack to share with his fellow merchants. Quite unexpectedly, the tangerines catch the attention of the locals who shower Wen Ruoxu in silver. On their way back to China, Ruoxu finds a giant tortoise shell on an uninhabited island; when the merchants arrive in Fujian to sell off their merchandise, a Persian dealer buys the shell for an obscene price; he later tells Ruoxu that the shell contains rare pearls that if sold in his native land are worth many times the amount he paid.

Ling Mengchu's story turns on a series of unexpected reversals in which something that is cheap in one context is dear in another: the tangerines that cost one tael per hundred catty in Suzhou but fetch a tael each in the foreign country of Jiling; the tortoise shell that is a worthless curio to the Chinese but is a rare treasure to the Persians. But as the narrator notes, these discrepancies that generated so much profit in this case are not indicative of a larger, legible system of value that can be understood or

10. Lope de Vega's play *The New World Discovered by Christopher Columbus (El nuevo mundo descubierto por Cristóbal Colón*, ca. 1598–1603) also features ocean-crossing merchant-explorers from the source culture landing on an island rich in gold, whose value is conceptualized vis-à-vis oranges and olives. For both the original text and the English translation, see Shannon, *El nuevo mundo descubierto por Cristóbal Colón*, 228–31.

11. The play's other narrative thread comes from the twelfth story in that collection, "Old Man Tao Takes in Visitors during a Rainstorm; Jiang Zhenqing Gets a Wife with Only a Few Words" 陶家翁大雨留賓, 蔣震卿片言得婦, which is based on a mid-Ming anecdote recorded by Zhu Yunming that Ling cites in the story itself.

exploited. When an imagined listener to the storyteller narrator asks why all merchants do not attempt to sell fruit to the people of Jiling, the narrator reproaches them:

> Dear audience, that is not the right way to think about this. This person came into this unexpected windfall entirely by chance. He went forth with these goods and happened upon great gain. Suppose he decided to go back a second time with more fruit. If the conditions were not favorable, by the third day or so the fruit will have started to rot.
>
> 看官，又不是這話。也是此人偶然有此橫財，帶去著了手。若是有心第二遭再帶去，三五日不遇巧，等得希爛。[12]

Aside from plugging narrative holes, the narrator is reiterating the point made in the introductory story, in which a man learns that the money he thought was his does not belong to him at all and can leave him at any moment for another "master." Wen Ruoxu similarly recognizes that he has no control over the movement of money. The other merchants urge Ruoxu to use his newly acquired silver as capital—to use it to purchase Chinese goods to then sell to the natives and thus turn his money into more money. Ruoxu, however, does not see the generation of money as the result of any process that can be understood. While the merchants make their arguments based on their understanding of the local economies—the relative values of silver coins, Chinese goods, and Jiling goods in both the domestic and foreign markets—Ruoxu, like the narrator above, dismisses this line of thinking. There is no economy, no system of surpluses and lacks that can be negotiated. There is only risk and chance, incommensurable value systems that accidentally intersect in a way that generates profit but could just as easily result in ruin.

A mid-story digression into Jiling's monetary system shows how even value itself has been rendered contingent. The people of Jiling use minted silver coins that all have the same weight (and

12. Ling Mengchu, *Pai'an jingqi*, 1:13b–14a.

would therefore be of equal value in China) and are assigned relative values based on the type of image etched on the coin's face. These face values follow a symbolic logic, with the dragon and phoenix coins worth more than the coins that depict humans, the human coins worth more than the animals, and the animals worth more than the trees. At the very bottom are the seaweed coins, which are worth one hundredth of the dragon and phoenix coins. The ludicrousness of such a system is clearly meant to skewer the Ming's reliance on fiat money that divorces face value from metallic content. But more than just recalling the more dysfunctional aspects of the Ming's copper coinage, these coins confront the reader with the contingency and instability of all forms of value. That the coins are silver—which so frequently comes to stand for value incarnate in the late imperial imagination—is a loaded choice, making the decoupling of money and meaning particularly jarring to a seventeenth-century audience.

Three Kinds of Happiness, even more so than the *huaben* on which it is based, paints the protagonist's path to riches as contingent. While Wen Ruoxu makes a measured decision to buy the Dongting tangerines due to their quality and cost-effectiveness, Jiang Chi grabs an abandoned barrel of unknown contents.[13] And while Ruoxu and his traveling companions arrive in a familiar country where they had previously done business, Jiang Chi and his olives land on an unknown island. As the bewildered helmsman asks Jiang Chi, "What kind of people are gathered there on the shore? I don't know if they are Japanese or Muslim" 岸上個星啥人，勿知倭子呢，勿知是回回.[14]

But if the conditions of Jiang Chi's arrival in Qiuci are even less governed by any sort of logic or plan, the exchange of fruit

13. The change from tangerines to olives is perhaps more consonant with performance needs, with olives being small enough that they do not need to be represented with any sort of prop. This change also heightens the contrast between value in Jiangnan and value abroad, with a single olive of unknown provenance being clearly less valuable than a ripe Dongting tangerine and yet still commanding over a tael of silver each.

14. Zhang Dafu, *Kuaihuo san*, 1:53b. *Huihui* 回回 being the generic term for any number of internal or foreign Muslims.

for silver does not similarly revel in the contingency of value. Rather, the money proffered for Jiang Chi's olives is entirely legible—while the silver that the natives throw at Jiang Chi are described as silver coins (lit. "silver copper cash" 銀銅錢) and thus clearly not the same monetary system as Ming China, there is no complex pictorial system that needs to be mastered. Though shaped like coins, there is no indication that this silver money is not also valued by weight as in China; or perhaps we would learn that there is some sort of nonequivalent system of value at work in this country, if this exchange were not immediately disrupted by an interpreter from the royal court who quickly shuts down this impromptu market in foreign olives: "All of you Muslims, listen: China indeed has unusual fruits; do not chaotically jostle like this. I must report this to the king, and you Muslims all need to disperse" 哟衆回回聽者，中華既有奇果，不許亂擠，須報與國王知道，番回回們都散去。[15]

After making his report to the king, the interpreter returns and whisks Jiang Chi away to the palace. The king of Qiuci has taken a particular interest in this foreign merchant and his unusual fruit. As he tells the audience, ever since he ascended the throne, his country has been peaceful and prosperous: "No alarms are sounded at sea and the mountains are full of rare treasures" 海無警報，山有奇珍. Nevertheless, he says, "while my body resides overseas, my heart longs for China" 咱身居海外，心慕中華思念。[16] This longing has "over time accumulated into a sickness" 日久積成一病, as he wastes away like a cold planet far from the sun.

This distance is overcome, and his illness cured, by ingesting a single olive grown on Chinese soil. The king's attention turns to a more metaphorical consumption of things Chinese, as he tells his advisors: "Today I have summoned the Chinese visitors to the palace to ask them about the Southern dynasty's

15. Ibid., 1:54a.

16. Ibid., 2:4b. While this declaration might seem to imply that the king was originally from China, there is no indication of this elsewhere in the play; his reliance on a translator to speak to the Chinese visitor and his ignorance of Chinese mythology supports the reading of the king as an outside admirer.

natural scenery" 寡人今日特召中華客哥上殿, 問他南朝山川風景.[17] The king seems to share Jiang Chi's appreciation of mountains and streams, a much-discussed obsession of his in the first part of the play; though Jiang Chi can slake his infatuation by traveling with his merchant friends, the king must rely on him for a virtual trip:

TRANSLATOR, played by the *xiaosheng*: I have received His Majesty's command. He asks the Chinese merchant who are the most important personages of the Southern dynasty? Where are the most perilous mountains and rivers? Please take your time to describe them, and I will translate for His Majesty.

JIANG CHI, played by the *sheng*: Hold on, he wants to ask me about the affairs of the Southern dynasty? How am I to answer? Bah! No one here can verify what I say, so I will just make up some nonsense. Listen to this: [To the tune "Sobering up Three Times"] Master Pangu was the first to rule over the universe. As for the mountains and rivers, listen and I will tell you. (*speaking*) Once Pangu divided clear heaven from the muddy earth, humans came into being. The Duke of Zhou established the rites, Confucius spoke about "achieving benevolence,"[18] and Mencius referred to "choosing righteousness."[19] Then heaven unexpectedly collapsed on the southeast side.[20] Luckily someone was there.

TRANSLATOR: Luckily who was there?

JIANG CHI, singing: Luckily there was Lady Nüwa who smelted stones to repair heaven. (*speaking*) At that time *yin* and *yang* had not yet

17. Ibid.

18. Reference to *Analects* 15.9, in which Confucius says that moral individuals "may sacrifice their lives to achieve benevolence" 有殺身以成仁. *Shisan jing zhushu*, 23:239.

19. Reference to *Mencius* 6A10, in which Mencius declares, "Life is something I desire. Righteousness is also something I desire. If I cannot have both, then I will give up my life and choose righteousness" 生亦我所欲也, 義亦我所欲也。二者不可得兼, 舍生而取義者也. *Shisan jing zhushu*, 25:363.

20. Jiang Chi here butchers the classic geographical formation "Heaven is collapsed in the northwest, and earth is caved in the southeast" 天傾西北, 地陷東南, which appears with variations across early texts such as *Master Huainan* (*Huainanzi* 淮南子), *Master Lie* (*Liezi* 列子), and *Classic of Mountains and Seas* (*Shanhai jing* 山海經).

divided. The nine suns appeared simultaneously in the sky, burning to death nine out of every ten people on earth. Luckily someone was there.

TRANSLATOR: Luckily who was there?

JIANG CHI: There was a man called Houyi. With his left hand he held an iron bow and with his right he drew a golden arrow, shooting the suns down one after another, leaving only one sun in the sky. (*singing*) This is Houyi shooting down the golden crows.[21] (*speaking*) With the sun and moon settled, unexpectedly the earth caved in in the northwest. Luckily there was someone at that time who broke apart the giant sea turtle's four legs to stabilize all under heaven. (*singing*) This is breaking the legs of the giant turtle to establish the poles and hold up the cosmos. (*speaking*) Heaven is measured in length, the earth is measured in *li*, the sun and moon are measured in waxing and waning, winter and summer are measured by the calendar. (*singing*) Analyzing the maps of the terrestrial poles of *yin* and *yang*, the land of China is ideal for excellence in both literary and military matters.

小生: 領旨。中華客哥, 大王問你, 南朝人物何人最高, 山川風景何地為險, 慢慢的說來, 我與你傳上去。

生: 且住, 他要問我南朝事體, 教我如何回答。呸, 左右沒對証的, 就亂說些天話便了。聽我道, 【解三酲】盤古氏首出御宇。山川景, 聽吾說與。(白) 纔分天清地濁, 那時就生出人來了。周公制禮, 孔子成仁, 孟軻取義。其時不想天傾了東南半邊。那時虧了一個人。

小生: 虧了那個。

生唱: 虧了那女媧氏, 煉石將天來補。(白) 其時陰陽未分, 九個日頭一齊並出, 十分人到晒死了九分。那時又虧了一人。

小生: 又虧了那個。

生: 那人喚名后羿, 左挽鐵胎弓, 右搭金鈚箭, 把那日頭一輪輪都射了下來, 只留輪在上。(唱) 這是后羿射落金烏。(白) 剛定得日月, 不想地又陷了西北一角。其時又虧了一人, 斷了海中巨鰲四足就定天下。(唱) 這是斷鰲立極將宇宙扶。(白) 我那裡天有度數, 地有里數, 日

21. A traditional figuration of the sun; in some versions of this myth, the suns became golden crows as they fell from the sky.

月有盈虧之數，寒暑有往來歷數。(唱)剖出陰陽地極圖，中華土真個是能文善武足智多謀。[22]

This grandiose bit of topographic history is then followed by an equally grandiose litany of the curative properties of the humble olive:

TRANSLATOR: I have received His Majesty's command. Brother Merchant, the king also wanted to ask you what the name is of the fruit that you brought?

JIANG CHI: This fruit is exceedingly rare in the world. The tree on which it grows has luxuriant foliage and flowers that bloom in five colors as big as bamboo baskets. Three thousand years pass before fruit is produced. Beneath the tree, *lingzhi* mushrooms reflect its brilliance, and phoenixes make their nests on top. It confers immortality and its flavor is balanced.

TRANSLATOR: How much do you want for one?

JIANG CHI: The price is one thousand pieces of gold each.

小生：領旨。客哥，大王又問你適纔的果兒叫什麼名兒。

生：此果世間絶少，枝葉甚是婆娑，花開五色大如籮，年過三千結果。下有靈芝相映，上多鸞鳳巢窠。長生不老味調和。

小生：要多少一個。

生：實價千金一個。[23]

Up until this moment we seem to be witnessing an effective if overly involved sales pitch that invests the olives with thousands of years of Chinese "history" so as to justify their price tag of thousands pieces of gold.[24] And the king buys everything the

22. Zhang Dafu, *Kuaihuo san*, 2:5a–6a.
23. Ibid., 2:6a–b.
24. This repackaging and upselling the olives, borrowing bits and pieces from stock narratives about the creation of the cosmos, echoes the production of the play itself, which, like many Suzhou circle plays, adapts and recuts well-known vernacular stories to sell to the literary consumer in another form.

merchant is selling, from questionable historiography to overpriced olives, though Jiang Chi gets more than he bargained for:

> TRANSLATOR: The king has decreed thus: He bestows on you one cart of gold ingots, one cart of silver ingots, and one cart each of pearls, agate, ivory, and rhinoceros horn, all of which will be sent to your residence. Tomorrow he will travel with you to China to present tribute.
>
> 小生：大王有旨，賜客哥馬蹄金一車，馬蹄銀一車，珍珠瑪瑙象牙犀角各載一車，送到公館住下。明日大王親自同你到南朝進貢哩。[25]

This moment echoes the final exchange in "A Chinese Man Changes His Luck," in which the Persian's purchase of the tortoise shell exceeds the bounds of a commercial exchange and starts to become something else. In that story, the nature of the overpayment is central to the moral calculations of the narrative. Despite the narrator's protestation that there is no advice to take away from this story aside from the axiom that all fortune is fated, there is nevertheless a clear moral logic to Wen Ruoxu's successes and failures. Before he sets out on his overseas adventure, Ruoxu tries to sell fans in Beijing. The narrator blames the failure of this venture on the unusually humid weather that ruined Ruoxu's merchandise. But what goes unremarked upon is the fundamentally antisocial nature of this venture. Ruoxu, we are told, sells three kinds of fans: fancy ones with inscriptions or paintings solicited from well-known literati, middling ones with imitations of the aforementioned literati's work, and cheap plain ones that he planned to sell for twice their purchase price. Though the commodification of amateur artistic production and social exchange, counterfeiting, and overcharging are fairly minor betrayals when placed in a world of raping and pillaging pirates, this can be seen as a distinction of degree and not kind.

If this earlier venture is marred by its undercutting of social trust, the later one is entirely dependent on rebuilding it. The tael of silver that Ruoxu uses to buy the tangerines was not the capital

25. Zhang Dafu, *Kuaihuo san*, 2:6b.

from a previous venture but a gift from a few fellow merchant friends. And Ruoxu does not buy the tangerines to sell but to enjoy and to share: "I can use my tael of silver to buy a little over a hundred catties of these tangerines, which I can use on the boat to quench my thirst, and I can also give one or two to my travel companions to thank them for helping me" 我一兩銀子買得百斤有餘，在船可以解渴，又可分送一二，答眾人助我之意. Enjoyment and pleasure—not profit—were also the impetus for Ruoxu's decision to take the tortoise shell from the uninhabited island. After his fellow shipmates tease him for lugging such a giant, worthless thing on board, Ruoxu explains that the shell is not a thing to sell but a personal thing and a social thing: a marvel to behold, a memento of his voyage to a strange land, a piece of evidence to show his friends who might doubt his wild stories.

Like the tangerines, the shell turns out to also be a valuable commodity, which Ruoxu offers to sell to the Persian dealer. But the Persian complicates the old dance between buyer and seller, first by refusing Ruoxu's initial offer as being too low and then by overcompensating the assembled merchants with gifts of silver, silks, and pearls. This exchange also begets another one—as the transport of the agreed-upon fifty thousand taels is complex and perilous, the Persian offers to sell Ruoxu his silk shop and the surrounding residence as a secure location to store the silver while arrangements are made to gradually ship it back to Suzhou. The shop, the Persian claims, has three thousand taels in capital invested therein, and the hundred-plus-room compound is worth two thousand taels, which he offers to sell at cost; in a departure from the earlier exchange, in which settling on a price for the tortoise shell involved guesses in the dark, here all is made transparent. And while that earlier exchange produced an impossible windfall for the Persian—who paid only one-twenty-fourth of what the "priceless treasure" 無價寶 was worth—here it is Ruoxu who purchases "profit without end" 利息無盡 by becoming the proprietor of a ready-made business.[26]

26. The Persian jokingly blurs the line between commercial transaction and social exchange by describing twenty-three of the twenty-four pearls as "gifts" 尊惠 from Wen Ruoxu in an attempt to paper over the unevenness of the sale.

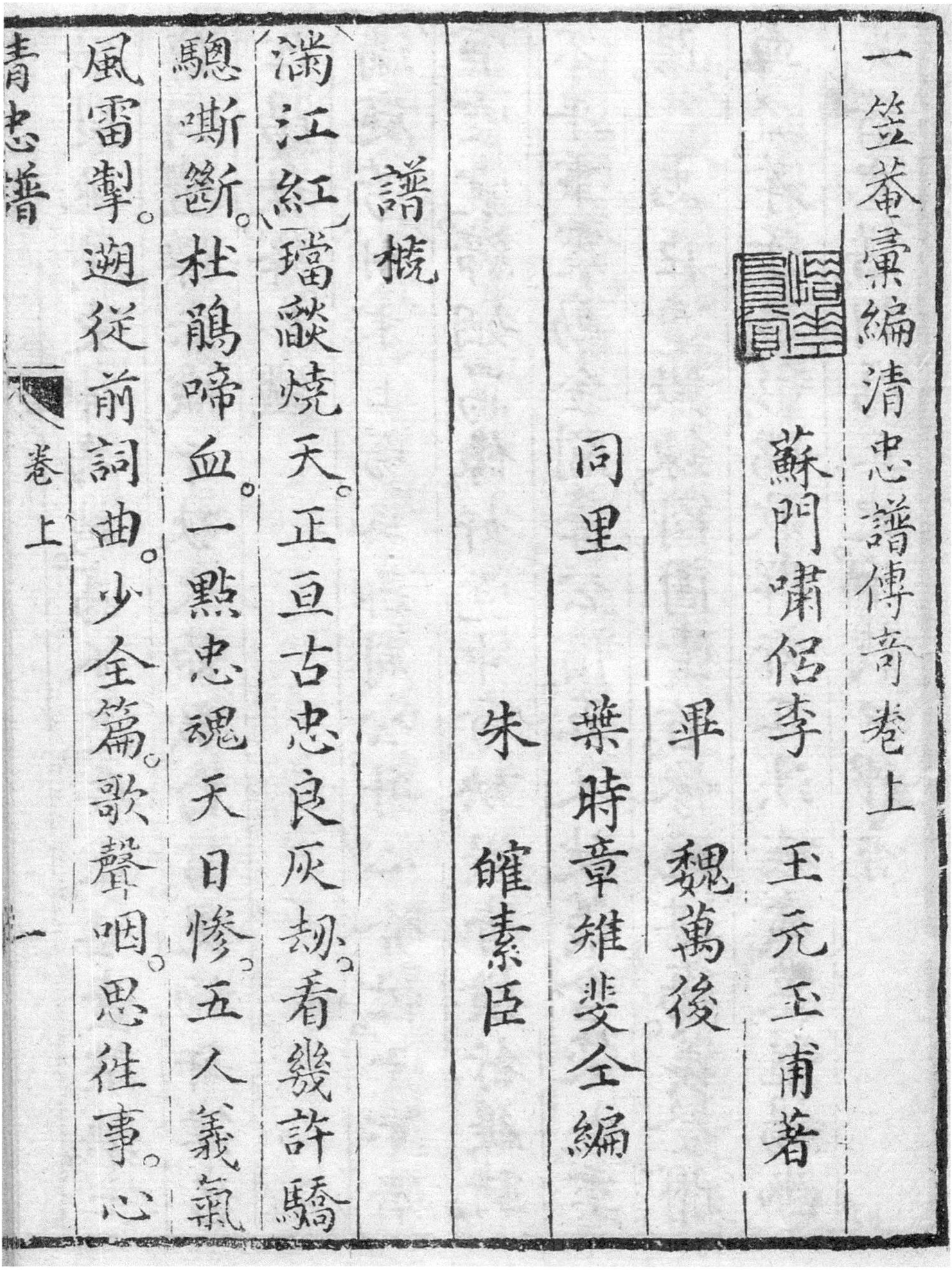

一笠菴彙編清忠譜傳奇卷上

蘇門嘯侶李　玉元玉甫著

畢　魏萬後

同里　葉時章雉斐仝編

朱　㿥素臣

譜概

【滿江紅】璫燄燒天。正亘古忠良灰刼。看幾許驕驄嘶斷。杜鵑啼血。一點忠魂天日慘。五人義氣風雷掣。遡從前詞曲。少全篇。歌聲咽。思往事。心

清忠譜　卷上　一

Plate 1. Title page of the Shunzhi-era woodblock edition of *Register of the Pure and Loyal*. Facsimile reprint in *Guben xiqu congkan sanji*. Reproduction courtesy of The University of Chicago Library.

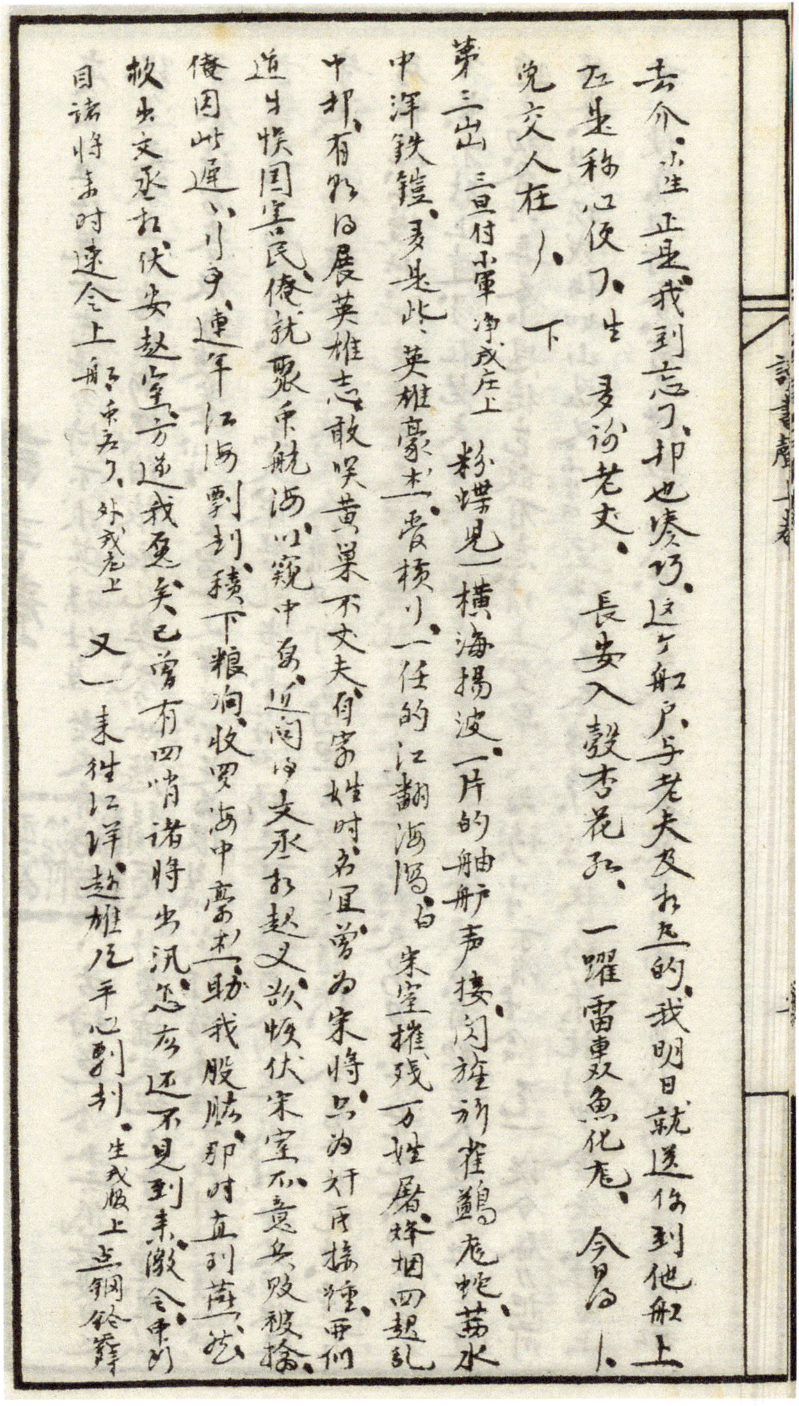

Plate 2. Page from an undated manuscript of *The Sound of Reading*. Facsimile reprint in *Guben xiqu congkan sanji*. Reproduction courtesy of The University of Chicago Library.

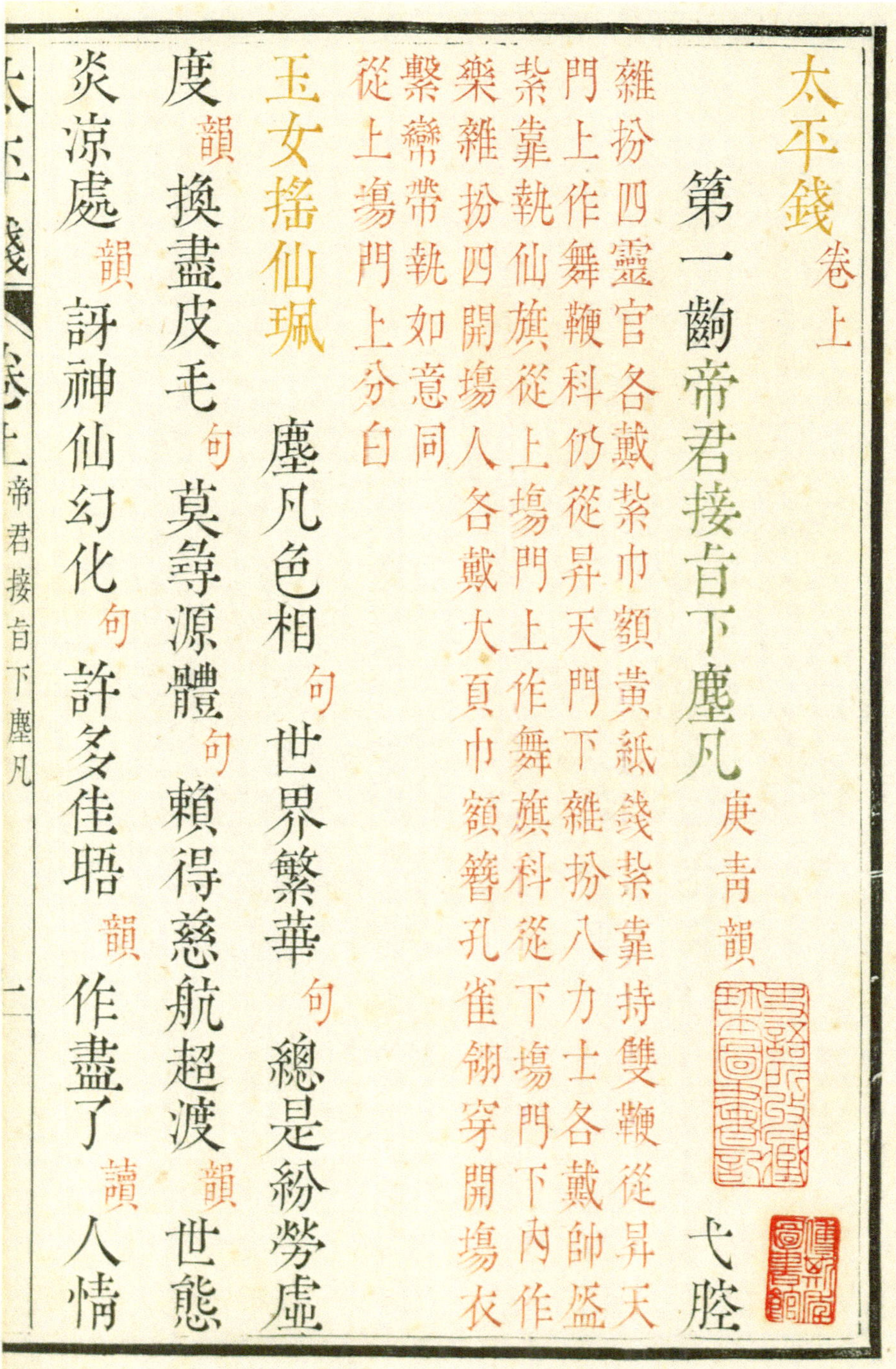

太平錢 卷上

第一齣帝君接旨下塵凡 庚青韻 弋腔

雜扮四靈官各戴紮巾額黄紙錢紮靠持雙鞭從昇天門上作舞鞭科仍從昇天門下雜扮八力士各戴帥盔紮靠執仙旗從上上場門上作舞旗科從下場門下內作樂雜扮四開場人各戴大頁巾額簪孔雀翎穿開場衣繫鑾帶執如意同從上場門上分白

玉女搖仙珮 塵凡色相 句 世界繁華 句 總是紛勞虛度 韻 換盡皮毛 句 莫尋源體 句 賴得慈航超渡 韻 世態炎涼處 韻 謌神仙幻化 句 許多佳瑭 韻 作盡了 讀 人情

太平錢 卷上 帝君接旨下塵凡 一

Plate 3. Title page of the mid-Qing palace manuscript edition of *Coins of Heavenly Peace*. Image courtesy of the Institute of History and Philology, Academia Sinica.

Plate 4. Illustration of the scene "Joining the Pair of Jades" from the Chongzhen-era woodblock edition of *Winning the Prize Courtesan*. Facsimile reprint in *Guben xiqu congkan sanji*. Reproduction courtesy of The University of Chicago Library.

Plate 5. Illustration of "Yang Balao's Extraordinary Encounter in the Kingdom of Yue" from a Tianqi-era woodblock edition of Feng Menglong's *Stories Old and New*. Image courtesy of Hosei University Library.

Plate 6. Detail from Xu Yang et al., *The Qianlong Emperor's Southern Inspection Tour, Scroll 6: Entering Suzhou along the Grand Canal* (1770). Handscroll; ink and color on silk. 68.8 × 1994 cm. The Metropolitan Museum of Art.

Plate 7. Workshop of Wang Junfu (fl. ca. 1660), *Shen Wansan's Cornucopia*. Woodblock print; ink and color on paper. 37.8 × 58.8 cm. Image courtesy of Tenri Central Library.

Plate 8. Illustration of the scene "Obtaining What Was Buried" from the Chongzhen-era woodblock edition of *Between Man and Beast*. Facsimile reprint in *Guben xiqu congkan sanji*. Reproduction courtesy of The University of Chicago Library.

Though the Persian suggests the shop as a temporary way station on Ruoxu's eventual journey back to his native Suzhou, Ruoxu decides instead to stay in Fujian and put down roots, eventually marrying and having children. As Tina Lu notes, "A Chinese Man Changes His Luck" presents the fantasy of the perfect market—what she characterizes as "economic wish fulfillment"—in which every party comes away with an impossible profit.[27] However, the perfect market as presented here is not merely an engine of seemingly infinite monetary gain, but rather something that is at once generated by and generative of social relations.

In *Three Kinds of Happiness*, Jiang Chi's foray into commerce is similarly presented as an organic extension of friendly sociality, an idyllic imagining of the very first market exchange: Jiang Chi offers the natives some of his olives and, in a spontaneous gesture of thanks, they throw silver coins his way. And as in "A Chinese Man Changes His Luck," these exchanges end in an overpayment that turns a commercial exchange into something else. Unlike the source story, however, what is being generated by this overpayment are not the horizontal relations of friends and kin, but the hierarchical positions of sovereign and subject, with the carts of ingots and ivory and agate given to Jiang Chi by the king functioning as an act of diplomacy. While Jiang Chi might have aggrandized the potency of the Chinese earth for the sake of shilling his wares, to the king of Qiuci it is understood as testimony to the natural sovereignty of the Ming. That the king himself will be traveling to China on the merchant ship—making the exact journey with the same crew but in reverse—makes explicit the formal affinities of (and easy slipperiness between) trade and tribute, merchant and diplomat.

The parameters of diplomacy and commerce are ultimately sorted out at court. Appearing before a court eunuch, Jiang Chi is announced as "the maritime merchant Jiang Chi" 泛海商人蔣痴, his single foreign adventure sufficient to mark this erstwhile

27. Tina Lu, *Accidental Incest, Filial Cannibalism, and Other Peculiar Encounters*, 34–38.

student as a merchant in the eyes of the state.[28] The eunuch then reads the emperor's proclamation: "Although Merchant Jiang Chi is a trader, he is indeed capable, so I bestow on him the status of 'presented scholar' and appoint him the prefect of Yangzhou. He will immediately take office and thank His Majesty for His beneficence" 商人蔣痴雖為商賈，信有辦才，欽賜進士出身，除授揚州刺史。即日走馬上任謝恩.[29] The emperor thus proclaims away Jiang's merchanthood—and the problematic loyalties of the subject who subjects himself to the hierarchies and economies of other lands—by reinscribing him within a feudal relation.

The eunuch then calls forward the king of Qiuci, who eagerly prostrates himself before the absent Ming emperor.[30] From the exhortation of *qiansui* 千歲 (one thousand years) that greets the king to the deferential *wansui* 萬歲 (ten thousand years) that the king wishes the emperor, the relationship between the king of Qiuci and the Ming emperor is already suffused with the hierarchical language of vassaldom even though no such relation between the two lands exists. The emperor approvingly notes that the foreign king has an intuitive understanding of China's cultural superiority, and by personally bringing tribute to the Ming court, the king recognizes the Ming's sovereignty over land and sea. For this display, the emperor bestows on him the title of grand commander-in-chief of sea transport 海道大總管 and invites him to a royal banquet.[31]

The fantasy of the self-subjugating foreign king, who instinctively recognizes the universal dominion of the Ming, must have been particularly seductive in the waning years of the dynasty, as threats to the Ming's mandate appeared from rebellions within

28. Zhang Dafu, *Kuaihuo san*, 2:12a.

29. Ibid., 2:12b–13a.

30. The appearance of an emperor character on stage was proscribed in both Ming and Qing legal statutes, though these laws were often ignored, and some plays like *Peony Pavilion* found a way around the prohibition by having emperors speak from the wings. See Tian Yuan Tan, "Prohibition of *Jiatou Zaju* in the Ming Dynasty and the Portrayal of the Emperor on Stage."

31. Hucker notes that the title *dazongguan* 大總管 is reserved for frontier positions. Hucker, *A Dictionary of Official Titles in Imperial China*, 473.

and foreign pressures without. While the pirates looting Ningbo raise the specter of a new maritime order outside of the state's control, the enfeoffment of the island king reasserts the state's mediation of overseas trade through the language of the tribute system.[32] With trade thus folded into diplomacy, commercial relations are reinscribed within tributary hierarchies; sovereignties are transformed into tributaries and foreign economies incorporated into domestic networks. While the Ling Mengchu story ends with the dragon pearls being sent back to Persia, *Three Kinds of Happiness* stages the shipment of cart after cart of treasure to China. Though foreign locales might be rich in jewels and silver, China is the source of true and enduring value, the center to which people and things must return and submit.

The Tongues of Shrikes

The impulse to reorient the horizontality of the marketplace into the verticality of tribute relations finds expression throughout *Three Kinds of Happiness* in the way linguistic difference is performed. When the king of Qiuci first appears on stage, he speaks to his court in Chinese, which the audience is meant to understand as being in Qiuci language. This device allows the king to function as any other *chuanqi* character—able to introduce himself to the audience and convey his thoughts through the direct address of the aria. In contrast to characters like the barbarian envoy in *Peony Pavilion*, who are from beginning to end unintelligible and unknowably other and thus permanently excluded from the possibility of sinicization, the king's self-expression in Chinese is at once a narrative convenience and a signal that the language proper to these thoughts is already somehow latent within him.

Once Jiang Chi is summoned before the court, the king and

32. On the fraught distinction between tribute and trade, see Hevia, *Cherishing Men from Afar*.

his translator speak to each other in Qiuci language, which is conveyed through gibberish interspersed with enough Chinese that the audience can follow the contours of the conversation:

KING, played by the *jing*: Translator, ask him ai ke ma ya gou bu de er ha duo sa li li meng chi chi.

淨：通事，你去問他愛刻麻牙茍不的兒哈多撒里里蒙赤赤。[33]

However, a couple scenes later, when the king of Qiuci appears in the Ming emperor's court, the need for a translator suddenly vanishes. Instead, the king speaks to the emperor (via his eunuch) in Chinese. While a reasonable explanation is not out of the question—perhaps Jiang Chi taught the king Chinese during their voyage to the capital—none is provided to the audience. Certainly the seriousness of the imperial court renders improper such comic performances as the gibberish arias we hear in the Qiuci court. However, this turn from the exotic color of the island language to the elevated *guanhua* 官話 (lit. language of officials) of the Chinese court is not merely a tonal shift, but an ideological one as well. Within the majestic ambit of the Ming court, that which is outside or beyond must be incorporated within; the act of translation would cede the emperor's sovereignty over meaning, reorienting the bestowal of imperial grace into a horizontal negotiation between two equivalent systems.[34]

Translation in this sense is not unlike commerce, in which two different things are rendered commensurable.[35] And just as these adventures in foreign markets reveal the imperfect alignment of different systems of value—the worth of a seaweed coin in Jiling

33. Zhang Dafu, *Kuaihuo san*, 2:5a.

34. On the role of heterolinguistic moments in the production of modern notions of sovereignty, see Lydia Liu, *The Clash of Empires*, 70–107.

35. Indeed, in this play commerce is treated as a kind of ur-language, with the silent exchange of olives for silver later mirrored in the linguistic exchanges between Jiang Chi and the Qiuci king. Elsewhere commerce is imagined to have its own language, as in *jianghu heihua* 江湖黑話, the secret language through which merchants and thieves were thought to communicate.

and Suzhou, the worth of an olive in Qiuci and Ningbo—so too does the negotiation between foreign languages threaten to expose the particularity of meaning. Such a possibility reappears in another late Ming drama of overseas adventure, *A Pair of Golden Placards* (*Shuang jinbang* 雙金榜), written by the much-praised dramatist and much-loathed official Ruan Dacheng.[36] The story of this play is set in motion by the ambitious pirate Mo Cifei, whom we first encounter plotting to steal a pearl possessed by the famous White Horse Monastery in Luoyang. This pearl, he tells us, is no ordinary pearl, but a numinous treasure that when smelted in a special alchemical process reveals its true power: all the creatures and kingdoms of the sea come to pay fealty to the holder of the pearl and shower him with rare treasures.

The magical pearl and the treasures it calls forth invoke the well-worn trope of the sea as the site of impossible riches—a trope that inflects "A Chinese Man Changes His Luck" and *Three Kinds of Happiness*'s depictions of the plenitude and favorability of the overseas market.[37] But unlike those stories in which a dragon prince or foreign king or Persian merchant bestows pearls and coral and gold on an outsider, this is not a gift of riches but an expropriation of power. As those from the edges of the ocean—the mermen and dragon girls, the kings of Laos and Java—come to pledge allegiance, the pirate on the margins of Chinese society finds himself suddenly in the center. The echoes of usurpation are not unintentional—that the pearl is an emblem of imperial power is clear from its associations with dragons and

36. A late Ming print edition of this play is preserved in the second series of the *Guben xiqu congkan*. On the dating of this play to ca. 1638–42, see Hu Jinwang, *Rensheng xiju yu xiju rensheng*, 164–65, 175. The golden placards of the title refer to the list of new *jinshi* 進士 (presented scholars), the successful candidates of the palace-level civil service examinations.

37. For the classic expression of this trope, see medieval classical tales such as "Liu Yi" 柳毅 and their later rearticulation in such dramatic works as Shang Zhongxian's 尚仲賢 *At Dongting Lake Liu Yi Delivers a Letter* (*Dongting hu Liu Yi chuanshu* 洞庭湖柳毅傳書) and Li Liweng's *The Tower in the Mirage* (*Shenzhong lou* 蜃中樓). Li Fang, comp., *Taiping guangji*, 419:3410–17; Zang Maoxun, ed., *Yuanqu xuan*, vol. 4; Li Yu, *Liweng chuanqi shizhong*, vol. 1. This trope, and *baomu* 寶母 (mother of treasures) like Mo Cifei's pearl, will be discussed further in the next chapter.

its explicitly political history. As Mo Cifei recounts, the pearl was given as tribute to the Tang court by emissaries from Zhenla 真臘 (Cambodia) and later donated to the monastery by the imperial consort Yang Guifei to adorn the head of a statue of the Śākyamuni Buddha, the former crown prince Siddhārtha.

Once in possession of the pearl, Mo Cifei decamps for Champa 占城, a historical kingdom located in present-day Vietnam. He recalls with regret how his plot embroiled the innocent Huangfu Dun, the play's morally upright protagonist. Mo Cifei sends a messenger to invite Huangfu Dun, who is now living in Guangdong, to a banquet in his honor. Huangfu Dun happily agrees, thinking that the banquet will be nearby in the Pearl River Delta and not realizing until too late that he will be traveling three thousand *li* away to Champa. Over dinner, Huangfu Dun and Cifei discuss what Cifei should do with his newfound power over the myriad barbarian countries and tribes. Huangfu Dun suggests that Cifei undertake a diplomatic mission of sorts ("If you wanted to do the work of a Fu Jiezi or a Zhang Qian, it would be as easy as turning over your hand" 倘作傅介子張騫之事，易如反掌耳) in order to "recruit and lead the four barbarians" 招率四夷.[38] Cifei thinks Huangfu Dun is better suited for this task than he is and asks him to stay for a short while in Champa to set up a school. Huangfu Dun agrees on the condition that someone is sent to fetch his family or, at the very least, inform them that he will be away for a few months. But in a tragic turn of events, Huangfu Dun's implication in a crime he did not commit has forced his family into hiding, and no one knows where they have gone.

When Huangfu Dun next appears on stage, it is eighteen years later and he is still in Champa. Today, he tells us, he is giving a special lecture to an audience of barbarian crown princes: his translator tells him that "the princes from Champa, Cambodia, Samboja, and Java are waiting at the top of the hall to attend the lecture; those others from Byzantium, Laos, Europe, and Portugal are prostrating themselves at the foot of the stairs" 是占城、真

38. Ruan Dacheng, *Shuang jinbang*, 2:11a. Fu Jiezi and Zhang Qian were officials known for their foreign exploits that furthered the interests of the Western Han.

臘、三佛齊、瓜哇，四處上堂領班。其餘拂菻、老撾、歐羅巴、佛狼機，都在階下頂禮.[39] What follows is a wide-ranging tour of the Chinese intellectual tradition: from trigrams to Confucius to the Cheng-Zhu school. As in *Three Kinds of Happiness*, a translator is employed, though, as in that play, not consistently. Here the translator translates in both directions—both instructions from Huangfu Dun to the princes and questions from the princes to Huangfu Dun:

> HUANGFU DUN, played by the *sheng*: I understand. Princes, listen to what I have to say.
>
> TRANSLATOR, to the foreign princes: Jida ci. Jia mangji, ta ya ti li.
>
> [. . .]
>
> FOREIGN PRINCE:[40] Jie xi hua, yaming lala de jiahun lao, hai ximo gong-gong *Jiagang*?
>
> TRANSLATOR: They have a rough understanding of what you just discussed; would you mind speaking a little about the *Book of Changes*?
>
> 生: 知道了。各王子聽我道夂。
>
> 通與番說介: 擠搭刺。甲茫擠塔啞剔黎。[41]
>
> [. . .]
>
> 番王: 借西滑, 啞名辣辣得假昏老, 還西抹拱拱押綱。
>
> 通: 說這些話, 他們略略的解分了, 煩師父講講易經。[42]

Ruan takes seriously the mechanics of translation in this scene, which is best reflected in his phonetic representation of a foreign

39. Ibid., 2:20b. This rather bizarre list indicates that Ruan was more familiar with his neighbors to the south than to the west. Corrected from the print edition, in which the grass radical is transposed over the 拂; the second character in Laos is given as 檛, and the 羅 and the 巴 in Europe are transposed.

40. The translator and foreign princes appear in the original print edition under these names and not their role types.

41. Ruan Dacheng, *Shuang jinbang*, 2:21a.

42. Ibid., 2:21b–22a.

language that enlists not some humorous gibberish but what often resembles Cantonese—though it is unclear if this is meant to signify a particular language like Cantonese per se (and its role as lingua franca across these Southeast Asian polities) or is to be understood as some unknown barbarian tongue.[43] However, despite this display of linguistic verisimilitude, large sections of the scene remain untranslated—while the dialogue before and the questions after are translated from Chinese into this other language, the arias that make up Huangfu Dun's lecture are not. Certainly such a move is in keeping with the requirements of dramatic economy; as the need for translation has been established, its actual depiction can be thus elided.

Although the audience does not hear the translation of the arias into a foreign language, they experience their translation in another sense. As Huangfu introduces his audience to the personages and texts of the Confucian tradition, he does so through the language of Buddhism, singing: "The wheel turned to the sage of Mount Ni [Confucius], who is the Buddha to Come" 直輪到一位尼山老，是當來佛. And: "The [Chan compendium] *Records of the Transmission of the Lamp* is merely the Four Poetic Modes, the Four Books, the Three Rites, and the Three Counsels [of the Confucian canon]" 傳燈錄則是四詩、四傳、三禮、三謨.[44] In this act of cultural translation, which reverses the historical transmission of Buddhism into China through the conceptual categories of Confucianism, Huangfu Dun opens up a space of equivalence and commensurability that is appropriate to his and Mo Cifei's roles as merchants of culture.

The potential of horizontality offered by these acts of translation is quickly overturned; much like Jiang Chi's disquisition for the foreign king in *Three Kinds of Happiness*, Huangfu Dun's lecture to the princes ends in submission. When he has finished speaking, and the students' final questions have been answered, Huangfu Dun has them practice a series of ritual obeisances and exclamations of *wansui*. Their transformation into good imperial

43. On the Cantonese (and possibly Malay) linguistic elements in the play, see Hardie, *The Many Faces of Ruan Dacheng*, 230n29.

44. Ruan Dacheng, *Shuang jinbang*, 2:21b.

subjects is complete by the penultimate scene of the play, when the four princes put their kowtowing practice to good use and enter into formal tributary relations with the Chinese court.

The foreign princes are not the only ones brought in from the margins. In the final scenes of the play, Mo Cifei submits both himself and the pearl to the court and is rewarded with an official position, and Huangfu Dun receives a full exoneration and an honorary title. As in *Three Kinds of Happiness*, these men on the periphery of Chinese society—failed students, fugitives, rebels—are seamlessly reincorporated into the imperial center.

In this ending the play diverges most strikingly from the story upon which it appears to be loosely based: "Yang Balao's Extraordinary Encounter in the Kingdom of Yue" 楊八老越國奇逢 from Feng Menglong's 1620 vernacular tale collection *Stories Old and New* (*Gujin xiaoshuo* 古今小說).[45] This *huaben* tells of a merchant named Yang Balao who is abducted by pirates and forced to live in Japan for nineteen years. Eventually Balao is brought back to China and must convince officials and family that he is not a Japanese pirate but a loyal Chinese subject. The parallels to *A Pair of Golden Placards* are clear: Huangfu Dun's innocent entanglement with pirates leads to a similarly long sojourn abroad; upon his return, Huangfu Dun is also suspected of being a pirate himself; like Yang Balao, he has two wives with two sons who are not aware of each other's existence, and both narratives end with reconciliation, reunion, and promotion.

While they begin and end in the same place, however, at the heart of "Yang Balao's Extraordinary Encounter" is a very different notion of how the sea can unmoor one's sense of self. Early in the vernacular tale, the narrator tells us about a particular strategy the pirates use in their raids that turns on the differences in appearance between Japanese pirates and Chinese commoners (plate 5):

45. Like many of the stories thought to be authored by Feng, an iteration of this story appears in his classical story collection *A History of Sentiment* (*Qingshi* 情史) as "Mr. Yang" 楊公, which is itself derived from the nearly identical story, "Mr. Nie and Mr. Yang Gain a Father" 蘖公楊公得父, from Wang Tonggui's 王同軌 (ca. 1530–after 1608) anecdotal collection *Tales Overheard* (*Ertan* 耳談).

> If a captive had a strong constitution, the pirates would shave and paint his head so that he could pass as Japanese. When fighting broke out, they would be sent off to the front lines. The government troops would get a reward for every enemy head they produced, so in the past, even regular Chinese folk who happened to be bald might find themselves beheaded by soldiers looking for a reward. How much more so for those captured during battle: whether they were real enemies or fake, no one cared—they would not be spared regardless. Since the fake Japanese with shaved heads knew that they were probably going to die anyway, they figured they might as well throw in their lot with the Japanese and perhaps live an extra few days, so they fought ferociously on the battlefield. The real Japanese would let the fake Japanese fend off the enemy on the front lines, only to charge forth from the rear once those in front had fallen. The government troops were repeatedly defeated by this tactic and were unable to gain the upper hand.
>
> 若是強壯的，就把來剃了頭髮，抹上油漆，假充倭子。每遇廝殺，便推他去當頭陣。官軍只要殺得一顆首級，便好領賞。平昔百姓中禿髮瘌痢，尚然被他割頭請功。況且見在戰陣上拿住，那管真假，定然不饒的。這些剃頭的假倭子，自知左右是死，索性靠著倭勢，還有捱過幾日之理，所以一般行兇出力。那些真倭子，只等假倭攩過頭陣，自己都尾其後而出，所以官軍屢墮其計，不能取勝。[46]

The tactic being employed here rests on an inversion of real and counterfeit that turns out to be at once meaningless and self-constituting. The ruse at first appears to turn on the physical disguise of Chinese commoners as Japanese pirates—that a bald head and a quick shellac of paint will sufficiently convince Chinese soldiers that the captives are Japanese. But the disguise need not be convincing to work, as the Chinese soldiers are not only incentivized to pass off these counterfeit Japanese pirates (or rather, their heads) to their superiors as the real thing, but they are also themselves occasional counterfeiters of Japanese pirate heads. In this chaotic war economy, in which the counterfeit has the same currency as the real, the only way for the captives not to be circulated as head-ingots is to become the very things they are faking.

46. Feng Menglong, ed., *Gujin xiaoshuo*, 20:672–73.

In their desire to live, to remain subjects in the face of the multi-directional forces trying to turn them into objects, the captives become Japanese pirates in the realest sense.

If, in that brief moment before their inevitable deaths, the counterfeit Japanese pirates somehow become genuine Japanese pirates, the narrator reveals that the "real" Japanese pirates are not so real after all:

> Actually the king of Japan generally was not aware of these pirate raids. In fact, these pirates were the poor folk of each island who joined together to make the overseas journey—just as with Chinese bandits, this was like a business venture. When they set out on their raids they would organize themselves into ranks under a self-proclaimed "great king." When they returned home, this title would be taboo. . . . If any were killed by the Chinese, it was just like a business losing capital.
>
> 原來倭奴入寇，國王多有不知者，乃是各島窮民，合夥泛海，如中國賊盜之類，彼處只如做買賣一般。其出掠亦各分部統，自稱大王之號。到回去，仍復隱諱了。. . . 如被中國人殺了，只作做買賣折本一般。[47]

The Japanese pirates are not exactly Japanese, nor are they properly understood as pirates. Their identities are organized, not around the country, but around the hyperlocal and the trans(proto)national—the poverty of their individual islands, the promise of their collective overseas enterprise. As their use of the term "great king" to describe their leaders demonstrates, the only sovereign kingdom in the open waters is the kingdom of silver. And though they are frequently referred to using the language of banditry, rather than the ragtag group of *haohan* 好漢 toughs such language might conjure, here these pirates are portrayed as well-organized businessmen who react to the deaths of their comrades not with cries of vengeance but with the cold calculation of a merchant adjusting his ledgers.

47. Ibid., 20:674–75.

In this way our antagonists are not so different from our protagonist. A failed student who turns to trade, Yang Balao is not immune from the ways in which a mercantile ethos transforms human relations into commercial transactions. Indeed, his initial resistance to taking a second wife is undone by his future mother-in-law's insistence that having a family in Fujian "would make it easier to do business" 做生意也是方便順溜的.[48] And like the Japanese pirates, once Balao leaves his homeland, his identity becomes unmoored from those of his countrymen. The narrator recounts the fate of men like Balao:

> Those young sturdy men that they captured were kept on as servants. They looked just like the Japanese, with their heads shaved and their feet unshod. They were given weapons and trained in fighting techniques. Terrified, the Chinese did not dare disobey. After about a year or so, they had gotten used to the foreign environment and learned the Japanese language—in the end they were no different from real Japanese people.
>
> 所擄得壯健男子，留作奴僕使喚。剃了頭，赤了兩腳，與本國一般模樣。給與刀仗，教他跳戰之法。中國人懼怕，不敢不從。過了一年半載，水土習服，學起倭話來，竟與真倭無異了。[49]

Unlike the slipshod disguises of those Chinese turned into "Japanese pirates" described earlier, these captives undergo a more involved transformation. While both transformations operate at the level of appearance, here the body is brought into what we might call culture—trained in new kinds of knowledge, exposed to new climates and foods, communicating through a new language. Such changes challenge the very constitution of identity: if one looks like a Japanese person, moves like a Japanese person, lives like a Japanese person, and speaks like a Japanese person, in what way is one still not-Japanese?[50] While the story is

48. Ibid., 20:667.
49. Ibid., 20:675.
50. This transformation "in place" echoes a similar one already undergone by the Persian merchant in Ling Mengchu's "A Chinese Man Changes His Luck," though in

ultimately unwilling to dispense with the notion of a fundamentally stable self, this moment in which the distinctions between real and fake, Chinese and Japanese, self and other collapse into "no difference" 無異 intimates another, more radical possibility: that one's identity is just a collection of gestures and bodily practices that can be learned and unlearned. In a rather dark reversal of the late Ming fascination with the self as a theatrical mode, here one does not fashion oneself through role-play but is fashioned under duress by others.

For Yang Balao, this troubling of self and other is dramatized by a moment of misrecognition when he catches his reflection in a mirror. If he has somehow become foreign to himself, he wonders, "how would other people be able to recognize him?" 他人如何認得. These fears are shown to be well founded. On a raiding trip to China, Yang Balao and twelve other men are taken prisoner by Yuan forces. Once in custody, "they all declared that they had been wronged and were not really Japanese, but no one paid them any attention" 衆人口稱冤枉, 都說不是真倭, 那里睬他.[51] Balao is eventually saved by his former servant, who no longer recognizes his face, but recognizes his story.

In *A Pair of Golden Placards*, Huangfu Dun does not learn the "shrike's tongue" 鴃舌, the incomprehensible twittering of his barbarian students, nor does his physical appearance change with the passage of time.[52] The sameness of the Huangfu Dun of scene 27 and the Huangfu Dun of scene 31 would have been reiterated and reinforced by the appearance of the *sheng* on stage still in the same (or at least, quite similar) robes as before—certainly not

---

that story there is a fundamental physicality that cannot be transformed: "As it turns out, the Persian had lived in China for so long that his clothing, speech, and gestures were not all that different from a Chinese person's. Only his shaved eyebrows and trimmed beard along with his deep-set eyes and high-bridged nose were a bit strange" 元來波斯胡住得在中華久了, 衣帽言動都與中華不大分別。只是剃眉剪鬚, 深目高鼻, 有些古怪. Ling, *Pai'an jingqi*, 1 57–58.

51. Feng Menglong, ed., *Gujin xiaoshuo*, 20:681.

52. Recalling the reference to taking a "shrike-tongued southern barbarian" 南蠻鴃舌 as one's teacher that appears in *Mencius* 3A4, Huangfu Dun sings, "When teaching in translation, you have disciples with shrike's tongues" 翻教授, 有鴃舌門徒. *Shisan jing zhushu*, 25:176–77; Ruan Dacheng, *Shuang jinbang*, 2:19a.

dressed in the manner of the barbarian translator or students, with whom he would make a striking visual contrast. He stays other, separate, above (quite literally, when delivering his lecture). Rather than reiterate the *huaben*'s unsettling narrative of a Chinese man becoming something foreign to himself, the play shows how a Chinese man domesticates the foreign, bringing it into the center until there is nothing left outside.

A Pair of Golden Placards was written by an influential and well-known literatus-official aligned with the powerful eunuch Wei Zhongxian 魏忠賢 (1568–1627). *Three Kinds of Happiness* is attributed to a relatively obscure commercially oriented playwright, whose associates in Suzhou seemed united around a shared loathing of Wei Zhongxian and his clique.[53] But despite these political and social chasms, both plays give voice to the late Ming fantasy of an infinitely expansive center that takes every horizontal exchange—every market interaction, every act of translation—and quickly reorients it. In *A Pair of Golden Placards*, the anxiety to reorient becomes neurotic; the final scenes repeatedly fixate on the gestures and bureaucratic processes of tribute, especially as it concerns Mo Cifei's return of himself and the pearl to imperial subjection. The reasons for Cifei's voluntary submission are never clear, though we are presumably meant to see his tremendous ambitions as the result of a personal failure to ascend the traditional ladder of success, a resentment that is easily dispatched when the emperor grants him a fancy title.[54]

This compulsion toward integration—itself a generic tendency of *chuanqi*—seems to foreclose any alternative sovereignty to that

53. Wei Zhongxian and his faction are the explicit villains of Li Yu's early Qing play *Register of the Pure and Loyal*, which recounts the 1626 uprising in Suzhou against Wei's persecution of the Donglin partisans. Other plays, like Qiu Yuan's *Stele of the Partisans* (*Dangren bei* 黨人碑), transpose these events into other contexts and times.

54. In an echo of the biography of the assassin Jing Ke 荊軻 in the *Record of the Historian*, Cifei laments: "I studied books and learned swordsmanship, but in half of my life I have achieved nothing" 小弟讀書擊劍, 半世無成. Ruan Dacheng, *Shuang jinbang*, 2:11a.

of the state. At the same time, the market and the expansive horizontality it makes possible are never fully subsumed, an ever-present possibility just below the surface. It is only after the fall of the Ming, when the fantasy of political and social integration promised by these plays becomes permanently untenable, that the structure of market exchange comes to offer something more.

Castaways

Ruan Dacheng, an architect of the short-lived Southern Ming, did not live to see the new order brought into being by Manchu rule. But Zhang Dafu did. *The Sound of Reading*, also attributed to Zhang Dafu, restages these late Ming voyages for a world that had been radically transformed.[55] In many ways, *The Sound of Reading* can be seen as a rewriting of *Three Kinds of Happiness*. Both plays are set in southeastern coastal cities thrown into chaos by pirate raids. Both feature scholarly protagonists who find themselves first on a merchant ship and then on a strange island. It is on this island, and not in the examination hall, that both

55. The only extant edition of *The Sound of Reading* is an incomplete and undated manuscript from the collection of the famous *jingju* male *dan* Cheng Yanqiu 程硯秋 (1904–58). As the first scene and part of the second are missing from the extant play text, it is unknown if an author was originally listed on the text. As with *Three Kinds of Happiness*, the consensus of the scholarly community on the attribution of the play to Zhang Dafu is based on a reference in Gao Yi's *New Southern Dramas* (in which it is listed as the fifteenth of Zhang's sixteen plays and thus presumably a later work; *Three Kinds of Happiness* appears seventh). However, while it is impossible to know if the extant undated manuscript is the same play as *The Sound of Reading* written by Zhang Dafu in the early Qing, the structure of the play and its use of Wu dialect and of source materials from Feng Menglong's collections are typical of the Suzhou circle. As I discuss later in this chapter, the content also speaks very specifically to the coastal crises and ethnopolitics of early Qing Jiangnan (and the political commitments of Zhang Dafu) such that even if the extant text does not itself date from the early Qing, it nevertheless bears the traces of a prior work produced in the early Qing. Scholars uniformly list the play as written in the early Qing. For example, Sun Shulei, *Ming mo Qing chu xiju yanjiu*, 33.

protagonists find success, and both parlay this extragovernmental achievement into state-bestowed status.[56]

However, in the early Qing moment, the imperialist optimism of *Three Kinds of Happiness* is untenable; while that earlier play stages a particularly late-Ming vision of a seamlessly expansive body politic, *The Sound of Reading* makes visible the violent exclusions that make such an expansion possible. In *The Sound of Reading*, the various hierarchies reaffirmed at the end of *Three Kinds of Happiness* are replaced with a more nuanced deconstruction of the distinctions between center and periphery, Chinese and barbarian, loyalist and traitor, merchant and scholar, and human and beast. If the work of *Three Kinds of Happiness* and *A Pair of Golden Placards* is to turn the horizontality of market relations into the legible verticality of the state, *The Sound of Reading* constantly trespasses and inverts the supposed order of things.

In the thirteenth act of *The Sound of Reading*, the poor orphaned student Song Ru finds himself alone on a strange and seemingly uninhabited island. He had arrived there on the merchant cargo ship of his father-in-law, Boatman Dai; they had stopped on the island to find some herbs to treat the ailing student's illness, but when Song Ru sees the ship sailing away, he realizes that he has been tricked and abandoned.[57] This turn of events

56. Many of these plot elements are also shared with *A Pair of Golden Placards*.

57. *The Sound of Reading* brings together two narrative threads. The first derives from a classical tale that is anthologized in Feng Menglong's *A History of Sentiment* as "Student Sun from Wusong" 吳淞孫生 and that was expanded into the vernacular story "Over Mistaken Accusations of Flirting, Mrs. Jia Curses Her Daughter; From a False Lawsuit, Mr. Sun Obtains a Wife" 錯調情賈母詈女, 誤告狀孫郎得妻 in Ling Mengchu's *Slapping the Table in Amazement, vol. 2* (*Erke pai'an jingqi* 二刻拍案驚奇, 1632). The second thread comes from a story in Wang Tonggui's *Tales Overheard*, that is anthologized in Feng Menglong's *A History of Sentiment* as "The Wife of Jin San" 金三妻. This story is given an expanded treatment in Feng's *Comprehensive Words to Warn the World* as the vernacular story "Mr. Song Brings about a Reunion by Means of a Tattered Felt Hat" 宋小官團圓破氈笠. This use of material from the collections of Feng Menglong and Ling Mengchu was common among the Suzhou circle, as was the intertwining of two narrative threads in the construction of a *chuanqi*. However, in a departure from many of the other plays attributed to the Suzhou circle, *The Sound of Reading* draws primarily from the classical anecdotes and not the elaborated

should not have come as a surprise, as Song Ru's marriage into the Dai family had been deeply fraught from the beginning. Earlier in the play, Song Ru sought passage on the Dais' boat in order to travel to the capital to sit for the civil service examination. When the Dais' daughter Run'er was caught eavesdropping on him reciting texts late at night—the enchanting "sound of reading" from which the play's title derives—her horrified parents accused her of impropriety; humiliated, she strangled herself with her sash. Blaming Song Ru for Run'er's death, her parents returned to land to file a lawsuit. When Run'er suddenly revived during the court hearing, the Haimen 海門 County magistrate dismissed the charges and compelled Boatman Dai to accept Song Ru as his son-in-law, which he did begrudgingly. Back at sea, Song Ru's illness provided the perfect pretext for the Dais to rid themselves of the "useless" student and marry their daughter to a sturdy boat hand.

Sick, freezing, and lost, with dusk turning to dark, Song Ru sees a looming figure approach. It is the *jing* "dressed as a savage" 扮野人, who grabs Song Ru and drags him offstage. The first half of the play comes to a dramatic close as we hear Song Ru cry out in despair, "Oh no, this is really bad!" 哎呀，不好了嚇.[58] While the appearance of this creature is a shock to Song Ru, the audience had already heard tell of a mysterious *renxiong* 人熊 (lit. human-bear).[59] Earlier in the third scene, a band of pirates lands on the island looking for a place to stash their ill-gotten treasure. After a commotion offstage, several of the men report to their leader, Shi Yi, that in the forest they encountered "a savage, extraordinarily fierce and strong" 一個野人，勇猛異常. They tried to kill the creature, but "neither cannon fire nor arrows nor spears and daggers were able to injure it" 火砲、葉箭、鎗刀俱傷他不得. Shi Yi explains that this was not just some wild animal:

---

huaben versions. The *renxiong* discussed below is an innovation of the play; no such creature appears in any of these source texts.

58. Zhang Dafu (attrib.), *Dushu sheng*, 1:21a.

59. Though the term *renxiong* is used in modern Chinese to refer to bears, in the late imperial period this was a term used to describe a type of creature with powers and possibilities that exceed what is conveyed by the term "bear" and will therefore remain untranslated here.

"I have heard that the *renxiong* is a most numinous beast; it cannot be harmed" 我聞人熊，乃至靈之獸，不可傷他.[60]

When Song Ru reappears a few scenes later, we learn the truth of what happened after the terrifying cliff-hanger. That fateful night, he tells us, "I saw something that was like a man but wasn't a man, like a beast but not a beast, that carried me to this cave" 只見一個似人非人，似獸非獸，負我到此山洞中.[61] Though Song Ru thought death was imminent, it turns out that the creature wanted to take him not as its meal but as its mate, "to perform the rites to become husband and wife" 欲我成其夫婦之禮. In the safety of the cave, the *renxiong* supplied him with medicinal plants, and he made a full recovery in a matter of days. As for the creature itself, Song Ru declares that "although this *renxiong* is a ferocious beast, it understands human feelings quite well" 只是那人熊雖則猛獸，亦頗解人意.[62] The *renxiong* has even taken on the role of teacher: every day, Song Ru tells us, whenever there is free time, it teaches him how to spar with spear and sword and he is now quite proficient.

Their quasi-domestic idyll is interrupted when Song Ru catches sight of the boat of an old friend. Song Ru quickly makes his way to the shore, overjoyed to be rescued at last. As he sails off, the *renxiong* chases after him; when it realizes he is gone for good, it throws itself into the ocean. The friend witnesses the *renxiong*'s suicide and mentions it to Song Ru, who is overcome with guilt: "Dear bear, it is I who heartlessly harmed you!" 熊熊，是小生無情害了你了.[63] Song Ru swears that if he ever attains fame and rank, he will have a memorial tablet erected in the *renxiong*'s honor.

This island interlude is the unexpected pivot on which the entire play turns, in which a seeming geographical and narrative dead end is actually a site of renewal and profit. The ailing student not only recovers his health but also gains martial skills that will

60. Zhang Dafu, *Dushu sheng*, 1:3b.
61. Ibid., 2:4b.
62. Ibid.
63. Ibid., 2:6a.

serve him well in the latter half of the play. And although dumped on the island like so much refuse, he leaves loaded with treasure: Song Ru had stumbled upon the pirates' hidden spoils, which he takes with him when he is rescued. When the Haimen magistrate is kidnapped by the pirates, Song Ru uses this booty to redeem the man who had once saved him and then joins the military effort to defeat the pirates once and for all. Song Ru's efforts are rewarded with a marriage to the magistrate's daughter and a reunion with his faithful first wife, Run'er. The play ends with a tribute to the creature that made all of this career and romantic success possible: "The achievements and the rank and riches I have today have been given to me by that *renxiong*. This is a debt that I must repay" 今日功成富貴，此人熊之賜也，不可不報.[64] Song Ru recalls his earlier promise and has a shrine for the *renxiong*'s spirit built on the island.

Song Ru's *renxiong* figures into a long imaginary of beings that occupy the liminal space between man and beast.[65] Though called a savage 野人, a beast 獸, and a bear 熊 and played by the *jing*, a painted face role typically reserved for male characters, the *renxiong's* large physical presence and terrifying painted exterior masks a surprising capacity for feeling. In its nursing of Song Ru back to health and its suicide upon being abandoned, the *renxiong* acts in ways not unlike a proper *chuanqi* heroine. The stage directions, though limited, reveal the *renxiong*'s final scene to be a bravura performance of heartbreak that cycles through desire, anger, and resignation: "The *jing* enters dressed as a savage and crying out" 淨扮野人叫上, and then, spotting the ship, gesticulates to the men sailing away, "making a beckoning gesture" 招介. When that does not work, it "angrily throws stones" 恨介擲石 before "throwing itself in the water and rolling off stage" 自投水滚行下.[66]

64. Ibid., 2:23a.

65. The uses and meanings of the *renxiong* in the late imperial imagination, and how its depiction here relates to the play's broader ethnopolitics, are further explored in Fox, "Exit, Pursued by a Bear."

66. Zhang Dafu, *Dushu sheng*, 2:6a.

The unexpected emotional performance given by the *renxiong* does not happen in isolation from the larger moral drama of the play. Rather, it can be seen as part of the play's overall project to expand a certain kind of personhood to those who would otherwise be considered objects and not subjects. Set in the early years of the Yuan dynasty, *The Sound of Reading* places at its center the ever-deepening reciprocal exchanges between two men whose relationship is freighted with nothing less than the weight of dynastic transition: Song Ru 宋儒 (lit. Song [dynasty] Confucian) and the Mongol magistrate of Haimen, Yelü Wulitiemu'er 耶律烏梨鐵木兒. Yelü grants Song Ru his freedom and his first wife; Song Ru buys Yelü's release and marries his daughter as his second wife. The path of their relationship from recognition—in which the magistrate sees the true character of the falsely accused student—to mentorship and ultimately kinship echoes the homosocial bonds that structure many late imperial *chuanqi*. That Magistrate Yelü is a member of the Mongol royal family brings this development of affinity (and affinal bonds) into the realm of ethnodynastic politics.[67]

However, while Yelü's blood and bureaucratic ties to the Mongol Yuan court are repeatedly mentioned, markers of ethnic difference are conspicuously absent. When Yelü, played by the *wai*, makes his first entrance, he is led onstage by a procession and is wearing a cap and belt as befitting a (Chinese) official, in a striking contrast to the ethnic others that often appear on the late Ming stage, like the foreign princes of *A Pair of Golden Placards*, who "enter dancing" 舞上 dressed in their foreign robes and "sit cross-legged on the floor" 盤腳坐介 or the Jurchen envoy in *Peony Pavilion*, who enters "on horseback, dressed as a barbarian general and brandishing a dagger" 扮番將帶刀騎馬.[68] While the princes and envoy speak in incomprehensible tongues, Yelü, as befitting a man of his position, speaks in *guanhua*, the standardized language

67. While this name does not appear to refer to a historical personage, Yelü 耶律 was the surname of a prominent Khitanese clan whose members attained high office during the Liao and Yuan dynasties.

68. Ruan Dacheng, *Shuang jinbang*, 2:20b–21a; Tang Xianzu, *Mudan ting*, 217.

of officialdom.[69] As Yelü insightfully adjudicates the case against Song Ru, the role that he embodies—the upright and perceptive judge—owes a significant debt to the Song dynasty personage-turned-legend Judge Bao.[70] And when Yelü is kidnapped, his daughter Maozhuan fully inhabits the role of the devoted Confucian child, willing to sell her own body to pay her father's ransom.

It is this daughter who will serve as the physical link between Magistrate Yelü and Song Ru, between the Yuan and the Song, between Mongol and Han, when she is given in marriage to Song Ru. That this marriage comes at the behest of the emperor himself, rather than a low-level official (as in Song Ru's earlier marriage, which was arranged by Yelü), highlights the larger symbolic significance of this union between the Mongol royal family and a "Confucian of the Song."[71]

The depiction of Yelü as an upright magistrate and his daughter Maozhuan as a filial exemplar does much to fold the Mongol other into what Peter Bol translates as "this culture of ours" (*siwen* 斯文)—an understanding of the received tradition that was articulated through one's scholarly practice, ethical behavior, and civil service.[72] Similarly, Run'er's refusal to remarry, despite parental pressure and strong financial incentive, demonstrates an innate

69. In this sense, Yelü recalls certain depictions found in the *huaben* tradition of assimilated others—the Persian merchant in "A Chinese Man Changes His Luck," who was in many respects "not all that different from a Chinese person," or the Chinese merchant-turned-Japanese-pirate in "Yang Balao's Extraordinary Encounter," who appeared "no different from a real Japanese person." However, in those cases, there remains something uncanny about this act of assimilation, some sense that it remains a surface-level act, and some core, stable identity (of Persian, of Chinese) lies below. The treatment of Yelü here contains none of this anxiety; no move is made to show that he does not belong in the cultural Sinosphere.

70. On the post-Song emulation of Bao Zheng 包拯 (999–1062) as the epitome of a "pure official" 清官, see Idema, *Judge Bao and the Rule of Law*, ix–xxxiv.

71. That Maozhuan is given as Song Ru's secondary wife 二夫人 perhaps reveals fault lines in this seemingly harmonious solution. While the marriage between Song Ru and Run'er certainly predates the union of Song Ru and Maozhuan, the final configuration whereby the daughter of a boatman is accorded a higher rank than the daughter of an aristocratic official serves as a comment on the increasing acceptability of marrying across status while perhaps expressing some unease with this post-conquest fantasy of an assimilated Sinosphere.

72. Bol, "This Culture of Ours," 1–5.

capacity among non-elites for a particularly Neo-Confucian performance of wifely chastity. In much the same way, the *renxiong* demonstrates an intuitive benevolence, revealing a truly human(e) heart in contrast to the villainous Dais, who are derided for having "the face of a human but the heart of a beast" 人面獸心.[73] Despite not being fully Chinese, fully elite, or fully human, Maozhuan, Run'er, and the *renxiong* become the play's exemplars of filiality, chastity, loyalty, and compassion, very much in keeping with the late Ming discourse of *qing* that lauds the spontaneous moral behavior of those outside the reach of traditional Confucian education.[74]

The play ends with a happy polygamous union between Song Ru, Run'er, and Maozhuan, the formation of new kinship relations bringing these women from the margins of elite culture into the center. That "a Confucian of the Song" marries the daughter of a boatman and the daughter of a Mongol would offer a particularly loaded lesson to an early Qing audience, showing how the imagined distance between scholar and merchant and between Chinese and barbarian can be overcome. But what of Song Ru's third "wife," the *renxiong*? Why can only the boundary between man and beast not be overcome? Perhaps it would be instructive to look at another character, also tied to the island in the middle of the sea, who cannot be assimilated into this new polity: the pirate leader, Shi Yi.

Pirates were not an infrequent presence on the late imperial stage. In *Three Kinds of Happiness*, they are terrifying sowers of disorder: the pirate leader, Hai Qiu'er 海鰍兒 ("Sea Loach"), makes his grand entrance singing of his stockpile of "a million spears and swords" 百萬鎗和劍 that his fearsome band of pirates will use to "turn heaven and earth upside down, bringing chaos everywhere" 地覆天翻，到處胡麻亂.[75] These pirates are not driven by any sort of political agenda; rather, in a bit of historical verisi-

73. Zhang Dafu, *Dushu sheng*, 2:22a.

74. For other such examples, see Goldman, *Opera and the City*, 145–74; Sibau, "Maids, Fishermen, and Storytellers"; Liu Chiung-yun, "Huanguan, xiaji, he nüyi."

75. Zhang Dafu, *Kuaihuo san*, 1:29a.

militude, these pirates "used to traffic in black-market salt" 向販私鹽 and are driven to looting when a government crackdown cuts into their business.[76] These erstwhile merchants are concerned only with the accumulation of riches; in the fourteenth scene, Hai Qiu'er orders Ying'er's old nursemaid killed when she is unable to provide them with anything of value. As the dark id of the maritime market, violently extracting value and in the process wresting people and things from their proper places and leaving a broken community in their wake, the pirates form a pointed contrast to the fantasy offered by the kingdom of Qiuci, in which trade is a natural extension of sociality, with gift exchange sliding seamlessly into market exchange and back again.

The pirate Mo Cifei of *A Pair of Golden Placards* is not as irredeemably vicious as Hai Qiu'er, though he is similarly motivated by an expansive acquisitiveness—once in possession of the magical pearl, "the sea market is fully in [his] grasp" 海市吾操總—and a destructive disregard for the lives that are caught up in his machinations.[77] And while his pearl plot sets him up as a regional rival to the Ming—collecting tribute from peoples who should be tributaries of the Ming—his ambitions stem not from a desire to reorganize or reallocate power but from a lack of recognition within the existing political structure, as he is easily and seamlessly brought back into the Ming bureaucracy.

In contrast to the grasping, acquisitive pirates of *Three Kinds of Happiness* and *A Pair of Golden Placards*, the pirates of *The Sound of Reading* are an entirely different ilk. Their leader is a former Song dynasty general who enters not bragging of the destruction he has wrought or the riches he hopes to accrue but bemoaning the dire state of affairs that drove him to the life of an outlaw: "The Song ruling house was destroyed, and ten thousand people were slaughtered" 宋室摧殘萬姓屠. In an echo of much of the (Qing-sanctioned) discourse surrounding the fall of the Ming,

76. Ibid. The salt market was controlled by a government monopoly administered through official certificates.

77. More bloodthirsty pirates figure significantly in another Ruan Dacheng play, *The Śākyamuni Pearls* (*Mouni he* 牟尼合), as the murderers of the main character.

he blames the collapse of the Song not on northern invaders but on "treacherous officials" 奸臣 who "undermined the state and harmed the people" 誤國害民. Shi Yi has gathered a band of "heroes and valiants" 英雄豪傑 who style themselves after the Liangshan outlaws. While the pirates in *Three Kinds of Happiness* and *A Pair of Golden Placards* are motivated by a crude acquisitiveness, the pirates in *The Sound of Reading* participate in shadowy overseas economies only for the sake of funding their loyalist activities.[78] In the third scene, one of Shi Yi's men presents him with "gold, pearls, jade, and silk; strange perfumes and unusual treasures from foreign lands" 金珠玉帛，外國奇香異寶.[79] These valuables are hidden on the abandoned island until the time is right to launch their attack on the capital.

The impetus to launch a land campaign arrives with the abduction and imprisonment of the historical martyr Wen Tianxiang 文天祥 (1236–83) in the capital Dadu (modern Beijing). Since the magistrate of Haimen is a member of the Yuan royal family, the pirates decide to loot the city, hold the magistrate for ransom, and from there continue inland to the capital. But this loyalist economy, through which the pirates fund their exploits, is also the source of their ruin. Song Ru steals their hidden treasure and uses it to pay the magistrate's ransom; when the pirates return to the island to retrieve this treasure, they discover that they have been tricked and pay with their lives.

When he is defeated by Song Ru and the formerly captive magistrate in battle, Shi Yi defiantly faces his imminent death, singing: "You were once a pheasant in my cage, but today I have become a dragon out of water.[80] There is nothing left for me but to die" 你曾作我籠中之雉，我今日成失水之龍，有死而已.[81] No attempt is made to recruit him to his enemy's side; unlike the bandit-rebels in Li Yu's early Qing play *Two of Beard and Brow*, Shi Yi's unwavering

78. Zhang Dafu, *Dushu sheng*, 1:2b.
79. Ibid., 1:3a.
80. Unlike in Western dragon iconography, Chinese dragons live in the water and are closely associated with both bodies of water and rain.
81. Zhang Dafu, *Dushu sheng*, 2:17b.

loyalty to the previous dynasty cannot be overcome.[82] Shi Yi's steadfast dedication to his cause is treated with a nuance not usually reserved for *chuanqi* antagonists, which can perhaps be attributed in part to the character's historical antecedents.[83] While the point of reference for the late Ming plays is the memory of the mid-Ming piracy crises (set in motion, as is depicted in *Three Kinds of Happiness*, by the restriction of maritime commerce), by the early Qing, piracy was inflected with a more political meaning—a "pirate" was no longer a merchant whose activities were not in the commercial interests of the state, but a subject whose activities had been deemed threatening to the state's very existence.

These references are barely below the surface of *The Sound of Reading*; Shi Yi is clearly meant to evoke the Ming general turned loyalist Zheng Chenggong 鄭成功 (aka Koxinga 國姓爺, 1624–62), with Shi Yi's attacks on the Mongol Yuan recalling Zheng's exploits against the Manchu Qing: Shi Yi's abortive campaign to retake the northern capital, Dadu, echoes Zheng Chenggong's failed attempt to take the southern capital, Nanjing, and just as Zheng retreated to Taiwan in the face of this defeat, Shi Yi flees to a remote island. The pirate's loaded name, Shi Yi 時宜, with its reference to "taking action according to the circumstances" 因時制宜, not only makes explicit the connection to the present day but also offers a justification of sorts: Shi Yi is resorting to piracy only as an expedient means in a time of grave crisis.

But while Shi Yi is treated sympathetically by the play, he is not the heroic redeemer of a fallen dynasty like other Zheng Chenggong proxies that appear in early Qing narratives, such as *Later Tales of Water Margin* (*Shuihu houzhuan* 水滸後傳).[84] As his name makes clear, it is Song Ru and not the loyalist pirate who is the true inheritor of the Song's cultural tradition. While Shi Yi's

82. For a discussion of this play and the distinction it makes between "local bandits," whose loyalty is a free-floating quality that could be redirected, and "roving bandits," who cannot be redeemed, see Wai-yee Li, *Women and National Trauma in Late Imperial Chinese Literature*, 254–68.

83. The real villains of *The Sound of Reading* turn out to be the treacherous Dais and a murderous boat hand.

84. On this novel, see Widmer, *The Margins of Utopia*.

loyalist commitments are treated with empathy and respect—which is to be expected from a *chuanqi* playwright emerging from mid-century Jiangnan—there is no place for him in the new order. His death is a necessary precondition for the formation of a post-transition community; as he says, he is a dragon out of water, a man out of joint with his time, who can do nothing but die.

The death of the *renxiong* is similarly one of resignation, of recognizing that the world of the protagonist has no room for a creature like it. Like Shi Yi, the *renxiong* fulfills a narrative function that allows the polity to be put back together again by delimiting what is inside and what is outside, where it begins and where it ends. In extending its community to include the barbarian but not the beast, the play disentangles the late imperial discourses that conflated the foreign and the subhuman—a conflation made visible on the late imperial stage in the pointed resemblance between the barbarian character dressed in furs and babbling incomprehensibly and the wild beast grunting and covered in hair.[85] Positioned against the depiction of Yelü Wulitiemu'er in Han clothes, speaking *guanhua* and inhabiting a familiar role, the *renxiong* allows the play to rescue the conquest dynasty from barbarity.[86]

The exclusion of the loyalist and the savage in order to construct a new community between the remnant and the barbar-

85. One passage frequently associated with the *renxiong* in late imperial texts comes from a description in the *Classic of Mountains and Seas* of the people from the foreign land of Xiaoyang Country 梟陽國. *Shanhai jing jiaozhu*, 319. The rhetorical slippage between barbarian and beast was common in the late Ming (see, e.g., Yuming He, *Home and the World*, 236–38), though perilous in the early Qing.

86. The text's attitude toward the ruling mandate of ethnic others, while unusual for a Suzhou circle play, accords with an attribution of the text to Zhang Dafu. Zeng Guoguo argues that the titles of Zhang's nonextant *zaju* seem to indicate that they were *zhushou xi* 祝壽戲 (birthday celebration plays) written for the Kangxi emperor or the empress dowager. Zeng also notes that Zhang's aria manual *Newly Established Southern Scores in the Nine Modes and Thirteen Tones from Cold Mountain Studio* lists his sons' courtesy names as Junfu 君輔 and Junzuo 君佐. These names, which Zeng argues were most likely given in the early Qing (and at the very least not changed by the time of the *qupu*'s publication during the Kangxi reign), demonstrate a commitment to helping the new regime (i.e., "assist the ruler with governing" 輔佐君王). Zeng Guoguo, "*Rushi guan* wei Zhang Dafu suo zuo xianyi," 50.

ian is necessary but not untroubled. Their deaths, treated with sympathy and regret, are experienced as losses, not gains; in resisting *chuanqi*'s compulsive restoration of wholeness, they gesture to the fractures and exclusions that made the restoration of order in the early Qing possible. There is no place in this world for the love of a *renxiong* except the bottom of the sea.

In *The Sound of Reading*, the categories that structured earlier *chuanqi* begin to break down; as characters move between hero and villain, pirate and soldier, loyalist and traitor, merchant and student, Chinese and other, the received hierarchical orientation of these categories is inverted, leveled, reoriented: a loyalist general-turned-pirate is alternately noble and mercenary, heroic and villainous; an ethnic Mongol of the Yuan royal clan assumes the mantle of the beloved Song dynasty judge Bao Zheng, meting out justice and upholding Confucian morality; the "Song Confucian" protagonist leads the rooting out of the Song hold-outs; and a savage beast shows itself to be a caring and virtuous helpmate, while the grasping in-laws lack all human feelings of compassion.

This porousness of identity—the fluid movement between one thing and another—is made possible by the liminal spaces created by the maritime economies of the South China coast. Much of *The Sound of Reading* is set in spaces like merchant boats, pirate ships, and uninhabited islands that slip the net of dynastic authority, the trauma of the Song-Yuan transition (a clear displacement for the Ming-Qing transition) set against the timeless pull of the ocean waves carrying people and things into unexpected places.

As in *Three Kinds of Happiness* and *A Pair of Golden Placards*, it is the ocean that brings new social relations into being. The ocean in these plays functions as a kind of stage—a space that acts as both a surface and a boundary, where characters can become something that they were not before. The formal similarities between ocean and stage can be glimpsed in those scenes where the stage "acts" as the ocean and the ocean "acts" as a stage. On the stage that becomes an ocean, characters pantomime sailing on and drowning in its waves, like the *renxiong* in *The Sound of Reading* rolling around the (ocean) floor. On the ocean that becomes a kind of stage, sea voyages turn characters into both figurative and literal actors, like the merchants aboard the ocean-going ship in *Three Kinds of Happiness*, who pass the time with an impromptu staging of a play, or the student Jiang Chi, whose ocean voyage leads him to play the roles of "merchant" and "Chinese expert" in the foreign court.

The ocean as it is enlisted in these plays as market and stage, as site of exchange and site of performance, is not just a metaphor; it is a lived experience. The imbrication of ocean and market and stage was visible in the Suzhou cityscape—the arterial waterways that connected the city to the Grand Canal, the Yangzi River, and the ocean beyond were sites of both bustling commerce and active performance. From outdoor canal-side stages or the decks of pleasure boats and performance barges, the voices of *kunqu* actors carried across the water's surface, intermingling with the sounds of hawkers selling their wares and longshoremen unloading cargo, making everyone at once performer and audience.[87]

For the playwrights of the Suzhou circle, who were writing for theatrical events in the waterways and temple markets of the city, this performance context frequently presents the possibility of self-referential staging—to perform *Winning the Prize Courtesan*'s pleasure boat scenes in the cabin of a pleasure boat, or the impromptu performance on the deck of a merchant vessel in *Three Kinds of Happiness* as an impromptu performance on the deck of a merchant vessel, such that those watching might realize that they themselves are also implicated in larger economies that radiate out from the canals to the delta and beyond, that they too are actors on the ocean-stage.

87. Sophie Volpp describes the theater barges of Suzhou, in which a larger vessel acts as the stage and the audience assembles around it in small boats. She notes the "mobile and participatory" nature of this kind of spectatorship, linking it to a larger kind of social spectatorship made possible by the late imperial theatrical imagination. Volpp, *Worldly Stage*, 73–75. For a treatment of waterborne theatrical entertainment, see Cervone, "Waterscapes."

Coda: Sea/Change

The waterways of Suzhou, where the city's commercial and cultural identities converged, posed problems of ideology and administration—this floating world that rejected the Neo-Confucian suspicion of profit and pleasure and that defied the neatly ordered jurisdictional boundaries of counties (and prefectures and provinces and states). The Kangxi emperor visited Suzhou in 1684 on his first southern tour, and the uncertainty over how to navigate this space is palpable in the official record. The emperor lodged for only one night within the city walls, it says; he visited temples to perform rites, but (officially, at least) kept his distance from the thrum of singing and selling outside of their gates.[88] But when his grandson, the Qianlong emperor, makes his southern tours, this anxious avoidance of the spaces of commerce and culture is replaced with a muscular embrace—the brightly painted boats and busy markets are now in line with the aesthetics and rhetoric of the "prosperous age" (*shengshi* 盛世) of the high Qing, and the direct engagement with the spaces of commerce are consonant with imperial ambitions to reassert sovereignty over an expanding maritime commercial realm and restrict the growing influence of powerful merchants from Suzhou and Yangzhou.[89]

In a panoramic reimagining of the Qianlong emperor's 1751 visit, his court painters depict a Suzhou lined with busy but orderly shops and dotted with over half a dozen stages in the city streets, along the water, and on boats (plate 6).[90] A number of townspeople

88. Chang, "Historical Narratives of the Kangxi Emperor's Inaugural Visit to Suzhou."

89. Chang, *A Court on Horseback*, 219–59.

90. Xu Yang 徐揚 (active ca. 1750–after 1776) et al., *The Qianlong Emperor's Southern Inspection Tour* (*Qianlong nanxun tu* 乾隆南巡圖, 1770). This detail is from the sixth scroll, *Entering Suzhou along the Grand Canal* (*Dayunhe zhi Suzhou* 大運河至蘇州). In seventh scroll of *The Kangxi Emperor's Southern Inspection Tour* (*Kangxi nanxun tu* 康熙南巡圖), a similarly imperially commissioned painting by Wang Hui 王翬 (1632–1717) and his assistants of the Kangxi emperor's visit to Suzhou, operatic performance, which appears in other sections, is conspicuously absent. For background on these paintings, see Hearn, "Document and Portrait."

go about their business, engaging with shopkeepers or stopping to watch the performances, which appear to be staged in celebration of the imperial visit.[91] However, in the dramatic focal points of the scroll—the empress dowager's barge and the emperor's entrance through Chang Gate on horseback—several opera performances attract no attention at all, as all eyes turn to the real performance. No longer sites of moral turpitude to be avoided as much as possible, the lanes and canals within and around the city become a stage for the grand spectacle of imperial power.

Drawing explicitly on *Along the River during the Qingming Festival* (*Qingming shanghe tu* 清明上河圖), this painting situates itself in the tradition of imperial appropriation and containment of urban commerce and culture.[92] A similar move can be seen in high Qing court theater, which compulsively stages ocean voyages through which the entire globe is brought into the physical and ontological boundaries of the empire. If seventeenth-century theatrical performance, from the market stages to the literati gardens to the imperial court, captured the experience of Chinese explorers venturing across the ocean to discover new things to buy and sell and new people to buy and sell with, during the eighteenth century the Dutch and British East India Companies reverse the directionality of discovery and, by the turn of the nineteenth century, of profit. Such a shift is reflected and reinscribed into legible and reassuring hierarchies in high Qing court plays such as *Ascendant Peace in the Four Seas* (*Sihai shengping* 四海昇平),

91. Cheng-hua Wang has written on the deployment of theatricality and spectatorship in high Qing court painting, noting both an attention to a variety of street performances and the turning of the street itself into a stage for the dramatization of everyday life. Cheng-hua Wang, "One Painting, Two Emperors," 87–94. On the theatrical performances held in Suzhou during the Kangxi and Qianlong tours, see Pei Xuelai, *Qingdai qianzhongqi Suzhou jutan yanjiu*, 170–85.

92. This appropriation and containment became quite literal inside the imperial retreat Yuanmingyuan 圓明園, where two southern-style *maimaijie* 買賣街 (commercial streets) were constructed. According to Qianlong-era Jesuit observers, these bustling simulacra employed palace eunuchs to staff shops and playact various urban denizens while members of the imperial family browsed the wares. For a translation of these sources, see Barmé, "A Garden of Perfect Brightness, A Life in Ruins," 119.

Arhat Crossing the Sea (*Luohan duhai* 羅漢渡海), and *Rainbow Bridge across the Ocean* (*Hongqiao xian dahai* 虹橋現大海), in which all manner of foreign subjects and creatures travel across the oceans to come to China and pay tribute.[93]

But even in the careful controlled spaces of the Qing court, ghosts of the past reappear. In the waning years of the Qing, the Empress Dowager Cixi arranged for three performances of a *pihuang* 皮簧 opera called *Marriage Affinity of Dragon and Horse* (*Longma yinyuan* 龍馬姻緣)—the first of which was in 1893, the year that Cixi is historically (mis)remembered for squandering the navy's money on a marble boat for the summer palace Yiheyuan 頤和園.[94] This play, itself adapted from the 1840 *pihuang Realm of Ultimate Bliss* (*Jile shijie* 極樂世界), has its roots not at the optimistic grandeur and imperial ambition of the high Qing nor in the increasingly frayed wish fulfillment of the late Qing, but in the oceanic imaginary of the seventeenth century.

The story on which the play is based is from Pu Songling's 蒲松齡 (1640–1715) classical tale collection *Records of the Strange from the Studio of Leisure* (*Liaozhai zhiyi* 聊齋誌異).[95] In the tale "The Rakshas and the Sea Market" 羅刹海市, the protagonist Ma Ji is, like Jiang Chi of *Three Kinds of Happiness*, an educated aesthete who is pressured by his family to join an overseas trade expedition. As in *Three Kinds of Happiness*, all of Ma Ji's fellow merchants are thrown overboard in a storm that deposits him on a strange land. What follows is a deeply satirical interlude in the Country of the Rakshas, where the handsome Ma Ji must smear his face with black paint to be seen as attractive and thus worthy of career success.[96] Once Ma Ji is ensconced as a court favorite,

93. Other examples include *Tributes from the Eight Corners of the Earth* (*Bafang xianghua* 八方向化), *A Meeting of Kings in an Era of Great Peace* (*Taiping wanghui* 太平王會), and *Ten Thousand Countries Pay Tribute* (*Wanguo laichao* 萬國來朝). On these plays, see Liana Chen, *Staging for the Emperors*, and Ye Xiaoqing, *Ascendant Peace in the Four Seas*.

94. Liana Chen, *Staging for the Emperors*, 237–38.

95. For a discussion of the ways this play adapts "The Rakshas and the Sea Market," see Liana Chen, *Staging for the Emperors*, 237–46. The play also draws from another thematically similar Pu Songling story, "Kingdom of the Yakshas" 夜叉國.

96. On the ways this story plays with the relativity of strangeness and normality, see Zeitlin, *Historian of the Strange*, 21.

jealous rivals begin plotting his demise; to save himself, he retires from his position and sets sail with the crew of a boat heading to the titular sea market—an isolated island city where "merfolk from the four seas gather to sell their pearls and jewels and people of the twelve kingdoms from all four directions come to trade with them" 四海鮫人, 集貨珠寶, 四方十二國, 均來貿易.[97]

The sea market's brief appearance in the story belies its narrative import (an import signaled by its inclusion in the title of the story if not by the amount of ink spilled on it). After the perverse inversions and destabilizing signs of the Country of the Rakshas—in which beauty is the signifier of talent, and ugliness (from the focalized perspective at least) is regarded as beauty—the sea market offers a cleansing return to legibility. Ma Ji, his face washed of the black paint, wanders the streets of the market, when suddenly he is approached by a young dragon prince on horseback. The prince sees that Ma Ji is no ordinary marketgoer, and brings him back with him to the palace of the dragon king deep below the sea. After charming the king with his literary skills, Ma Ji is given the king's daughter in marriage and a position in his court.

The encounter in the market thus functions as an important pivot from the first half of the story, which presents the bewildering prospect of the subjective and unstable nature of value, to the second half, where we are returned to a notion of worth that is universal and self-evident—that there are things in the world that should be valued and ways that that value can be identified. That this happens in the middle of a market is not a coincidence; as a corrective to the unexpected inversions and reversals of the Raksha court, the market promises a place where treasures (a dazzling pearl, a sprig of bright coral, a talented man) can be properly displayed, assessed, and obtained.[98]

As in the plays above, the market is a space that affords entry

97. Pu Songling, *Quanben xinzhu Liaozhai zhiyi*, 1:467.

98. Indeed, the way the prince describes the encounter to his father employs language that turns Ma Ji into another piece of merchandise: "I traveled to the market and obtained a Chinese man of merit" 臣游市廛, 得中華賢士. Ibid.

into new kinds of political and social relations—unlike the warped relations predicated on disguise, dishonesty, and degradation that characterize the first part of the story, those generated out of the encounter in the marketplace are a fantasy of transparent recognition and well-deserved reward: the subject to a sovereign who recognizes his worth, the husband to a wife who is as loyal as she is lovely. In a departure from plays like *Three Kinds of Happiness* and *A Pair of Golden Placards*, this is not a fantasy of domination but one of submission—here the overseas merchant seeks not to transform the strange beings he encounters into objects of empire, but to find a place worthy of his subjection.[99]

Ultimately, however, this fantasy of such a place—where one's worth is treated at face value—is revealed to be just that. As the Historian of the Strange's end comment makes clear, the place where legible value and stable meaning can be relocated is but a *haishi* 海市, a watery mirage. The promise of this market, where everything can be found and possessed, quickly dissolves and the story ends with loss and longing on both sides. Out of homesickness and a sense of filial duty to his parents, Ma Ji returns home with instructions from his pregnant wife to return to the sea in three years, at which time she delivers their twins to him. The children grow up but not out of their profound sense of dislocation. As toddlers, they beg their father to take them back to a place that can no longer be found. Years later the son "could not stop thinking about his mother; one day out of the blue he jumped into the sea, and only after several days did he return" 輒思其母, 忽自投入海, 數日始還.[100] The daughter's gendered cloistering prevents her from trying like her brother to physically close this distance; instead, her mother comes to her and reminds her that a woman's life is always one of rupture and unbelonging, in which she must inevitably leave her natal family: "You will soon be married; what

99. This impulse toward submission becomes the focal point for a tradition that reads the bodily deformation that Ma Ji must undergo in order to serve in the Raksha court as a gesture to the forced queue of the Manchus. See, for example, Barr's suggestion that the story satirizes twice-serving officials. Barr, "Pu Songling and *Liaozhai zhiyi*," 304n41.

100. Pu Songling, *Quanben xinzhu Liaozhai zhiyi*, 1:470.

reason is there to cry?" 兒自成家，哭泣何為。[101] The story closes on an image of Ma Ji, rushing into the room, grasping his long-lost wife's hand, only for her to vanish as a loud clap of thunder rocks the house.

Like many of Pu Songling's more lyrical stories, "The Rakshas and the Sea Market" captures the momentary permeability of the membrane separating this and other worlds. In positioning this marketplace on the edges of the edge—even the elites in the faraway Country of the Rakshas find the market too distant and perilous to visit—Pu Songling evokes the long tradition in classical tales of imagining the market as a liminal space between worlds, where the foreign and the supernatural intersect.[102] In the end, though, we are left with the irreconcilability of this-worldness and fantasy, of Chinese and other, of human and superhuman, and the impossibility of communication and return. Though it begins in the same place as *Three Kinds of Happiness*, "The Rakshas and the Sea Market" ends with the melancholic impossibility of having all three kinds of happiness. By the time a transfigured version of this story is performed in Cixi's court (on the cusp of another dynastic rupture), Ma Ji has been finally given his happy ending of career success, family reunification, and religious transcendence. Though in an ironic twist, it is in its original form that the story anticipates the dislocation and dissipation wrought by three centuries of transoceanic trade. Our merchant protagonist returns from his foreign adventure loaded with treasure—gems and pearls and children—yet he is still lost at sea.

101. Ibid.

102. As in medieval tales such as "The Story of Miss Ren" 任氏傳, where the Chang'an market is the locus of *hu* 狐 (fox spirits) and *hu* 胡 (barbarians). Li Fang, comp., *Taiping guangji*, 452:3692–97.

FOUR

Staging the Endless Surplus

Early in the play *Cornucopia*, attributed to the Suzhou circle playwright Zhu Suchen, a fisherman gently places a clam back in the water.[1] Though the fisherman imagines his action as an impromptu gesture of compassion, as with much in this play, things are often not what they appear. Indeed, what is intended as a release is instead revealed to be a further entanglement in the nets connecting heaven and Earth, human and divine, within which everyone is already caught. The clam is no ordinary clam but a clam spirit named Che E, who has cultivated her essence over thousands of years. She had become marooned on the banks of the Sanmao River near Suzhou while fleeing the attack of an evil dragon, who desired the pearl she is gestating in order to become a flying dragon.[2] Observing all of this are two goddesses

1. *Cornucopia* is attributed to Zhu Suchen in Gao Yi's *New Southern Dramas*, as well as in Wu Zhensheng's 吳震生 (1695–1769) *Lige's Critiques of Old Plays* (*Lige piping jiu ximu* 笠閣批評舊戲目, 1762?), in which the play is ranked as *shangxia* 上下, the lowest group of the highest quality of plays. See Yang Jialuo, *Lidai shishi changbian erji*. The undated scripts from both Xu Zhiheng's and Fu Xihua's collections list "Zhu Suchen of Wu County from the early Qing" 清初吳縣朱素臣 as the author. Several full and fragmentary performance-oriented manuscripts are extant; differences across these editions are relatively minor. I am drawing primarily on the edition from Mei Lanfang's collection that was reprinted in the third series of the *Guben xiqu congkan*, though the scripts from Xu Zhiheng's and Fu Xihua's collections, as well as fragments housed at the Traditional Drama Research Institute at the Chinese National Academy of Arts have also been consulted. Guo Yingde has cited a Qianlong-Jiaqing edition, but it is unclear if it is still extant.

2. Evil dragons 孽龍 are often associated with flooding. One such creature plays an important role in *Journey to the West* (*Xiyou ji* 西遊記); after he eats Xuanzang's white horse, he is transformed by Guanyin into a replacement horse called White Dragon Horse.

of wind and moon, who decide to petition the Jade Emperor to punish the evil dragon and give the worthy Che E the elixir of immortality. Before they embark on their bureaucratic mission, the moon goddess uses her power of foresight to see that the fisherman will save Che E. After all, he is no ordinary fisherman, but the Star of Wealth reborn into the world of men. So, the goddess declares, she will "borrow this bit of karmic debt to give a lesson in the root causes of fortune and position" 借此一點因果，好教發跡始緣之根也。[3]

The fisherman, a man from Suzhou named Shen Wansan, had first glimpsed the clam while taking shelter from a sudden thunderstorm with his brother-in-law, the woodcutter Zhang You'er. You'er figures that a clam of that size was sure to contain a valuable pearl and suggests breaking it open. Wansan, transfixed by the clam's dazzling aura and a sudden chill in the air, stops You'er's axe: "From ancient times, the ten thousand things were formed through Heaven's nurture. Even insects and plants have a divine spark. How could you so lightly propose to do it harm?" 自古萬物造化，皆天宮化育。昆蟲草木，亦有所靈。豈可輕舉妄害。[4]

This is of course a rather strange disquisition to come from a fisherman, whose livelihood depends on the killing of aquatic creatures. It is not, however, strange for a reincarnated god to recognize the divinity in a similarly divine creature or to intuit the skein that connects all beings great and small. But Shen Wansan is destined not only to become a god but also to become a rich merchant. His refusal of profit—and of the conceptual basis of his livelihood—echoes those gallant merchants and mongers who appear elsewhere in Suzhou circle plays, giving away their money and their wares only to gain many times more in return. That Wansan's very first act on stage is to preserve the spark of life anticipates the ways that the play locates a new kind of generativity in the imbrication of the commercial and the divine.

3. Zhu Suchen (attrib.), *Jubaopen*, 2b.

4. Ibid., 4a. Corrected with Xu Zhiheng edition. *Suizhong Wushi cang chaoben gaoben xiqu congkan*, 12:357.

Safely returned to the water, the clam spirit Che E wishes to give Shen Wansan a reward, so she takes on human form and asks if he will help her across a single-plank bridge. After he gets her safely across, she tells him that she forgot a package on the other side. He recrosses the bridge and picks up the package, but when he turns around, she is gone. Wansan takes the package and returns home, fishless, to his hungry and long-suffering wife. When she asks what is in the package he tells her that, funnily enough, it is just a plain clay bowl. His wife is unimpressed:

> WIFE, played by the *dan*: Here I had assumed it was something valuable, seeing how pleased you are. But this could have only cost a couple pennies. What use is it? (*picks up bowl*) Moreover, encountering ghosts and spirits in broad daylight means this could be an unlucky object. Let's just smash it to pieces.
>
> 旦: 我只道什麼直錢的東西, 這等喜歡。買他不過幾文, 要他何用。(拿盆) 況青天白日見神見鬼, 敢是不祥之物, 拿來摔碎了罷。[5]

Wansan insists that this is unnecessary, and they should just use it to put things in. But what? An opportunity presents itself when a dog runs onstage to beg for food—his wife fills the bowl with scraps and sets it down on the ground. After a few minutes, they notice something rather odd:

> WANSAN, played by the *sheng*: Oh, how strange! This dog has been eating for a while now. How come there's just as much food in the bowl as before?
>
> WIFE: Actually, it's overflowing!
>
> BOTH, singing: In a flash, filled over the brim; manifold transformations out of thin air.
>
> 生: 呀, 好奇怪, 這狗攢食多時, 怎麼這盆中分毫不減。

5. Ibid., 10a.

旦: 卻還擁將出來。

合唱: 霎時溢滿, 平白地變幻多端。[6]

Wansan is convinced the bowl is some sort of treasure, but his ever-skeptical wife is not so sure: "Husband, from what we've seen, it might be a treasure but we can't say for certain. I have a coin here—you can put it inside to test it and see what happens" 官人, 這等看來, 或者是件寶物也未可知。我有一文錢在此, 你可頃下去, 試看分曉則個.[7] The results are similarly astounding:

WANSAN: What on earth! I just threw the coin in, and in a flash the bowl is filled with coins!

生: 咦咦, 才投下去, 霎時盆中堆起錢來了。[8]

As it turns out, just as the humble appearance of clam and fisherman belie their true place in the cosmic order, this simple clay bowl is actually a magical object from the palace of the Dragon King—a *jubaopen*, a basin that gathers treasures. Shen Wansan and his wife quickly produce a small fortune and move to Nanjing to start a new life as wealthy merchants.

A Man of Fortune

Cornucopia is crafted from the myriad narratives about Shen Wansan 沈萬三 in circulation since the early Ming, interweaving elements from histories, classical tales, local gazetteers, miscellanies, and oral lore. According to a number of these accounts, Wansan was a wealthy shipping magnate who was persecuted by Zhu Yuanzhang 朱元璋 (1328–98, r. 1368–98), the first emperor of the Ming dynasty. Zhu Yuanzhang was himself from a struggling

6. Ibid., 10b.
7. Ibid.
8. Ibid.

peasant household and had a natural suspicion of merchants as parasitically profiting off the back of agrarian production. To deal with major deficits early in his reign and to diminish the local power of wealthy merchants, Zhu Yuanzhang embarked on a series of confiscations and forced relocations. Shen Wansan was apparently targeted in these campaigns; according to some accounts he was banished to the frontier, in others he is executed by soldiers in the streets of Nanjing.[9]

While there are a few tomb inscriptions that reference the Shen family fortune in the early Ming, detailed written accounts involving Shen Wansan and his fabulous wealth do not appear until the late fifteenth century, when a number of local elites begin to record stories circulating around the lower Yangzi region about the true source of Wansan's wealth.[10] Many of these accounts gesture back to earlier oral tradition by prefacing their story with variations on the phrase "as passed down by legend" (舊傳, 俗傳, 相傳). Though most of these earlier accounts originate in the Wu 吳 region, especially around places such as Zhouzhuang, Suzhou, and Nanjing that figure prominently in Shen Wansan lore, by the late Ming, his fame had spread far and wide. So wide, in fact, that in *Plum in the Golden Vase*, his name is invoked as something known by all under heaven. As Pan Jinlian intones when revealing something thought to be a secret: "Just as Nanjing has its Shen Wansan, Beijing has its withered willows; just as a man has his reputation, a tree has its shadow" 南京沈萬三, 北京枯柳樹。人的名兒, 樹的影兒.[11] But while his name clearly had purchase in the late Ming (and perhaps a particular resonance for a grasping

9. For example, in the *History of the Ming* (*Ming shi* 明史), the empress intervenes when Zhu Yuanzhang wants to execute Shen Wansan, so instead he is sent to Yunnan. Zhang Tingyu et al., *Ming shi*, 12:3506.

10. See, for example, the tomb inscription for Shen Wansan's nephew Shen Hanjie 沈漢傑 (1320–1371) in Liu Sanwu, *Tanzhai wenji*, 2:26a–28a. These inscriptions have been used to argue that Shen Wansan was either dead or quite elderly at the start of the Ming, casting doubt on the various narratives about his conflicts with Zhu Yuanzhang.

11. Xiaoxiaosheng, *Jin Ping Mei cihua jiaozhu*, 2:888; Roy, *The Plum in the Golden Vase, or Chin P'ing Mei*, vol. 2, 325. This reference, which Jinlian repeats in chapter 72, is anachronistic for the Northern Song setting.

consumer of pleasure like Pan Jinlian), precisely what Shen Wansan was known for beyond his wealth and association with Nanjing is less obvious, as a number of radically different versions of his story circulated simultaneously.

The one commonality across these various narratives is Shen Wansan's tremendous wealth, with which his name became synonymous. Several early versions of the story attribute his wealth to his connections to a certain Lu Daoyuan.[12] In the *Wujiang Gazetteer* (*Wujiang zhi* 吳江志) published in 1488, Lu is recorded as giving his property to the Shen family before becoming a Daoist adept; a similar version can be found in Yang Xunji's 楊循吉 (1456–1544) *Suzhou Stories* (*Su tan* 蘇談), written around the same time.[13] A more fantastical origin for Lu Daoyuan's wealth is provided in Zhu Yunming's *Mr. Zhu's Record of the Strange* (*Zhuzi zhiguai lu* 祝子志怪錄).[14] In this telling, Lu had recently moved to Suzhou and had taken up residence in a haunted house. A confrontation with a pair of female spirits leads him to discover two jars of gold buried in the courtyard; it is this fortune that is then inherited by Shen Wansan, who had formerly served as Lu Daoyuan's wealth manager.

As Shen Wansan stories proliferated in the late Ming, so too did explanations for his vast wealth. Tian Yiheng 田藝蘅 (fl. 1570) mentions the Lu inheritance in *Daily Jottings to Preserve the Past* (*Liuqing rizha* 留青日札), but also credits the Shen family fortune to Wansan's father, who expertly and tirelessly managed their fields.[15] Other accounts attribute Wansan's riches to knowledge of alchemy. In *Diary from the Pavilion of Tasting Water* (*Weishuixuan riji* 味水軒日記), Li Rihua 李日華 (1565–1635) records a conversation about Wansan's use (or rather, misuse) of cinnabar.[16] Tian Yiheng and Xie Zhaozhe 謝肇淛 (1567–1634) both repeat rumors that Wansan's descendants had knowledge of alchemical arts.

A number of late Ming origin stories hinge on Wansan's

12. His name is alternatively given in these materials as Deyuan and Daopan.

13. *Wujiang zhi*, 7:4b; Yang Xunji, *Su tan*, 13a–b.

14. Zhu Yunming, *Zhuzi zhiguai lu*, 4:19a–20a. This story is retold with minor changes in Lü Bi, *Mingchao xiaoshi*, 9:785.

15. Tian Yiheng, *Liuqing rizha*, 35:1a–2b.

16. Li Rihua, *Weishuixuan riji*, 285.

discovery of a strange object that appears humble but is in fact exceedingly valuable. In the 1618 edition of *Recorded Anecdotes from Yunjiao Hall* (*Yunjiao guan jitan* 雲蕉館紀談), Kong Er 孔邇 offers two such origin stories.[17] In one, a mysterious old man gives Wansan seven nets filled with silver. In another, Wansan finds a trove of stones that turn out to be highly prized by connoisseurs. Kong Er tells us how the strange stones are appraised by someone with knowledge of the luxury market as being worth tens of thousands of cash each, and it is this cash that funds Wansan's lucrative overseas trading network. While a few sources directly attribute Wansan's fortune to mercantile activity, such as the Jiajing-era edition of the *Wujiang County Gazetteer* (*Wujiang xian zhi* 吳江縣志) that credits Wansan's wealth to foreign trade, more frequently trade is a consequence of (rather than the source of) wealth.[18] It is only after fantastic wealth or treasures have been accumulated that Wansan becomes a merchant—the supernatural and the strange transformed into commodities and capital.

This transformation of the rare, incommensurable object into discrete, saleable, and multipliable commodities also appears in a popular story about the afterlife of one of Wansan's treasures. Shen Zhou 沈周 (1427–1509) tells an early version of this story, in which an agate wine vessel, confiscated from Wansan's collection, is found approximately one hundred years later floating in a ditch by a lowly tutor named Li Ming.[19] Li Ming colludes with an associate to give the vessel to a powerful eunuch in exchange for rights to the salt monopoly. While transporting the prefecture's salt tickets, Li Ming's boat capsizes and the tickets are destroyed. The prefect insists that they reimburse the government for the value of the tickets. As a result, Li dies in prison and his associate goes bankrupt. Though this story is

17. Kong Er, *Yunjiao guan jitan*, 49–56.

18. An account from the final years of the Yuan tells of "a certain Mr. Shen from Dachang in Jiading prefecture who became rich by trading with foreigners" 嘉定州大場沈氏, 因下番買賣致巨富. Tao Zongyi, *Nancun chuogeng lu*, 379.

19. Shen Zhou, *Kezuo xinwen*, j. 6. The vessel is described in Shen Maoguan, *Huayi huamu niaoshou zhenwan kao*, 8:11b. This story also appears in Zhu Guozhen, *Yong chuang xiaopin*, 398, and Wang Tonggui, *Er'tan leizeng*, 11:2a.

only tangentially about Wansan, it rehearses many of the same tropes that come to define that narrative: the discovery of a strange object by someone of low social standing that precipitates his entry into mercantile activities, and the underlying logic that the generation and proliferation of wealth leads inexorably to financial ruin and death.

Of these various origins of Wansan's wealth, the one that most captures the imagination of late imperial writers is the *jubaopen*. In an early account, He Mengchun 何孟春 (1474–1536) writes:

> The tale of the *jubaopen* possessed by Shen Wansan's family has been passed down since olden times. According to the legend, whenever Shen placed a small amount of any object inside the *jubaopen*, the next day it would be filled to the brim. Every object he put inside had the same result. When other people tried to use it, it would not work. The Hongwu emperor heard about this and had the *jubaopen* brought to him. The emperor tried to use it, but it did not work, so he returned it to Shen. After Shen's property was confiscated, the *jubaopen* was brought back to the palace. I am doubtful that such an object existed in the world. How could such a thing be?
>
> 舊傳沈萬三家有聚寶盆事，云在沈氏貯少物，物經宿輒滿，百物皆然，他人試之不驗。事聞太祖，取入試不驗，遂還沈氏，後沈氏籍沒，乃復歸禁中。嘗疑世豈有此物，物安有是理。[20]

This account of a magical basin that would reproduce whatever was placed inside and that only Shen Wansan could operate was repeated by many late Ming writers and became the predominant imagination of the source of his vast wealth.[21] It is this version of the story that appeared in the studies of drama aficionados and on the stages of Jiangnan as at least two *chuanqi*, *Cornucopia* and the nonextant *Pavilion of the Heavenly Beacon* (*Tiansui ge* 天燧閣). Over the course of the Qing, Shen Wansan comes to be revered as a god of wealth with his endlessly productive basin figured as an

20. He Mengchun, *Yudong xulu*, 52:8.

21. For examples, see *Mige yuan gui zhengyao*, j. 7; Wang Kentang, *Yugangzhai bizhu*, 3:50a–51a; and Xie Zhaozhe, *Wu zazu*, 12:32b.

auspicious icon—an icon that continues to adorn New Year's prints, propaganda posters, and brand logos to this day.

Basins That Gather Treasures

Although this specific thing called a *jubaopen* only emerges during the late imperial period and only in conjunction with the stories surrounding Shen Wansan, it is one of a handful of "treasure-gathering" 聚寶 objects that were in literary circulation in the late imperial period.[22] These magical objects emerged as a popular trope in late medieval narratives, often within the well-established beats of the treasure tale, in which a seemingly worthless object, often found in or near a body of water, is recognized by a foreigner as something of great value.

One such object appears in a story included in *Extensive Records from the Taiping Era* (*Taiping guangji* 太平廣記, 978) and attributed to the collection *Record of the Origin of Transformation* (*Yuanhua ji* 原化記, ca. 840). In this story, a man finds a strange rock on the shore that looks like a colorful shard of pottery. He ends up showing the rock to a group of Persian merchants at their annual "treasure banquet" 寶會. The senior merchant buys it from him—after first insisting that he raise the price tenfold—and explains that it is an important treasure in his country. On the fifteenth day of each month, the king sets it on an altar in the sea,

22. Significantly, the identification of objects as "treasure-gathering" 聚寶 appears to have happened only in the late imperial period and usually as part of a discussion of Shen Wansan's *jubaopen*. The Song dynasty traces discussed below only become part of a coherent history of the *jubaopen* retrospectively; in this sense the *jubaopen* does not emerge out of a preexisting discourse so much as it reorients the discourse of treasure gathering around itself as late imperial writers seek its origins. For example, we are told that the abbot's bowl "is called the treasure-gathering bowl" 謂之聚寶碗 and the shepherd's vase "is named the treasure-gathering vase" 名曰聚寶瓶 not in any Song source but in later Qing collections such as Yuan Dong, *Shuyin congshuo*, 4:21b. Similarly, in the story discussed below, Ling Mengchu gives a magic mirror the name "treasure-gathering mirror" 聚寶鏡, which does not appear in the Hong Mai source text.

and "overnight, all manner of treasures like bright pearls and precious shells will have gathered. For this reason it is called the Mother of Treasures, as it produces riches many times the original investment" 一夕, 明珠寶貝等皆自聚, 故名寶母也, 生得財倍其先資也.[23] A similar object appears in a brief account found in Zeng Zao's 曾慥 (1091–1155) collection *Classified Tales* (*Leishuo* 類說), in which a man finds a large stone that a maritime merchant buys for a hefty sum. The merchant explains, "This is a gold-helper stone. You hang it in the ocean overnight, and when you pull it out, there is certain to be gold attached to it" 此協金石, 垂之海中, 經夕引出, 上必有金.[24]

Hong Mai expands upon these tropes in an account included in his *Records of Yijian* (*Yijian zhi* 夷堅志) collection. In "The Strange Bamboo of Ocean Mountain" 海山異竹, a Wenzhou merchant named Zhang Yuan gets lost at sea and makes a brief stop on an island covered with large stalks of bamboo, some of which he takes back with him. When he returns to harbor, Japanese and Kunlun merchants are shocked to see the bamboo and vie to buy it. After a Kunlun trader secures it with five thousand strings, Zhang Yuan learns why it is so valuable: "It is treasure-gathering bamboo from Baojia Mountain. If you stick it in a large body of water, then all manner of treasures will be drawn to it" 此乃寶伽山聚寶竹, 每立竹於巨浸中, 則諸寶不采而聚.[25]

As in the stories above, this account draws on the long imagination of the sea as the locus of treasure, with pearls and coral brought forth from within its depths and gold and silver from distant lands traveling its surface. In these treasure-gathering stories, however, access to the treasures of the sea requires a deeper discernment, here manifested in the recognition of an unassuming object that subverts all known indicators of worth. In order to obtain the limitless riches promised by overseas trade,

23. "Wei Sheng" 魏生, in Li Fang, comp., *Taiping guangji*, 403:3253.

24. Zeng Zao, *Leishuo*, 2:1359; this story also appears in Lu Yinglong, *Xianchuang kuoyi zhi*, 14:26a. Some later texts attribute it to Li Mei's 李玫 (fl. mid-ninth c.) *Compiling the Extraordinary* (*Zuanyi ji* 纂異記).

25. Hong Mai, *Yijian zhi*, 3:986–87.

these stories argue, one needs to master a more esoteric knowledge, not about what is universally, visibly valuable, like pearls and gold, but about the invisible powers contained within the object, the deeper currents underneath.

For one who lacks such knowledge, the possibility of profiting from overseas trade is accidental, and that profit is always limited. The Chinese subject transacts with the foreign other and perhaps becomes rich, but the promise of boundless profit is always out of reach. As that kind of profit requires knowledge not about the commodities themselves but the thing that brings the commodities together, the Chinese subject becomes the owner of great wealth, but not the master of the economy in which that wealth circulates.[26] The Chinese subject is shown to play an intermediary role in a larger drama, the contours of which remain just out of view, as if he were a minor character in a play, appearing on stage only during the final reunion scene having witnessed none of what came before. It is this sense of exclusion, of relegation to the margins of some larger story or economy, that Hong Mai's tale surfaces by ending on a note of quiet regret: "Zhang Yuan then let out a sigh and handed the bamboo over" 愿始嗟嘆而付之.[27]

In another story from *Records of Yijian*, this sigh is not an ending but a point of departure—what if the Chinese subject acted on his regret? In "The Mirror in Jiazhou River" 嘉州江中鏡, Wang Jia, a fisherman of humble means, pulls an ancient mirror out of the water:

> He brought the mirror home and consequently his business started booming; with no particular effort, the money would roll in. After two years, it was as if cash were raining down from heaven or being transported by spirits: their shabby room was filled to the brim with hundreds of thousands of strings of cash.

26. In some stories anthologized in *Extensive Records from the Taiping Era*, such as "Wei Yan" 韋弇 and "Mr. Cen" 岑氏, the reason for the objects' hypervaluation remains unknowable; we never learn where they come from and what if anything they do. The local knowledge is never disclosed to the Chinese character/reader; all we are offered is the tautology of an object being a treasure because it is treasured. Li Fang, comp., *Taiping guangji*, 33:209–10, 404:3261.

27. Hong Mai, *Yijian zhi*, 987.

持歸家，因此生計浸豐，不假經營，而錢自至。越兩歲，如天雨鬼輸，盈塞敗屋，幾滿十萬緡。[28]

But this newfound prosperity quickly becomes a source of anxiety for Wang Jia:

> From my grandfather on down, my family has fished for a living, making no more than a hundred cash a day. Since I have obtained this precious mirror, I can't have made less than one thousand times that amount. What sort of person am I that I have become suddenly wealthy like this? To receive such a fortune without labor, heaven surely must bring disaster to me.
>
> 我家從父祖以來，漁釣為活，極不過日得百錢。自獲寶鏡以來，何啻千倍。念本何人，而暴富乃爾。無勞受福，天必殃之。[29]

To avoid such a disaster, he decides to donate the mirror to a Buddhist temple, but after quickly falling back into poverty, Wang Jia, like Zhang Yuan, is soon sighing in regret. So Wang Jia returns to the temple to ask for the mirror back, but unbeknownst to him, the greedy abbot had a copy made and keeps the real mirror for himself. Rumors about the source of the temple's newfound riches reach the ears of a corrupt official, who has the abbot arrested and beaten to death. The abbot's disciple flees with the mirror, but abandons it when he is first confronted by an immortal in gold armor and then attacked by a tiger. We are told that the mirror was never seen again.

Wang Jia's mirror gathers not only treasures but also greed. There is something bankrupting about the mirror, leaving the Wang family poor, the abbot dead, the disciple terrified, the official disappointed. The personal tragedies and social ruptures left in the mirror's wake are anticipated by the operation of the mirror itself, which Wang Jia had sensed was dangerously dislocating. As Wang Jia himself tells it, because of the mirror he

28. Hong Mai, *Yijian zhi*, 3:1124.
29. Ibid.

abandons the honorable work of fishing—work that roots him to his family and its history—for easy money that accumulates "without labor" 無勞, "without needing to be managed" 不假經營. Like the treasure-gathering bamboo, the mirror can be read as a proxy for a new mode of accumulation that seems to generate money out of thin air, and for entanglements in invisible economies that remain largely beyond the ken of the individual actor. But whereas the bamboo circulates within the transoceanic economy that it represents, here the connection of cornucopian object and commerce is entirely divorced from the merchant and his markets, as any explicit reference to the commercial economy and its actors is absent. There are no foreign lands or Chinese merchants here; instead this is a story that happens between nonmerchants: fishermen, monks, officials, and runners. What remains is a deep unease over parasitic accumulation and the sudden ruptures it introduces into what had been "generations and generations that fished as an occupation" 世世以捕魚為業. As indicated by the immortal in gold armor, this is an object that does not belong in the human realm, a kind of wealth without labor that should not be loosed on honest men.

These Song-era stories, written at a moment when market specialization and long-distance maritime trade had begun to radically restructure the possibilities and mechanisms of wealth, find a new resonance in the late Ming. The sixteenth-century publishing boom made newly available many of these earlier collections, such as *Extensive Records from the Taiping Era*, *Records of Yijian*, and *Classified Tales*, while individual stories were frequently recompiled in new collections such as Wang Shizhen's 王世貞 (1526–90) *Compendium of the Beautiful and Strange* (*Yanyi bian* 豔異編).[30]

Elements from these earlier narratives also reappear in newly written stories and plays, as in the Mother of Treasures pearl that the pirate Mo Cifei steals in *A Pair of Golden Placards*, discussed

30. *Classified Tales* was printed in 1626; on the publication history of *Records of Yijian*, see Inglis, "A Textual History of Hong Mai's *Yijian zhi*."

in chapter 3.[31] Two of the most prominent reworkings of these motifs appear in the vernacular stories of Ling Mengchu. Ling's "A Chinese Man Changes His Luck," also discussed in the previous chapter, rehearses many of the beats from Hong Mai's "The Strange Bamboo of Ocean Mountain": the ocean as the locus of treasures; the foreign land found by accident; the strange yet seemingly worthless object that can only be identified by those with esoteric knowledge; the treasure banquet with ranked attendees; the offense taken by the foreign buyer toward the Chinese seller's undervaluing of his treasure. However, Ling's version ends not in disappointment and regret, but excess and overfulfilment: the Chinese protagonist receives not a one-time payment but a business in which to invest his capital, which we are told begets generations of wealth.

Ling similarly rewrites "The Mirror in Jiazhou River" in a way that preserves much of the original narrative while emplotting it in a distinctly late Ming ontology of wealth.[32] Whereas the Hong Mai version offers no explanation for the fisherman's discovery of the treasure-gathering mirror, Ling's narrators tells us that "it is only because Wang Jia and his wife were good people and had a predestined fate from a previous life to be rich that the mirror appeared to them and they were able to take it home" 只為王甲夫妻好善，也是夙世前緣，合該興旺，故此物出現，卻得取了回家. Wang Jia was not merely predestined to find the mirror, but also to lose it: as the immortal in gold armor tells Wang Jia, the mirror is a "divine treasure" 神天之寶 and is only temporarily

31. Such an object is also mentioned in passing at the treasure banquet in the play *The Appearance of the Star of Literature*, attributed to Zhu Suchen.

32. "Fisherman Wang Gives Up a Mirror to Worship the Three Treasures; A Monk from White Water Temple Steals the Mirror and Loses Two Lives" 王漁翁舍鏡崇三寶，白水僧盜物喪雙生, in Ling Mengchu, *Erke pai'an jingqi*. Ling inserts into the Hong Mai story episodes drawn from other medieval treasure stories collected in the *Extensive Records from the Taiping Era*. The stones echo those in "Mr. Cen" and the gold and silver men from stories such as "Gong Bo" 龔播 and "Chen Jun" 陳浚. Li Fang, comp., *Taiping guangji*, 404:3261, 401:3225, 3227. The panic about wealth leaving or transforming again is the focus of stories such as "A Commoner from Yichun Prefecture" 宜春郡民 and Hong Mai's "Zhang Gongzhi's Silver" 張拱之銀. Li Fang, comp., *Taiping guangji*, 401:3225; Hong Mai, *Yijian zhi*, 3:1084.

appearing in the human world for the sake of making them rich. Though the mirror has returned to its proper place in heaven, the immortal leads Wang Jia to a cart filled with precious objects gathered by the mirror that will support him for the rest of his life. As in Ling's "A Chinese Man Changes His Luck," the story ends with the protagonist in a state of blissful surplus.

If the source material emphasized the loss of the treasure-producing object, in these rewritings that loss is incidental. Here it is revealed that it is not the object itself that produces wealth but the fate that delivered the object into their hands in the first place. It is an awareness of this larger system through which the object circulates that shifts the reaction toward surplus from anxious disavowal to acceptance of one's fate. Hong Mai's Wang Jia worries that his accidental windfall will earn heavenly censure; Ling Mengchu's Wang Jia learns that no windfall is accidental. In the late imperial imagination, there is a logic that governs the circulation of things, and there is no amount of money that is not tied up in this karmic economy.

Basins that Generate Treasures

Shen Wansan's cornucopia and Zhu Suchen's *Cornucopia* emerge out of this treasure-gathering lineage, though with some significant departures. In the above stories, objects are "treasure-gathering" in a literal sense, pulling treasures toward their holders like a magnet. That these objects are found in or around bodies of water, and occasionally must be placed back into the water in order to be efficacious, literalizes the invisible forces drawing new and strange commodities to Chinese shores from distant lands. Underpinning this imagination of treasure-gathering is a limit: by pulling in the existing treasures of the world, at some point there will be nothing left to pull. None of these stories ever reaches this limit—the object always exits the narrative before such a point—but the logic remains distinctly zero-sum and proto-mercantilist. In the middle-period stories, each exchange of money for object has a winner in whose favor the balance of trade shifts; the losers are the protagonist and the readers reading through him, who are left with half-answered questions. The late Ming rewritings attempt to overcome this loss through extreme recompense—bestowing on the treasure-loser more riches than he could use in several lifetimes and satisfying the reader with detailed information on the treasure's origin and operations.

Despite its name, the *jubaopen* does not gather treasures in the same way as these other treasure-gathering objects. Rather than pulling existing objects from elsewhere, the *jubaopen* needs to be seeded with a thing that it then multiplies. This reproduction of kind from kind echoes the ways that the accumulation of wealth is frequently articulated within the symbolic language of the natural world. In early and medieval Chinese culture, a range of icons—the money tree, the golden toad, the coin-spitting dragon, the coin-festooned bug—stand in for the sudden accumulation of wealth and function as totems or charms bringing such wealth into being. In this imagination of riches, the object of value is reinvested with the very embodied liveliness that was lost in the transition to specie from earlier currencies of shells, pelts, and silk. In the treasure-gathering stories discussed above, the organic foundness of the treasure-gathering stone and bamboo, the treasure mirror netted in the river like a fish, and the reproductive symbolism of the Mother of Treasures evoke a similar impulse to naturalize and enliven the origin of value.

But unlike the money tree or the coin-spitting dragon, the *jubaopen* does not generate money in a way immediately analogous to living things, like the way plants grow flowers or animals produce saliva. Rather, the grammar of the *jubaopen*'s unceasing replication resembles not so much agrarian production or mammalian reproduction—which earlier representations of wealth share with the Hellenistic cornucopia—but the market. In its automatic production of money from money, the *jubaopen* perfectly embodies even as it mystifies the process of mercantile accumulation in which there is no profit without capital investment, in which this capital begets more capital, in which the end is not commodities but monetary surplus. As articulated by Shen Wansan's wife in the scene above, a bowl that reproduces food is a novelty—but it is only when it reproduces money from money that it can be deemed a treasure.

In its operations, the *jubaopen* requires a level of human involvement and direction that is absent in other treasure-gathering stories. Ling Mengchu's story of the treasure-gathering mirror stresses how the will of its possessors is incidental to its operation:

> Once Wang Jia and his wife obtained the mirror, riches would arrive without any effort to seek them. If they swept the floor at home, they would sweep up bits of gold; if they tilled their fields, they would uncover deposits of silver; if they cast a net on a boat, they would pull in a net full of treasures; if they cracked open a clam, they would find a shining pearl.
>
> 自得此鏡之後，財物不求而至。在家裡掃地，也掃出金屑來。墾田，也墾出銀窖來。船上去撒網，也牽起珍寶來。剖蚌，也剖出明珠來。

Rather than imposing itself on those it enriches, the *jubaopen* only operates through the exertion of human will: specific treasures are gathered when its owner decides to gather them. In this sense the *jubaopen* resembles another legendary object, the "as you wish" (*ruyi* 如意) treasure that derives from the Buddhistic *cintāmaṇi* (*ruyi zhu* 如意珠 or wish-fulfilling jewel) and appears in medieval tales in various forms such as the bones of a beloved pet fish, the heart of a golden-winged bird, or a jade wine flask that materialize the desires of their owners.[33]

33. See Duan Chengshi, *Youyang zazu, xuji* 續集 1:2b–4a; Dong Kang, ed., *Quhai zongmu tiyao*, 2:1322; "Mr. Yuan and Mr. Liu" 元柳二公, in Li Fang, comp., *Taiping guangji*, 25:166–69.

Significantly, for the *jubaopen*, the materializing of the desired object is an act of will without labor. Some treasure-gathering objects reiterate the connection between human labor and value production, like the golden awl that appears in the ninth-century *Miscellaneous Accounts from Youyang* (*Youyang zazu* 酉陽雜俎) that its holder can use to carve out of stone whatever he wishes,[34] or Ling's description of how the mirror's treasures are obtained through the work of sweeping, tilling, and fishing.[35] The *jubaopen*, however, is mechanistic and automatic, its inputs and outputs controlled and predictable and the operator's labor virtually nonexistent: a coin goes in, many coins come out. Value is here produced not by human labor but from an investment that is simultaneously figured as karmic and monetary: the good act that earned the *jubaopen*, the coin that earned the other coins.

Shen Wansan's *jubaopen* is not the first magical receptacle that promises such a return on investment. Though rare, a handful of stories about *jubaopen*-like objects appear alongside other kinds of treasure-gathering or as-you-wish objects in Song dynasty collections (and are often included in late Ming discussions of Wansan's *jubaopen*). In one story that appears in

34. In a story set in Silla, a poor but industrious man encounters a group of strange children in the mountains who use a golden awl to carve the wine and food that he desires; he takes the awl back home and uses it to become rich. Here it is not a gathering or a reproduction but an act of work that literalizes the connection between labor and wealth: to labor with one's hands produces some intermediary commodity that is exchanged for money that is exchanged for a desired thing. In this story the intermediaries vanish but the logic is the same: one labors to get what one wants. Duan Chengshi, *Youyang zazu*, *xuji* 1:1a–2a.

35. Such a logic can also be seen in the story "The Pure Maiden from Clear Water" 白水素女, in which an immortal disguised as a snail secretly cooks for a young man who has neither family nor wife. Once he uncovers the source of his magical meals, she must leave, but first she gifts him her shell, telling him: "Use it to store your grain and you will never run out" 以貯米谷，常可不乏. In the first part of the story, the *jubaopen* is female domestic labor; the food and fire that appeared day after day did not materialize out of nowhere but were the result of the invisible labor of the pseudo-wife. In the second part, the shell promises endless grain, but it was the orphan's hard work in the fields that earned him the treasure, and the immortal instructs him to continue to "labor hard in the fields and fish and collect firewood to make a living" 勤於田作，漁採治生. Li Fang, comp., *Taiping guangji*, 62:387–88.

Classified Tales, an abbot finds a celadon bowl by the water's edge.[36] After returning to his temple,

> he cuts a flower and places it in the bowl in front of a statue of the Buddha. The next morning, the bowl is full of flowers. The abbot then places a little rice in the bowl, and overnight the bowl filled with rice. He tried this with coins as well as silver and gold and the results were all the same.
>
> 折花置佛像前，明日花滿其中，更置少米，經宿米亦滿碗，以錢及金銀置之皆然。[37]

From then on, the abbot uses the bowl to enrich his monastery. Years later when he is close to death, the abbot throws the bowl into a river, explaining to his befuddled disciples that he "does not want it to cause [them] to further accumulate sin" 不欲使爾增罪累. In a version of this story that appears in Wang Xiangzhi's 王象之 (1163–1230) *Records of Famous Places* (*Yudi jisheng* 輿地紀勝), the *jubaopen*—here described as a stone basin 石盂—was originally pulled from the river by a fisherman.[38] When the dying abbot throws it back in, his disciples desperately enlist fishermen to try to pull it back out, but all to no avail.

The chaotic potential of such an object loosed on the world is illustrated by another Song-era story included in Shao Bo's 邵博 (d. 1158) *Later Records of Things Heard and Seen by Mr. Shao* (*Shaoshi wenjian houlu* 邵氏聞見後錄). A young shepherd in a village in Shandong wanders into an old tomb looking for his sheep when he finds a plain-looking yellow vase.[39] When he uses the vase to store some newly harvested peapods, he discovers that the vase is immediately full. Startled, he tells his friends and they

36. This story later appears in the third *juan* of Xie Zhaozhe's *Fivefold Miscellany* (*Wu zazu* 五雜組). He Mengchun and later Feng Menglong attribute this story to Wu Shu's nonextant Song dynasty collection *Idle Talk from the Secret Pavilion* (*Mige xiantan* 秘閣閑談).

37. Zeng Zao, *Leishuo*, 5:3428–29.

38. Wang Xiangzhi, *Yudi jisheng*, 187:5479.

39. Written by Shao Bo as a continuation of his father Shao Bowen's 邵伯溫 (1057–1134) *Shaoshi wenjian lu* 邵氏聞見錄. Shao Bo, *Shaoshi wenjian houlu*, 27:1a.

test the vase several times, all with the same result. A passerby witnesses this and throws a coin inside—when he sees the money piling up, he snatches the vase from the boy and flees. The shepherd cries out to his father, who grabs his hoe and confronts the thief. In the ensuing fracas, the vase is smashed.[40]

Fundamental to these stories is the sense of crisis brought on by the treasure-generating receptacle: this strange object that has the potential to create an unrecoverable imbalance in the world's goods will either destroy those who seek to use it or be destroyed by its own productive capacity. Shen Wansan's *jubaopen* similarly invites danger for its owner, who in many tellings ends up exiled or dead. But unlike those earlier objects, the *jubaopen* also offers a path out of the danger, with its surplus functioning as a corrective that rebalances moral and monetary orders.

Through its imbrication of the commercial and the divine, the story of Shen Wansan and his *jubaopen* makes possible a redemptive reading of mercantile accumulation. Unlike those other putative sources of Wansan's wealth—those buried stores of gold or sacks of silver—the *jubaopen* is figured not as a hoard but as a flow, a dynamic force whose logic of capital investment begetting more capital would be highly recognizable to those living in the urban centers of the lower Yangzi region.

This dynamism is captured in images that attempt to represent the constant flux of the *jubaopen*'s operations. In a woodblock illustration from the workshop of Wang Junfu 王君甫 (fl. ca. 1660), Shen Wansan and his wives watch from a balcony while treasure is carried from a ship into his courtyard (plate 7).[41] Near

40. We are told the vase shards are later shown to Zhufu Qixian 主父齊賢 (a historical personage who appears in the *History of the Song*), who then tells this story to the scholar Wang Zhi 王銍 (fl. 1130–43).

41. On Wang Junfu's commercial prints, see Wang Cheng-hua, "Qingdai chuzhongqi zuowei chanye de Suzhou banhua yu qi shangye mianxiang," 11–12. In this image, a banner on the ship identifies the men carrying the *jubaopen* as "Eight Barbarians Presenting Treasures" 八蠻進寶, a common motif in Qing visual culture. Unlike the stories about the *jubaopen* discussed above in which it is not coded as a foreign object, the *jubaopen*'s depiction in Qing dynasty commercial prints often enlisted a syncretic iconography that referenced a tradition of tribute gifts from foreign lands. For a discussion of this history of representation, see Fox, "Southern Capital," 207–21.

the center of the print the *jubaopen* emits billowing waves, surrounded by a bevy of auspicious motifs: children frolic and shake the branches of a money tree, while servants convey a platter of ingots and a basin of coral into the house. A frenzy of activity crowds the frame, with people and things foreign and divine flowing in and out of Wansan's gates.

The *jubaopen* thus functions not only as the literal engine of Shen Wansan's commercial operations, but as a heuristic for imagining the infinitely expansive possibilities of the newly global market, with the silver that appears in his basin *ex nihilo* a mystical and mystified displacement of the unfathomable quantities of silver that seemed to materialize in Jiangnan's ports from distant lands, drawn by some unseen power into the hands of merchants like Wansan.

Even as stories about Shen Wansan's cornucopia reorient the locus of accumulation toward the waterways of Suzhou and the humble investment of a commoner, the *jubaopen* provides an iconographic link to the wider world in which Suzhou was enmeshed. The cornucopia as symbol of the boundless profit promised by global trade had purchase not just in the cities of the lower Yangzi but across the commercial centers with which it had become increasingly interconnected. In London, Amsterdam, Antwerp, and Venice, the Hellenistic horn of plenty appeared on buildings and murals, frontispieces and objets d'art. Paired with the globe, the cornucopia's classical association with the divinely bestowed abundance of the Earth was given new meaning as the icon of the expansive, extractive merchant-state seeking out new markets and colonies.[42]

But if in Europe the cornucopia served as a symbol that folded the mercantile into the body politic, the stories around Shen

42. On the cornucopia as a civic icon, see Ufer, "Imagining Social Change in Early-Modern Amsterdam," 33–34. For a reproduction and discussion of a 1671 illustration by Romeijn de Hooghe, in which a horn of plenty and a treasure chest (born by the Maiden of China) are deposited in the lap of a Dutch river god in the shadow of a giant globe, see Keulemans, "Tales of an Open World," 197–99. For other examples, see William Hoyle's frontispiece for Michael Drayton, *Poly-Olbion* (London, 1612); Pieter Isaacsz, harpsichord lid with *Allegory of Amsterdam as the Center of World Trade* (ca. 1604–7), Amsterdam, Rijksmuseum; and Peter Paul Rubens, *The Exchange of the Princesses* (ca. 1622–25), Paris, Musée du Louvre.

Wansan and his *jubaopen* point to a fundamental tension between the imperial state and the market.[43] This is a tension that is only exacerbated in the early Qing when the urban south continued to resist Manchu rule, when merchant-pirates used overseas trading networks to fund loyalist activities, and when the new court in Beijing relied on the tax revenue of the prosperous south to fund its expenditures. It is this tension between the imperial state and the borderless market that *Cornucopia* brings to the fore.

Settling Accounts

After moving to Nanjing, the now very rich Shen Wansan builds a massive residential complex and establishes an array of commercial operations. Before long he attracts the attention of the newly installed Hongwu emperor, Zhu Yuanzhang, whose treasury has been nearly bankrupted by expensive military expeditions. The emperor and his ministers come up with a number of pretexts to have Wansan pay for state expenses, such as providing a banquet for the troops or building a section of the city wall, but none of these plots seem to make a dent in Wansan's great wealth and the state's great need. So the emperor decides to bestow upon Wansan the position of minister of revenue along with a single coin. But while the language of bestowal (*ci* 賜) seems to indicate a form of gift, the imperial edict quickly clarifies that the coin is actually a loan, and a rather predatory one at that: "Every day the interest will compound, and in this way the state treasury will be replenished" 逐日對合取利, 以充國庫.[44]

One month later, Wansan is recalled to court, where an official from the Ministry of Revenue is summoned to determine

43. Like the European iconography of the cornucopia, the Mother of Treasures pearl in Ruan Dacheng's *A Pair of Golden Placards* is enlisted to recontain the impulses of the market. The pearl, which promises to bring its holder the bounty of the ocean market, has its origins in a tribute gift to the Chinese court and must ultimately be returned to the court as tribute.

44. Zhu Suchen, *Jubaopen*, 32b–33a.

what is owed. In a bravura performance of accounting, the interest on this coin is calculated by the official on stage:

> MINISTRY OF REVENUE OFFICIAL, played by the *jing*, pantomimes calculating: [To the tune "Rider of a Lucky Horse"] The preparations are made to calculate the total figure; counting each bead as it rolls across the abacus, the sum becomes known. (*speaking*) Sheesh, these figures are hard to calculate! (*singing*) Do not confuse multiplying and dividing, counting and summing up. To adhere to the law there is a new requirement; how could ten-thousandfold interest on a loan be forgiven?
>
> 淨算寫介:【福馬郎】算此全盤準備早, 歷歷盤珠滾數分曉。(白) 咦, 這一盤數目好難算也。(唱) 乘除計總不淆, 歸法有新條, 萬倍利怎相饒。[45]

The official then makes his report to the emperor:

> The principal was one cash coin, and interest accrued by doubling the total amount every day. On the first day he owed two cash, on the second day he owed four cash, on the third day he owed eight, on the fourth day he owed sixteen, on the fifth day he owed thirty-two, on the tenth day he owed 1,024, on the twentieth day he owed 1,048,576. Today a month of thirty days has passed, so altogether he owes 1,073,741,724 cash.[46] Since one cash is the equivalent of one mace of silver, then we can calculate the principal and interested owed in silver as 107,374,172 taels and four mace.
>
> 本錢一文, 每日對合起利, 第一日該二文, 第二日該四文, 第三日該八文, 第四日該十六文, 第五日該三十二文, 第十日該一千二十四文, 二十日該一百四萬八千五百七十六文。經今一月三十日, 共該十萬七千三百七十四萬一千七百二十四文。每文重一錢, 算該本利銀一億七百三十七萬四千一百七十二兩四錢整。[47]

45. Ibid, 35b. Aria corrected with Xu Zhiheng edition. *Suizhong Wushi cang chaoben gaoben xiqu congkan*, 12:443.

46. This figure is calculated incorrectly; the final three digits should be 824 not 724; this error occurs in the *Guben xiqu congkan*, Xu Zhiheng, and Fu Xihua editions.

47. Zhu Suchen, *Jubaopen*, 36a. It is through ledgers that Wansan is both bankrupted and redeemed. While this scene is structured around an appraisal of Wansan's

At this point in the play, Wansan's *jubaopen* had been stolen by the conniving former woodcutter Zhang You'er. As Wansan is unable to pay the entire debt in cash, the emperor has his property appraised by an official from the Ministry of Works:

> According to the calculations of the Ministry of Revenue, principal and interest in the amount of 107,374,172 taels and four mace is owed. A survey of Shen Wansan's property has found that there are ten cellars of gold ingots appraised at ten million taels, one hundred cellars of silver ingots totaling 300,000 taels, five hundred chests of pearls, jade, silks, and other valuables worth ten million taels, 800,000 substantial articles of daily use appraised at ten million taels, one hundred gold and silver utensils worth twenty million taels, land and commercial holdings along with various official business accounts worth twenty-seven million taels, one residence appraised at 300,000 taels, and household staff worth 74,000 taels. The value of the above items is 107,374,000 taels, which is 172 taels and four mace short of what he owes.
>
> 據戶部臣實算，該本利一億七百三十七萬四千一百七十二兩四錢。盤得沈萬三家產，金錠十窖估價一千萬兩，銀錠百窖計重三十萬兩，珠玉細軟五百箱估價一千萬兩，粗重什物共八十萬件估價銀一千萬兩，金銀器皿一百扛估價兩千萬兩，田產房業及京省各項帳目估價兩千七百萬兩，住房一所估價三十萬兩，又抄仆從家業估價七萬四千兩。以上共計估價一億七百三十七萬四千兩，照原算本利尚虧一百七十二兩四錢。[48]

After much remonstrating from his officials, the emperor forgives Wansan the outstanding 172.4 taels, contenting himself with confiscating all of Wansan's property and stripping him of his official post.

---

debts and assets, a later scene hinges on an accounting of his loyalty. In the twenty-ninth scene, Zhu Yuanzhang discovers a ledger in the Tiansui Pavilion that details the frequency and expenses of the rituals performed in honor of the imperial family and the funds given to Zhang You'er. Like the ledgers of merit and demerit popular among Qing dynasty literati, this ledger collapses the distinction between fiscal and moral accounting.

48. Zhu Suchen, *Jubaopen*, 36b.

The extreme amount of wealth the emperor generates from loaning a single coin—and the rapidity with which this amount accumulates—clearly mimics the work of Wansan's cornucopia, which spits out an unending stream of coins for every one placed inside. Thus, against the merchant's cornucopia is positioned the emperor's cornucopia: usury, which generates surplus through mathematical magic.

Although both cornucopias turn money into more money, they present contrasting visions of capital accumulation. The emperor's usury depends upon deceptive abstractions and false equivalencies. The *wen* coin itself does not produce the interest; rather, value is generated by the monetization of the loan period. Here phantom agreements and (mis)calculations are commuted into material objects through monetized time. The two "tallying" passages quoted above convey the shocking contrast between the imaginary work of accounting (numbers begetting numbers) and the very real spoils of ingots, silks, buildings, and bodies; the generative process of usury, in which abstracted value reproduces itself, is uncannily "both logically impossible and empirically real."[49]

Shen Wansan's cornucopia attempts no such transfiguration: a coin does not produce a trove of ingots; numbers do not turn into jewels. Rather, kind generates kind; a hoard of silver can only be produced by silver. While the language of usury turns on the metaphor of reproduction (the interest or "child" 息 is "born" 生 from the "mother" 母 principal), it is Wansan's accumulation—not the emperor's usury—that is generation in the sense of producing within the same species.

The way this scene of high stakes accounting unfolds foregrounds the unnaturalness of usurious accumulation. The emperor does not merely ask for the total figures. Rather, he stages these acts of enumeration, calling forth his accountant to play his abacus for the court like a singer accompanying herself on the zither and to recite from his ledgers like an actor from a script. The calculation of the interest and the appraisal of property are made into

49. Hawkes, *The Culture of Usury in Renaissance England*, 5.

self-consciously theatrical entertainments, with the artifice of these performances drawing attention to the sham loan that forces the wealthy Wansan to play the role of borrower.

The emperor's usury is not only "unnatural" but also finite. After computing the amount owed, the emperor runs up against the limit of existing wealth: Wansan is 172.4 taels short. While the emperor is merely expropriating existing resources, Wansan's cornucopia presents the possibility of endless accumulation. The figuration of Wansan's wealth as natural and infinite—as a bringing into being, rather than a taking away; as productive rather than parasitic—recurs across the Suzhou stage. In plays like *Fifteen Strings of Cash* and *Three Kinds of Happiness*, the merchant-hero produces something real while the usurious or exploitative aspects of mercantile accumulation are pushed onto other, nonmerchant characters.

The infinite expansion of value that Wansan's cornucopia makes possible is thus defined against the very modes of mercantile abstraction that enabled the growth of the global economy in this period and that were the historical sources of wealth for men like Wansan.[50] Indeed, in an anecdote recorded by Dong Gu 董穀 (*juren* 1516), the emperor devises the loan not to expropriate Wansan's wealth, but to teach the usurer Wansan a lesson about setting fair interest rates:

> The Ming founder once summoned Wansan on the first day of the month and gave him one Hongwu coin, saying: "I shall trouble you to bear interest for me over the course of a month. Starting on the second day and ending on the thirtieth, every day I will receive double the total." Wansan happily thanked him for giving him this task.

50. The reputation of Shen Wansan as a usurer makes sense in the context of the Ming credit economy, in which lenders were often wealthy merchants. Unlike the fraught position of usury in the early modern West, interest-bearing loans were considered an acceptable practice in seventeenth-century Jiangnan, though loans such as the one described above that far exceeded government-set interest rates were frequently condemned. While there were specialized shops that dealt with such loans, officials, local elites, and merchants also engaged in usury. See Liu Qiugen, *Ming Qing gaolidai ziben*, 28–72.

Once he had left and began to think through the arrangement, he realized the difficult position in which he was placed. He would owe 536,870,912 cash; since 160 Hongwu cash weighed one catty and 16,000 cash equaled one stone, by calculating in stone, he would owe 33,554 stone and forty-three catties.[51] Although Wansan was wealthy, how could he manage this in such a short time? The emperor's reason for this exercise was to demonstrate that the interest rate should be capped (at 30 percent), and even if the loan period ran on for many months or years, the accumulated interest should never exceed the amount of the principal. This was why this was written into law.

太祖高皇帝嘗於月朔召秀，以洪武錢一文與之，曰：煩汝為我生利，只以一月為期，初二日起至三十日止，每日取一對合。秀欣然拜命，出而籌之，始知其難矣。蓋該錢五萬三千六百八十七萬零九百一十二文。今按洪武錢每一百六十文重一斤，則一萬六千文為一石。以石計之，亦該錢三萬三千五百五十四石四十三斤零。沈雖富，豈能遽辦此哉。聖祖緣是利息(只以三分)為率，年月雖多，不得過一本一利，著於律令者，此也。[52]

Here the emperor is only temporarily, pedagogically donning the mantle of the predatory usurer to give Wansan a fitting comeuppance. In *Cornucopia*, however, the emperor is entirely serious about collecting on his loan. This is in keeping with his broader role in the play, in which the emperor is repeatedly aligned with the abstractions of finance, as in an earlier scene in which he visits a teashop incognito and pays for his silver-denominated bill with the very first *baochao* 寶鈔 (paper currency) minted by his court. By making the circulation of fiat money and the enforcement of predatory loans into machinations of the Ming emperor and his court, the play is able to rescue merchant capital accumulation from its unsavory historical practices, recasting it as a force of

51. The discrepancy between this amount and the amount given in *Cornucopia* is due to this loan accruing interest starting on day two of the loan period whereas the play's loan starts accruing on day one.

52. Dong Gu, *Bili zacun*, 8a–9a. Parentheses indicate half-size characters in the woodblock print. "One unit of interest for one unit of principal" is a long-standing legal metric that predates Hongwu. See Bernhardt and Huang, eds., *Civil Law in Qing and Republican China*, 77.

nature, something fated and divine, outside of the authority of the state and its mints.

The Usurer and the Alchemist

That the cornucopia and its functions rightfully belong to the merchant is reiterated through the conventions of southern drama. In late Ming and early Qing *chuanqi*, the play's eponymous object—the peony pavilion, the peach blossom fan—often serves as a conduit through which social relations are generated, solidified, and recovered. In *Cornucopia*, the eponymous object is not the conduit but rather the end in itself; Shen Wansan's relationship with the cornucopia is at the very heart of the play. Like a pair of romantic heroes, the merchant and the cornucopia find each other as if by fate, only to be separated by scheming rivals, supernatural forces, and the vagaries of history. When the *jubaopen* is stolen, like a chaste maiden refusing to submit to her captors, it ceases to work. The grand reunion scene, the emotional catharsis of the play, reunites not husband and wife, but, as its title "Reunion with the Treasure" 寶圓 indicates, Wansan and his cornucopia. In recognition that it is no mere object but some sort of numinous subject, Wansan addresses it directly thanking it for its service: "Oh treasure basin, you have served me as a faithful minister from beginning to end" 寶盆嚇，你是我沈萬三的始終功臣了.[53] Eager to replenish his coffers, Wansan has a servant bring him two ingots, one gold and one silver. Placing them in the basin, he and the various members of his household sing an excessive ode to excess:

> ALL: [Variation on previous tune] Gleaming metals pile up on the ground, eclipsing mountains and tidal waves, surpassing the wealth that Guo Ju dug up.[54] See its smelted radiance, the brilliant pearls and

53. Zhu Suchen, *Jubaopen*, 56a.

54. Reference to a story that appears in *Records of the Search for Spirits* (*Soushen ji* 搜神記) and was later canonized in *Twenty-Four Filial Exemplars* (*Ershisi xiao* 二

jade! As time passes, all of that gold befuddles the eye; it could fill a mountain and choke the streams. We laugh with pleasure; in an instant, small pieces of money fill the cellar, piled high with treasures and jade.

合:【換頭】光鋆遍地堆積, 羡如山海湧, 勝郭巨羸基。看鎔鎔燦爛, 光耀珠琪。時移黃金眼望迷, 錢山貯滿渠。笑欣頤, 頃刻錙銖盈穴, 珍堆玉砌。[55]

As servents cart away these riches, Che E returns and reveals her true self. After explaining that Wansan is the earthly incarnation of the god of wealth, she leaves him a recipe for immortality. Endless wealth and endless life are thus tied together in a larger cosmological economy of karmic debt at the center of which sits the cornucopia that renders accumulation divine and the merchant a god. In his anticipated apotheosis, the merchant-god becomes a cornucopia himself, the source of "riches and honor without end, blessings and virtue that reach the ends of the earth" 富貴無極, 福德彌涯.

While perhaps reflecting rising popular worship of Wansan as a "living god of wealth" 活財神, this ending is certainly not preordained by the story, as most circulating legends end with Wansan's exile or death.[56] Even within the genre of *chuanqi* drama, which is formally structured around reunion and resolution, an appropriate ending for Wansan could take a radically different form. An instructive comparison can be found in a *chuanqi* play on the same subject, *Pavilion of the Heavenly Beacon*, which is not extant but is extensively summarized in the *Catalogue of Summaries from the Ocean of Song*.[57] Though the contours of the story remain largely

---

十四孝) about a man who decides to bury his son alive in order to have enough food for his mother; while digging he discovers a jar of gold.

55. Zhu Suchen, *Jubaopen*, 56a.

56. On representations of a deified Shen Wansan in popular prints from the mid-Qing to the Republican era, see Laing, "'Living Wealth Gods' in the Chinese Popular Print Tradition."

57. According to Wang Wenjun, *Pavilion of the Heavenly Beacon* appears in the ninth or tenth *ce* 冊 of the National Library of China manuscript of *Yuefu kaolüe* 樂府考略, which served as the basis of *Quhai zongmu tiyao*. Wang Wenjun, "Guojia tushuguan suo cang *Yuefu kaolüe*," 90.

the same, this play supposedly ends with Shen Wansan smashing the basin to pieces and "with his wife and concubine living peacefully and working contentedly until the end of his life" 遂與妻妾，安居樂業，以終其身.[58] Here the *jubaopen* is treated with the suspicion that characterized earlier stories about treasure-gathering objects—that extreme wealth causes suffering and chaos, that the parasitic accumulation of wealth without work is tainted. Happiness is the refusal of infinitude, either of riches or of life, and the embrace of a happy industriousness that only ends in one's natural death.

Cornucopia's ending not only casts the merchant's endless surplus as divine but also offers a way out of the question of loyalty that hangs over the play. The nature of Wansan's allegiance to the Ming court remains problematically obscure to the end. In his introduction, Wansan tells the audience that his father was a high-ranking official under the Yuan; when the rebel leader Zhang Shicheng 張士誠 (1321–67) takes control of Suzhou, his father dies a martyr. In a description that evokes the remnant subjects of the Ming, Wansan narrates his predicament: "Left behind all alone without any connections, I had no choice but to forget my feelings among hills and vales and hide my traces among rivers and lakes. Back and forth on the Wusong and Sanmao Rivers, I make my living by fishing" 遺下卑人一身無繫，只得忘情丘壑，遁跡江湖，往來吳松三泖之間，捕魚為活.[59]

While earlier textual antecedents note Wansan's humble beginnings, *Cornucopia*'s insertion of the loyalist father-official does not merely make Wansan into a proper *chuanqi* leading man, but also frames his livelihood as a loaded choice. When the cornucopia brings Wansan back into the political regime from which he had disengaged, his allegiances are viewed with understandable skepticism. The Tiansui Pavilion 天遂閣 that Wansan built becomes the focal point of this skepticism. With its reference to "heaven fulfilling" the desire of men, the name of the towering structure contains the possibilities of both submission and subver-

58. Dong Kang, ed., *Quhai zongmu tiyao*, 2:1319.
59. Zhu Suchen, *Jubaopen*, 2b–3a.

sion: its intended reading as a blessing onto the imperial family and its misreading as a seditious curse.[60] The wise advisor Liu Bowen 劉伯溫 (1311–75) encourages Wansan to build this pavilion and to house within it the records of sacrifices to the imperial family as a form of exonerating evidence that can be used against later charges of treason. To an audience in the early Qing, such strategic loyalty echoes the fraught decisions of literati-officials who struggled to negotiate the expectations of the new regime, their own experience of trauma, and their responsibilities to history. Indeed, such a resonance is foregrounded by having the twice-serving official Liu Bowen, whose difficulties both before and after the fall of the Yuan were a source of poignant self-recognition for many early Qing literati, suggest this display.[61]

While Liu Bowen's advice ultimately saves Wansan, this neat and satisfying resolution—in which the two remnant subjects prove their loyalty to the current regime while extracting an admission of wrong-doing from the emperor—is in self-conscious tension with the horrors of history. Just as the darker versions of Wansan's story that were circulating in the mid-seventeenth century would have provided a stark contrast to the triumphant ending of the play, the historical Liu Bowen's sad end (slandered as a traitor, stripped of his position by Zhu Yuanzhang) would have been known to any early Qing literatus in the audience.[62]

In the final scene of the play, Wansan slips the net of dynastic fealty entirely: by being elevated to the position of immortal-in-waiting, Wansan is absolved of any obligation to the current regime.[63]

60. Shen Wansan's villainous brother-in-law explains to the emperor that the name is "nothing less than a desire to curse the emperor to death; it means 'heaven fulfills' man's wish" 無非要咒殺勾皇帝, 天遂人願勾意思嘛. The Fu Xihua edition uses a different character with a similar meaning (*sui* 隨 "to follow or comply with"), which allows for similarly opposed readings: "[Man] follows Heaven" and "Heaven follows [the will of man]." *Fu Xihua cang gudian xiqu zhenben congkan*, 19:251. The nonextant play *Pavilion of the Heavenly Beacon* uses a third *sui* 燧 that means signal fire; *Catalogue of Summaries from the Ocean of Song* explains that this name derives from the twinkling light of a lantern hung at the top of the pavilion.

61. Kang-i Sun Chang, "Qian Qianyi and His Place in History," 208.

62. Zhao Yuan, *Ming Qing zhiji shidafu yanjiu*, 275–76.

63. This ending echoes that of Li Yu's *Coins of Heavenly Peace*, discussed in

Just as the merchant, enmeshed within a complex web of surpluses and needs that reach across administrative borders, frequently trespasses the edge of empire, so too does Wansan participate in a larger economy of karmic obligations that transcends state actors or actions.

In its anticipation of Wansan's ascension, the play's ending connects mercantile accumulation to the divine by way of *waidan* 外丹 (outer alchemy) practices, in which precious metals are transformed into elixirs of immortality.[64] While alchemy is often figured as a progenitor of or metaphor for usury—as they both generate value out of absence—Chinese alchemical practice, unlike usury, turns not on the abstraction of forms of value, but on the material transformation of a thing into the perfected thing it always had the potential to become. Within the Daoist worldview that everything is composed of the same, constantly fluctuating *qi* 氣, the act of transforming cinnabar into gold and compounding gold into an elixir is merely a channeling of an already present nature—not unlike Shen Wansan's transfiguration into the deity he has always been.

Like the merchant's ship and the alchemist's brazier, Wansan's cornucopia functions as an extragovernmental mint, bringing forth into circulation gleaming piles of unregulated bullion.[65] Although Wansan is often described by later writers as having "wealth that rivals that of the state" 富可敵國, with these riches implicitly making him a rival power, the emperor realizes that Wansan's threat lies not in his wealth per se but in his ability to generate wealth. As the emperor wonders, indignantly: "No matter how cleverly he mints copper from Mount Shu, how can the great authority of the emperor be divided?" 憑伊巧鑄蜀山

chapter 1, in which an immortal flies away, ignoring the entreaties of the emperor to return and serve in his court.

64. In the late imperial period, the "inner" alchemy of bodily cultivation and "outer" alchemy of elixir preparation were deeply interwoven in the Daoist quest for eternal life. On the properties and transmutations of metals, see Li Shizhen, *Bencao gangmu*, vols. 7–11.

65. Scholars have suggested that some early anticounterfeiting edicts were directed at alchemical practitioners. Pregadio, *Great Clarity*, 27–28.

銅，怎分得天王權重.[66] In an articulation of what Schumpeter termed theoretical cartalism, the production of monetary value is here characterized as the preserve of the sovereign, a right enshrined in "golden precepts and jade laws" 金科玉律, a stock saying that evokes, once again, the emperor's transformation of abstractions (precepts, laws) into precious stuff (gold, jade).[67] As a warning to those who do not respect this authority, the emperor darkly alludes to the fate of Golden Valley Garden 金谷園, the lavish estate of the wealthy Shi Chong 石崇 (249–300), who was undone by political machinations. But Shen Wansan is not executed like Shi Chong, nor does his beloved courtesan jump from the top of the Tiansui Pavilion. Within the logic of the play, Wansan's minting of the unminted may violate the emperor's edicts but not Heaven's or the market's. In the heavenly market of the merchant-god, the causation of value is reversed: it is not that the laws are golden but that gold is the law.

As it circulates through the hands of the merchant-god, unminted bullion imbricates the numinous and the everyday, its hypervaluation overdetermined by the practices of Daoist alchemy and the bimetallic late imperial marketplace. In these overlapping discourses, the thing-in-itself-ness of bullion—as both symbol and material of value—makes its worth appear legible, natural, universal, and constant. Unlike specie, an unminted ingot is valued by weight, by a mass in the world that is unchanged by whatever marks or stamps are placed on it or whatever exchange rates to which it is subjected. The danger of this mass that slips between dynasties and borders was reiterated in the periodic promulgation of (infrequently enforced) state policies that outlawed or limited the circulation of silver as legal tender.

Government fiat money, by contrast, is value situated in dynastic time, value made legible by the reign name on its face. But from the Ming founder's nonconvertible fiat money to the increasingly desperate attempts by the last three Ming emperors

66. Zhu Suchen, *Jubaopen*, 20a.

67. Schumpeter, *History of Economic Analysis*, 288. On the purchase of cartalism within early Chinese monetary thinking, see Von Glahn, *Fountain of Fortune*, 23–28.

to artificially adjust the value of debased government issue, the constantly changing monetary regimes destabilized the correspondences between the face value, the official value, and the market value of government money. Wansan's impulse in the final scene to replicate an ingot of silver rather than government-issued specie bespeaks the status of unminted silver as both the preferred currency of commercial exchange and the engine of international trade and merchant wealth, as well as the lack of confidence in government fiat money as a stable measure of value.[68] Indeed, the status of coins and bills is such that throughout the play they are only used by the emperor, who is perhaps the only remaining person with confidence in his authority over value.

By positioning the emperor as one who intrudes on the cosmic pairing of a merchant-god and his ever-expanding piles of money, the play discredits the state's totalizing claims of authority over value. At every turn, the power of the emperor is subordinated to a market he can no longer control; his various attempts to regain fiscal control—minting abstract and dematerialized currency, creating a culture of credit and usury—are depicted as morally bankrupt and economically ruinous.

The implicit critique of the emperor-usurer can be seen as a displacement of a larger mid-seventeenth-century discourse on the limits of imperial sovereignty. The disastrous fiscal policies of the crumbling Ming state that attempted to extract revenue from the flourishing urban centers and hinterland industries of Jiangnan made economic autarky a compelling possibility and, in some areas, a foregone conclusion during the years of dynastic transition. The notion of imperial ownership over the land and the materials produced therein was increasingly questioned by such contemporary observers as Huang Zongxi 黃宗羲 (1610–95) and Gu Yanwu 顧炎武 (1613–82), who called for the devolution of central authority—a devolution that, ironically, traces its roots to the policies of the historical Zhu Yuanzhang. It is within such a

68. The play's concern with silver is anachronistic for the early Ming but would appear as the natural order of things to a seventeenth-century audience.

milieu that *Cornucopia* could invert the dominant figuration of the merchant as usurer and counterfeiter, and instead cast the emperor as the purveyor of spurious commodities and truths and the endless regenerating surplus of merchant capital as an expression of divine will that supersedes the claims of the state.

Coda: An Audience of Money-Slaves

Like many of the Suzhou circle plays, *Cornucopia* survives in undated manuscripts whose performance-oriented form indicates an intended staging, though little is known about how and when such a performance might have taken place.[69] One indication might be found in a *ci* 詞 (lyric) by the Shandong literatus An Zhiyuan 安致遠 (1628–1701). The lyric, set to the tune "Whole River Red" 滿江紅, is titled "Watching a Play with Cao Liangfu" 同曹梁父觀劇, to which a note is appended: "The performance that day was of the Shen Wansan story" 是日演沈萬三故事.[70]

It is unclear which play about Shen Wansan was performed that day, whether it was *Cornucopia*, the nonextant *Pavilion of the Heavenly Beacon*, or some other *chuanqi* now entirely lost to us. However, the details of this performance match what one would expect for a performance of *Cornucopia*. The performance took place during the two months that An Zhiyuan traveled throughout Jiangnan during the summer of 1667, during which he saw the well-connected Cao Guyong 曹賈勇 (d. before 1671), courtesy

69. While the play does not appear in eighteenth-century collections of opera excerpts like *Coat of Patched Fur*, some of the extant scripts likely date from the mid- to late Qing, indicating a continuing tradition on the *kunqu* stage.

70. An Zhiyuan, *Wujiang you xiao*, 5b–6a. An Zhiyuan (*zi* Jingzi 靜子) received the *xiucai* 秀才 degree in 1645 and eventually became a tribute student, but he repeatedly failed to pass at the provincial level. He remained active in literary circles and edited the 1698 gazetteer for Shouguang 壽光. On his biography, see Barr, "Marriage and Mourning in Early Qing Tributes to Wives." His volume of *ci* poetry, *Whistling While Traveling through Wujiang* (*Wujiang lü xiao* 吳江旅嘯), in which this poem is found, was published posthumously by his son in 1702 and was later compiled in the *Siku quanshu*. Yuan Min, "An Zhiyuan wenji diaoban yicun kaolüe," 25–26.

name Liangfu, who hailed from Zongyang 樅陽 in Anqing 安慶 prefecture.[71] The date of this performance is precisely in the middle of the only two dateable pieces from Zhu Suchen's literary output: Li Yu's *Register of the Pure and Loyal*, for which Zhu is listed as an editor, was published circa 1659, and Zhu's *Moon over the Qin Tower* was written during the late 1670s.[72]

That this Shen Wansan play was performed for an audience that included literati also accords with expectations for a play by one of the Suzhou circle playwrights. For this particular audience to enjoy a play by Zhu Suchen is also not an unreasonable assumption, as the social worlds in which An Zhiyuan and Cao Liangfu circulated had multiple points of overlap with Zhu Suchen's: Cao Liangfu was known to be good friends with Fang Yizhi 方以智 (1611–71) and An Zhiyuan was championed by Wang Shizhen 王士禎 (1634–1711);[73] both Fang and Wang were friends with Wu Weiye, who personally knew Li Yu and wrote prefaces to his *Expanded and Standardized Formulary of Northern-Style Lyrics* and the play *Register of the Pure and Loyal*. Chen Weisong 陳維崧 (1626–82), whose work was supported by Wu Weiye and whose father was friends with Fang Yizhi, also contributed to Zhu Suchen's *Moon over the Qin Tower*.[74] Wang Shizhen, Wu Weiye, and Chen Weisong were also acquainted with Wu Qi, who was friends with both Zhu Suchen and Li Yu and wrote the preface and inscription to Zhu's *Moon over the Qin Tower*.[75]

The existence of this poem points both to the fact that the Shen Wansan story appeared in some form on the early Qing stage and to the multiplicity of reactions such a performance could

71. On the dating of this trip, see Ding Peng, "Qingdai Shanzuo citan yanjiu," 19n11.

72. On the dating of these plays, see chapter 2.

73. Barr, "Marriage and Mourning in Early Qing Tributes to Wives," 141–49.

74. On these relationships, see Volpp, "The Literary Circulation of Actors in Seventeenth-Century China," 955.

75. The friendship between Li Yu and Wu Qi is evidenced by the latter's *ci* "Written to the 'Chu orchids' rhyme, for Yuanyu" 次楚畹韻贈元玉, in Wu Qi, *Linhui tang ji*, 25:4a–b. On Chen Weisong's literary activities with Wu Qi and Wang Shizhen, see Meyer-Fong, *Building Culture in Early Qing Yangzhou*, 225n25. On Wu Qi's interactions with Wu Weiye, Zhu Suchen, and others, see Wang Chaohong, *Wu Qi nianpu*, 110–39.

generate. It is the tension among these responses that structures An's poem:

同曹梁父觀劇	Watching a Play with Cao Liangfu
(是日演沈萬三故事)	(the performance that day was of the Shen Wansan story)
四座財奴	The audience of money-slaves,
醉朦懂	muddle-headed in their drunken stupor,
真須醒起	needs to be awakened.
笑千古	I laugh at those throughout the ages
錢神滋味	who hanker for the god of money;
大抵如此	most are like this.
眼底賺來黃馘計	If one were content with the meager earnings of the "sallow faced,"[76]
樓頭不用綠珠死	then Green Pearl need not have fallen to her death from the tower.[77]
解連環	Undoing the interlocking rings,
瑣屑青田翁	a trifling trick of the old man from Qingtian
偶然耳	is just a matter of chance.[78]
一斗酒新豐市	A jug of fine wine from Xinfeng,[79]

76. A reference to a story in the *Zhuangzi*, in which an envoy returns from abroad with a hundred carriages. He tells Zhuangzi that he is bad at being poor and sallow faced but good at winning favor (and riches) from heads of state. *Zhuangzi jishi*, 4:1049.

77. An Zhiyuan's linking of Shen Wansan and Shi Chong, whose wealth was confiscated and whose favorite concubine committed suicide, is quite apt, as the conflation of the Shen Wansan story and that of Shi Chong was common in the seventeenth-century imagination. In a version of the Shi Chong story that is told in "Song the Fourth Torments Miser Zhang" 宋四公大鬧禁魂張 from Feng Menglong's *Stories Old and New*, Shi comes into his fortune by saving the life of a divine aquatic creature. In "Lü Dalang Returns the Money and Recovers His Flesh and Blood" from Feng's *Comprehensive Words to Warn the World*, a lyric references Shi Chong as the owner of the *jubaopen*.

78. A reference to Liu Bowen, who hailed from Qingtian and whose schemes save Shen Wansan from the fate of Shi Chong.

79. Xinfeng was known for good wine, as referenced in Wang Wei's 王維 (701–761) "Ballad of Youth" 少年行. For a translation, see Pauline Yu, *The Poetry of Wang Wei*, 69.

一闕曲臨邛婢	a song of a servant girl from Linqiong.[80]
且題詩畫壁	Let us inscribe poems on the wall,
旗亭徵妓	and engage the wineshop singing girls to sing.[81]
雙髻排成鬼谷隊	Pairs of chignons lined up as in Master Guigu's battle array,[82]
全身混入天魔裏	their bodies swirling in the Dance of the Heavenly Demon.[83]
正江南	Here in Jiangnan
倦客愁無聊	the weary traveler is vexed with worries,
思歸矣	thinking only of returning home.

In the opening line, An Zhiyuan is alone in a crowd. His fellow spectators have become a spectacle to him—their obliviousness no different from that of the characters on stage or the legions of money-hungry ghosts who haunt the past. An Zhiyuan's moral drama centers not around the endlessly generative cornucopia but its inverse, a vacuum of bankruptcy and alienation. Here, through reference to the tragic fate of Shi Chong, an alternative ending to the Shen Wansan story is imagined (or, considering the fate of Shen Wansan in the historical tradition, is read back into the play) that dead-ends in persecution, confiscation, and death. Any notion of money as divinely willed is excised, any possibility of escaping political machinations is laughable; it is only by sheer chance that anyone makes it out of wealth alive.

80. Linqiong is located in Sichuan; this is perhaps a reference to Zhuo Wenjun 卓文君, who was from Linqiong and opened a wine shop with the Western Han poet Sima Xiangru 司馬相如, who won her over with a song.

81. A reference to the wine shop competition between the Tang poets Wang Zhihuan 王之渙, Wang Changling 王昌齡, and Gao Shi 高適 to see whose compositions would be sung the most by performers, which appears in Xue Yongruo's 薛用弱 (fl. ninth c.) *Record of Collected Anomalies* (*Jiyi ji* 集異記). Xue, *Jiyi ji*, 11–12.

82. *Master Guigu* (*Guiguzi* 鬼谷子), supposedly written during the Warring States period, is a treatise on political philosophy that contains discussions of military strategy.

83. The Dance of the Heavenly Demon is described in the *History of the Yuan* (*Yuan shi* 元史) as an elaborate sixteen-person ritual dance popular in the court of the last emperor. Song Lian et al., *Yuan shi*, 2:918–19.

Against this tension between making and taking money, in the second half of the poem, An Zhiyuan attempts to create a separate sphere of sociality and creativity that lies beyond the commercial and the political. These lines cast An and his companions in the roles of men from "the ages" 千古 at whom he does not laugh: Wang Wei drinking his fine wine; Sima Xiangru singing his alluring song; Wang Zhihuan, Wang Changling, and Gao Shi scribbling on the inn wall; Su Shi longing for home.

These men are no slaves, or so they would say—though in every line the commercial underpinnings of their nonslavery bubble below the surface (someone must buy the wine, own the servant, pay the singing and dancing girls, fund the voyage to Jiangnan and back). Despite his participation in these performances of literati selfhood and sociality, by the end of the poem, An finds himself once more an alienated observer of others. Just as the first half of the poem enfolds an ever-widening swath of humanity into its moral drama, the performances of the second half grow increasingly crowded—from one singer to three poets to a phalanx of dancers. This metastasizing performance crescendos in a spectacle that is by turns warlike and demonic, until it exhausts itself and all that remains is the bone-tired narrator-traveler longing for home.

But what An perhaps sees as a decadent too-muchness—these performances of abundant surplus—cannot simply be left behind. Rather, they are part of a larger shift in the second half of the seventeenth century, through which the possibilities of ever-expanding ambits of commerce are not something to be mystified, dismissed, or suppressed but rather become their own kind of aesthetics and their own kind of politics. An Zhiyuan imagined that he was leaving all of this behind in Jiangnan, but it followed him—along with rice, silks, and the latest plays—back to Shandong along the Grand Canal.[84] In fact it was already there to meet him.

84. On the interregional trade between Jiangnan and Shandong in the late Ming, see Brook, "The Merchant Network in 16th-Century China," 195–96.

Conclusion

The Cornucopian Stage

Stages of Plenty

Shen Wansan's endlessly generative cornucopia not only serves as a particularly apt symbol of the lower Yangzi region's entry into the early modern global economy but also captures the maximalist sensibility of the Suzhou circle plays. Indeed, the Suzhou stage operated as a kind of cornucopia, pouring forth strings of coin, jars of gold, and carts of silver; people and things that appear barren or worthless reveal themselves to be obscenely productive. In *Between Man and Beast*, an indebted man unearths ten thousand taels of silver buried in a humble garden. In *Coins of Heavenly Peace*, a poor gardener produces ten thousand strings of rare palace coins out of thin air. In *Three Kinds of Happiness*, a shipwrecked merchant trades a barrel of olives for piles of silver. In *The Sound of Reading*, an impoverished student stranded on an uninhabited island stumbles upon dozens of trunks of pirate booty.

In these plays, written at the tail end of China's silver century, money is uncovered, dug up, brought to the surface of the stage where it grows and multiplies, doubling and tripling before the audience's eyes. While most of these plays traffic in extreme amounts, even more humble quantities are subject to the same logic. In *Winning the Prize Courtesan*, a peddler pays twelve taels of silver to spend the night with a courtesan who ends up giving him twenty taels in return. In *Fifteen Strings of Cash*, much confusion is generated because there is not one set of the eponymous fifteen strings in circulation but three. There is always more money than it first seems.

And there is often more money than there was before. Most of these plays have their roots in recently published vernacular stories and classical tales, but when adapted for the Suzhou stage, the amount of money in circulation tends to multiply. *Between Man and Beast*, one of Li Yu's earliest plays, closely follows the *huaben* "Squire Gui Repents at the End of His Rope" 桂員外途窮懺悔 from Feng Menglong's 1624 collection *Comprehensive Words to Warn the World*.[1] Both Feng's *huaben* and Li Yu's *Between Man and Beast* open with a loan of three hundred taels of silver made to a failed merchant who is deeply in debt.[2] In the *huaben*, the man digs up fifteen hundred taels of silver that a miser had buried in his garden; it is later discovered that an additional two thousand taels were buried in his bedroom, with other, unquantified amounts found elsewhere on his property. *Between Man and Beast* uncovers significantly more—ten thousand taels found in the garden alone—and assigns a number to the grand total unearthed: an astronomical half a million taels.[3]

It is not simply the amount of money that has been enlarged in the shift from page to stage, but also the narrative space that the money takes up. Here the generic possibilities of *chuanqi* are put to use to generate effects not possible in *huaben*. While *huaben* may use the insertion of a poem or the voice of the storyteller-narrator to bracket or slow down the pace of a significant scene, the generic impetus of *huaben*, as written by Feng and his ilk, tends toward a propulsive momentum that allows for only a para-

1. This *huaben* was itself based on a classical tale that appears in Shao Jingzhan's 邵景詹 *Stories Told While Searching for the Lamp* (*Mideng yinhua* 覓燈因話, 1592). *Between Man and Beast* appeared in print during the Chongzhen period and was revised and reprinted by Feng Menglong before his death in 1646.

2. In the classical tale, the loan is for twenty ingots (of which two are later repaid).

3. The classical tale describes only vaguely the amount of money uncovered in the garden as "a cache of buried silver" 白金一藏, and no additional monies are discovered. Shao Jingzhan, *Mideng yinhua*, 1:3a.

graph or two of such indulgences. *Chuanqi*, however, is built around the poles of extreme expansion and extreme compression. Within the economy of the *chuanqi* play, in which (sung) emotional introspection is privileged over (spoken) narrative momentum, an aria can languidly unfurl the contours of a fleeting moment, while the space between scenes can traverse the passage of months or years. The discovery and experience of monetary excess is always given this expansive treatment as the climactic centerpiece of a scene. The narrative space occupied by this excess is made literal in the stage space by the performance conventions of *chuanqi* drama: according to stage directions, ingots, coins, and bills (either as physically present props or as physically conjured pantomimes) are snatched up, examined, and counted.[4] Large quantities are lugged around the stage in bags, hoisted on backs, or pushed around in carriages, as characters sigh, "Oh, how heavy!" 阿呀好重嗄 or poetically describe the rattling wheels as "sounding like the crashing waves of the ocean" 聲如海潮.[5]

Such an expansive treatment of excess can be found in the ninth scene of *Between Man and Beast*, "Obtaining What Was Buried" 獲藏 (plate 8). The scene opens with a prologue of sorts, in which a heavenly official in charge of buried treasure recounts how he was ordered by Guanyin to reveal a cache of one hundred thousand taels of silver to a man named Gui Xin as a test of his character. With the anticipation of the discovery thus seeded, the scene turns to Gui Xin and his wife, who are returning that evening to their humble home in their benefactor's garden. Their son had fallen asleep inside, so they bang on the door and call out to him to open it up. Awaking with a start, the boy looks out and sees a yellow snake and a white rat burrowing under a tree in the

4. Though evidence on props on the seventeenth-century stage is limited, in the prop list for *Peach Blossom Fan*, Kong Shangren includes several pieces of prop money.

5. *Shiwu guan*, 1:43b; *Taiping qian*, 2:23a. Stage directions in Qing-era scripts of *Fifteen Strings of Cash* include instructions to "act out taking out the money" 取錢介, but it is unclear how such actions were staged. Since the 1956 rewriting and abridgement of *Fifteen Strings of Cash*, performance practice involves the actors draping the strings over one shoulder.

garden. Gui Xin suggests that the boy was dreaming, but his wife takes this as a sign of buried treasure; though skeptical, Gui Xin agrees to start digging. So he digs and sings and digs; he grows weary, but his wife urges him to press on ("If you desire wealth and rank, then you must work to the limit!" 欲求生富貴，須下死功夫), threatening to do it herself if he lacks the willpower.[6] Finally he hits something: "a jar of big silver pieces!" 一罎大銀子.[7] His wife presses him for details: "How much silver is in each jar and how many jars are there total?" 一罎內有多少銀子，共總有幾罎.[8] He investigates further:

> Gui Xin, played by the *jing*, takes hold of one of the jars: [To the previous tune] Peering inside the jar, I see it is full; peering inside the jar, I see it is full. (*picks up an ingot and examines it*) The finest silver bullion. A single ingot weighs a full fifty taels! Each jar has twenty pieces. (*counts the jars*) I count five pairs of jars, I count five pairs of jars. Carefully calculating what is stored inside, it's exactly ten thousand taels!
>
> 淨搬介：【前腔】覷罎中滿裝，覷罎中滿裝。(將錠看介) 細絲白鏹。一個元寶，足有五十兩重哩。每罎廿個都一樣 (數罎介) 數罎兒五雙，數罎兒五雙。細算內中藏，剛剛一萬兩。[9]

This scene captures not only the pleasure of uncovering and then reveling in the bounty of the stage-earth but also the pleasure in quantifying it.[10] Arias of calculation like this recur both throughout this play and across the Suzhou circle plays more generally. In the abacus-tallying and inventory-taking performances of *Cornucopia* and the daily savings plan the poor oil seller lays out in *Winning the Prize Courtesan*, one experiences the satisfaction of adding it up, of numbers and objects that

6. Li Yu, *Renshou guan*, 1:33b.
7. Ibid.
8. Ibid., 1:33b–34a.
9. Ibid., 1:34a.
10. All three of them take turns touching and fondling, including the son, who playfully "grabs an ingot and clowns around" 搶一錠，諢介. Ibid.

multiply. These acts of accounting are not just a source of aesthetic pleasure but of potential salvation. In *Cornucopia*, Shen Wansan's assiduously kept registers of sacrifices in honor of the imperial family rescue him from charges of disloyalty. In *Winning the Prize Courtesan*, the oil seller's financial planning allows him to buy his family back into existence. A similar ending is staged in *Between Man and Beast*, when a dead man's careful record of his savings reveals the crimes of the wicked and rewards those who suffered injustice.

In their intertwining of the pleasure of accumulation and the rectitude of accounting, arias of calculation capture the dual nature of the seventeenth-century enthusiasm for ledgers as systems of monetary and moral account. The increasing numerical complexity of everyday urban life—the credits and debits, revenue and liabilities, assets and taxes—required enterprises large and small to make use of a range of accounting techniques to quickly tally up what was owed or what was received. It was through the mastery of the multi-legged ledger as well specialized numerals and abacus counting systems that such enterprises could grasp at any given moment their place in the flow of money and goods into and out of their doors.[11]

There was a similar impulse to locate the self within the various debts and repayments of what could be called the karmic economy. This impulse most clearly found expression in the increasingly sophisticated ledgers of merit and demerit that were in vogue among literati across the seventeenth century.[12] By recording and assigning value to one's good and bad deeds, these ledgers asserted new equivalences across things, actions, and ideas: saving one hundred ants has equal merit to saving a man; drinking to excess is worth three demerit points less than break-

11. While some scholars have asserted that a native double-entry bookkeeping system ("dragon-gate bookkeeping" 龍門賬) emerged in the mid-seventeenth century, there is little archival evidence to support such claims. For an overview of the scholarship on late imperial accounting, as well as the earliest evidence of a native double-entry system in mid-nineteenth century account books, see Lowenstein and Cac, "Business Accounting at Fengshengtai."

12. See Brokaw, *The Ledgers of Merit and Demerit*.

ing a promise. In making one's moral choices quantifiable they were thus rendered commensurable—not only formally similar to but interchangeable with the pieces of silver or strings of coin that could purchase expiation through donation.

In concretizing the twin abstractions of capital and karma, the ledger fetish of the seventeenth century rendered the complexity of everyday life legible, knowable, even controllable. This is the work of the arias of calculation that appear throughout the Suzhou circle plays: if the troves of treasure uncovered by the protagonist dramatize the influx of goods and money made possible by an expanding trade network, the arias of calculation perform the forms of knowledge that make such a world meaningful and navigable.

Worlds of Plenty

On the cornucopian stage, the arithmetic of profit is not simply a theme but an aesthetic and an ethic—an argument about the perfect functioning of the world and the self within it. This optimistic cornucopianism is not limited to the narrative unfolding within the diegetic space of these plays but also describes the relation between the play and the extratheatrical world in which it is embedded. Through their many metatheatrical gestures, these plays extend this ethos to the spectators, who are revealed to themselves as bound up and bound together in the proliferating economic relations mediated by the performances happening before and around them.

Further offstage but no less enmeshed are the Suzhou circle playwrights themselves, whose sheer productivity far outstripped most of their predecessors and contemporaries: against Tang Xianzu's five *chuanqi*, Ruan Dacheng's four, and Kong Shangren's one, at least nineteen plays are attributed to Li Yu, thirteen were supposedly penned by Zhu Suchen, while twenty are attributed to his brother Zhu Zuochao and at least ten were written by Zhang

Dafu. Very few late imperial playwrights, such as the similarly enterprising Li Liweng, with ten *chuanqi* dramas and several additional scenes to his credit, even come close. The plays of the Suzhou circle were not only plentiful but profitable; actors and aficionados competed to buy their latest plays, and commercially minded publishers rushed to print revised editions.[13]

But while the Suzhou circle playwrights were outliers among their elite Jiangnan contemporaries, they had long-lost half-siblings all over the world. Over the long seventeenth century, in cities such as London, Amsterdam, and Osaka, an early modern repertoire emerged in newly established commercial theaters that centered the tastes and experiences of a socially diverse urban audience.[14] Written, often collaboratively, by professional playwrights and inhabited by the socially anxious and financially volatile—destitute nobles and rich merchants, small-time scammers and intercontinental fortune hunters—these plays mine the precarity and the possibility of the early modern margins.

These plays from around the globe are rooted in an imagination of the city as a commercial space and the self as a commercial actor. It is in this transactional horizontality that both the city and the self reach outward beyond themselves in ways that interweave the local and the transoceanic. In English city comedies, as in Tokugawa *jōruri* 浄瑠璃, the rhythm of everyday life beats in time with global commodity flows: domestic bliss is inextricably linked to the sale of Dutch cargo, a New World gold rush, the smuggling of Chinese goods.[15] There is no sphere untouched and no relation uncolored by the imperatives of global commerce. And that includes the theater itself, where the play text and its production were commodities and commercial events with their own trans-

13. Feng Menglong, ed., *Mohanzhai chongding Yong tuanyuan chuanqi*, *xu* 2a–b.

14. During the period from the end of sixteenth century to the middle of the seventeenth century, permanent commercial theaters were established for the first time in London, Madrid, Venice, Amsterdam, Tokyo, and Osaka. Suzhou did not have permanent commercial theaters, though such structures flourished earlier and later.

15. Dekker's *The Shoemaker's Holiday* (1599); Chapman, Jonson, and Marston's *Eastward Ho* (1605); Chikamatsu's *The Girl from Hakata Spends the Night at Sea* (*Hakata kojorō namimakura* 博多小女郎波枕, 1719).

regional circuits, like the sixty Spanish *comedias* that were performed on the seventeenth-century Amsterdam stage or Jan Vos's 1638 rewriting of Shakespeare's *Titus Andronicus*, which was a smash hit throughout northern Europe.[16]

With plots that frequently feature doubles and disguises, this early modern repertoire enlists metatheater as a tool to make visible the kinds of role play and self-alienation that characterize life within a highly commercialized society. Role play is of course internal to the forms of market exchange, which require a kind of theatrical inhabiting of stock roles in which each party performs from a shared social script. In plays such as Gaspar Aguilar's *The Merchant Lover* (*El mercader amante*, before 1605) and Thomas Middleton's *A Trick to Catch the Old One* (1608), we see that as the marketplace expands beyond the boundaries of a discrete "place" and instead suffuses all aspects of life, these roles of buyer and seller, investor and dupe spill over into the "pristine" spheres of romance and domesticity, transforming affective bonds into a zero-sum competition for resources. Other plays, like Gerbrand Bredero's *The Spanish Brabanter* (*Spaanschen Brabander*, 1617), Philip Massinger's *A New Way to Pay Old Debts* (1626), Molière's *Tartuffe, or The Imposter* (*Tartuffe, ou l'Imposteur*, 1664), and Joost van Breen's *Farce of Jean de la Roy, or The Imagined Rich Man* (*Klucht van Jean de la Roy, of dingebeelde rijke*, 1665), survey the cast of unknowns that move through the commercial city and its social hierarchies; in a time of rapidly shifting fortunes, it becomes increasingly difficult to know if the stranger you pass on the street or meet in an inn is who he says he is or just pretending.

From Edo to Madrid, theater served as an apt metaphor for the duplicity that sits at the heart of the commercially engaged early modern world: the commoner actor who plays a king and wields a wooden prop sword formally echoes the scammer who invents personae and traffics in counterfeit goods and the nouveau riche upstart who purchases titles and profits from the fictitious value of official fiat currencies. But while many of these

16. Blom, "Enemy Treasures," 121; Helmers, "The Politics of Mobility," 345.

plays give voice to the anxious experience of navigating an unstable social world, there are also convergences with the Suzhou circle playwrights' more productive approach to metatheater. By surfacing the ways that the performance space is a commercial space and everyone inside an economic actor, the staging of these plays makes possible the inhabitance of new roles that are born of this theatrical-qua-commercial alienation but are not socially destructive.

One such mode of metatheatrical productivity is the centering of merchant characters whose merchant-ness is not framed as a moral problem but as a universal figuration of the urban experience. As in *Jean de la Roy* or *The Merchant Lover* or many of Chikamatsu's *sewamono* 世話物 (current events) dramas, the narrative is focalized through the experience of flawed yet ultimately sympathetic merchants. The universalizing of a mercantile consciousness as a feature of the emerging early modern subject appears even when the merchant himself is subject to condemnation, as in Lope de Vega's *Brazil Restored* (*El Brasil restituido*, 1625). Here a commoner soldier is engaged in a constant hustle in which all personal relations are leveraged for profit; as he declares when selling his protection to a rich woman, "These are times when everything is for sale" (que el tiempo vende las cosas).[17] But underneath his sardonic and base clownishness is a loyal and valiant subject of crown and church, a strong contrast with the actual merchants—the traitorous Jews and their heretical allies in the Dutch West India Company—against whom he fights; his heroics in battle (and subsequent profit from these heroics) ultimately demonstrate a morally and politically sound navigation of the socially transformative possibilities of a New World economy.[18]

17. Stackhouse, *Translations of the American Plays of Lope de Vega*, 509 (original), 510 (translation). Literally, "time sells all things."

18. The *gracioso* (clown role type) typically hails from the lower classes and acts as a servant of and apologist for his aristocratic masters. Here, in his shrewd navigation of the New World market, the *gracioso* embodies not the aristocratic values of Madrid but a new hybrid transatlantic subjectivity. See Sánchez, "The Subject of the King and a Mercantile Ideology in Early Modern Spain."

The resonance of these figures on stage, in which sympathetic characterization elicits empathetic self-recognition, is aided by the frequent dramatization of events in living memory, as in Joost Van Den Vondel's *Zungchin* (1667), which dramatizes the fall of the Ming two decades prior;[19] Chikamatsu's *The Girl from Hakata Spends the Night at Sea*, which relates a smuggling episode involving the China trade that took place the previous year; and *Brazil Restored*, which tells of the recapturing of Brazil by Spanish-Portuguese forces a few months earlier.[20] This turn to current settings and current events gives expression to the way a developing commercial economy impels the speeding up of circulation and thus gives rise to an acceleration of the time scale of everyday life and a notion of simultaneity that bridges near and far. At the same time, recency acts as a form of metatheater, as the unfolding of a recent event on stage recalls the spectator's prior consumption of said event: how he had read the news of that colonial war or overheard the gossip about that scandal. In watching the performance of actors reading news or hearing gossip, he becomes the self-aware spectator of his own spectating, an experience that is simultaneously alienating and self-constituting: he is alienated from his own specific memory at the same time that the abstracting and universalizing of this experience interpellates him into a collective subjecthood.

Just as these plays depict faraway events in which the local is deeply implicated, the early modern subject that is articulated and instantiated through the act of communal spectatorship is at once deeply of his specific urban locale—a citizen of London, a *chōnin* of Osaka—and fully enmeshed in irreducibly global circuits of exchange. Like the fantastical overseas (and underseas) markets discussed in chapter 3, these circuits promise the early modern man wealth without end: the gold bars the indigenous islanders offer up to Columbus; the ships that arrive in the port of Moji

19. "Zungchin" is an attempted romanization of [the] Chongzhen [emperor]. On this play see Kuruppath, *Staging Asia*, 61–115.

20. Lope's play was performed for an audience that likely included men who fought in the campaign depicted. Stackhouse, *Translations of the American Plays of Lope de Vega*, lviii.

"every day laden with thousands of *kanme*, tens of thousands of *kanme*; gold coins race about and silver flies through the air" 日に千貫目萬貫目，小判走れば銀が飛ぶ.[21]

This is a surplus that comes invariably from somewhere else—or rather everywhere else, as the globe becomes one endless market. In Jan Vos's theatrical poem *The Expansion of Amsterdam* (*Vergrooting van Amsterdam*, 1662), which was recited by over eighty performers at the Amsterdam Theater in celebration of the expansion of the city's canal ring, the merchant-state is showered with riches from across the cornucopian Earth. A personification of Blessing is described as borne by eagles to the Amstel River, where "mild Trade and lavish Surplus suckled from her rich breast a fountain of treasures" (De milde Neering en de weelig' Overvloedt, die uit haar rijke borst een bron van schatten zoogen).[22] The sites of this trade and the origins of these treasures are given form in the figure of the World, who appears before the city of Amsterdam

> accompanied by her daughters of great value: yellow America, full of gold and silver mines; turbaned Asia, covering most of the earth; black-roasted Africa, full of tigers, dragons, lions; and town-rich Europe, famed for its cleverness.
>
> Zy was verzelschapt van haar dochters, groot van waardt: Het geel' Amerika, vol goudt en zilvermijnen; 't Getulbandt Azia, het grootste deel van d'aardt; Het zwart' gebraad' Afrijk', vol tygers, draaken, leeuwen; En 't steederijk Euroop, beroemt door schranderheidt.[23]

This imagination of the world presenting its bounty in tribute is a common source of resolution on the early modern stage, from

21. Lope de Vega, *The New World Discovered by Christopher Columbus* in Shannon, *El nuevo mundo descubierto por Cristóbal Colón*, 208 (original), 209 (translation); Chikamatsu Monzaemon, *The Girl from Hakata Spends the Night at Sea* in Chikamatsu, *Chikamatsu jōrurishū*, 1:325, translation adapted from Keene, *Major Plays of Chikamatsu*, 352. The Japanese weight measurement of *kanme* 貫目 is the equivalent of 100 Chinese taels. The gold coins are *koban* 小判, an official currency of the Tokugawa shogunate equal to one *ryō* 両 (approximately six Chinese taels).

22. Vos, *Vergrooting van Amsterdam*, 833–34.

23. Ibid., 836–37.

the "six newly arrived, half-naked and painted Indians" (seis indios bozales medio desnudos, pintados) brought to the Spanish court in Lope's *The New World Discovered by Christopher Columbus* to the kowtowing foreign princes in Ruan Dacheng's *A Pair of Golden Placards*.[24] Here the threat that the borderless empire of silver poses to the bounded sovereign state is effaced, as are the messy dynamics of overseas exchange, the dangerous voyages and financial risks, the violence of colonial extraction.

But elsewhere the various costs, human and otherwise, are tallied. Often the surplus of the cornucopian Earth is felt more in its absence than its presence, like Antonio's cargo ships, the status of which remains vexingly out of reach for much of *Merchant of Venice*, silently trawling the vast expenses between Tripoli, Barbary, Mexico, England, and India. In this vacuum of uncertainty and unpredictability, what proliferates on stage are mortgages, loans, and promissory notes—gambles on a promised bounty, the failure or deliverance of which separates tragedy from comedy. A shadow surplus generated by usury and alchemy takes center stage, as in Chapman, Jonson, and Marston's *Eastward Ho* (1605): when the promise of a gold-paved Virginia ends in a shipwreck, a goldsmith decides to "blanch copper so cunningly that it shall endure all proofes" and thereby fabricate his own New World fortune.[25]

Though counterfeits and deficits, risks and losses, similarly abound on the Suzhou stage, there is always profit to be had closer to home. Money—real, hard money—can be found in the most quotidian spaces: in the water and the dirt, in clay jars and rats' nests, stuffed in the eaves and buried in gardens. The surplus that surfaces on the Suzhou stage—in plays such as *Between Man and Beast*, *Fifteen Strings of Cash*, *Winning the Prize Courtesan*, *Coins of Heavenly Peace*, and *Cornucopia*—is a surplus that originates

24. Shannon, *El nuevo mundo descubierto por Cristóbal Colón*, 276 (original), 277 (translation).

25. Chapman, Jonson, and Marston, *Eastward Ho*, act 4, sc. 1, lines 258–59. A similar treatment of alchemy as an elaborate scam that enervates as much as it proliferates appears in Jonson's *The Alchemist* (1610), in which credulous seekers of the cornucopian philosopher's stone are swindled out of their money.

and belongs there. Unlike those aforementioned plays of debt and lack, in which money comes from—and invariably departs for—someplace else, the Suzhou circle plays orchestrate a fantastical reimagining of the historical flow of bullion from New World and Japanese mines into southern China. This bullion is naturalized in both senses of the word, written into urban Jiangnan's prehistory (often courtesy of the local gods) and given permanent residency within its walls. On Suzhou's cornucopian stage, riches are not a device but a birthright and an investment. Tens of thousands of coins and bills and ingots are deposited into the hands of urban commoners, to whom value always already belonged, and funneled into their shops and ships, performing and instantiating the utopian possibility of a new order in which they sit at the center.

Bibliography

Agnew, Jean-Christophe. *Worlds Apart: The Market and the Theater in Anglo-American Thought, 1550–1750*. New York: Cambridge University Press, 1986.

Aina Jushi 艾衲居士. *Doupeng xianhua* 豆棚閒話. Facsimile reprint of Hanhai lou 翰海樓 edition in *Guben xiaoshuo jicheng* 古本小說集成, vol. 331. Shanghai: Shanghai guji chubanshe, 1990.

Altenburger, Roland. *The Sword or the Needle: The Female Knight-Errant (xia) in Traditional Chinese Narrative*. Bern: Peter Lang, 2009.

An Zhiyuan 安致遠. *Wujiang lü xiao* 吳江旅嘯. In *An Jingzi ji* 安靜子集. Shouguang: Zizu yuan, 1863.

Bao Qizhen 包啓禎. *Bao Yinhe shiji* 包飲和詩集, preface 1632. In *Taiwan zhencang shanben congkan, Gu chaoben Mingdai shiwen ji* 台灣珍藏善本叢刊, 古鈔本明代詩文集, vol. 5. Edited by Wang Guoliang 王國良 et al. Taibei: Xinwenfeng chuban, 2013.

Barmé, Geramie R. "A Garden of Perfect Brightness, a Life in Ruins." *East Asian History* 11 (1996): 111–58.

Barr, Allan. "Marriage and Mourning in Early Qing Tributes to Wives." *Nan Nü: Men, Women and Gender in China* 15.1 (2013): 137–78.

———. "Pu Songling and *Liaozhai zhiyi*: A Study of Textual Transmission, Biographical Background, and Literary Antecedents." PhD diss., Oxford University, 1983.

Bernhardt, Kathryn, and Philip C. C. Huang, eds. *Civil Law in Qing and Republican China*. Stanford, CA: Stanford University Press, 1994.

Birge, Bettine. *Women, Property, and Confucian Reaction in Sung and Yüan China (960–1368)*. Cambridge: Cambridge University Press, 2002.

Blom, Frans. "Enemy Treasures: The Making and Marketing of Spanish *Comedia* in the Amsterdam Schouwburg." In *Literary Hispanophobia and Hispanophilia in Britain and the Low Countries (1550–1850)*, edited by Yolanda Rodríguez Pérez, 115–44. Amsterdam: Amsterdam University Press, 2020.

Bol, Peter K. *"This Culture of Ours": Intellectual Transitions in T'ang and Sung China*. Stanford, CA: Stanford University Press, 1992.

Bourdieu, Pierre. *The Logic of Practice*. Translated by Richard Nice. Stanford, CA: Stanford University Press, 1990.

Brokaw, Cynthia. *Ledgers of Merit and Demerit: Social Change and Moral Order in Late Imperial China*. Princeton, NJ: Princeton University Press, 1993.

Brook, Timothy. *The Confusions of Pleasure: Commerce and Culture in Ming China*. Berkeley: University of California Press, 1998.

———. *Geographical Sources of Ming-Qing History*. Ann Arbor: University of Michigan Center for Chinese Studies, 1988.

———. "The Merchant Network in 16th-Century China: A Discussion and Translation of Zhang Han's 'On Merchants.'" *Journal of the Economic and Social History of the Orient* 24.2 (1981): 165–214.

Brown, Bill. "Thing Theory." *Critical Inquiry* 28.1 (2001): 1–22.

Bruster, Douglas. *Drama and the Market in the Age of Shakespeare*. Cambridge: Cambridge University Press, 1992.

Cervone, Einor Keinan. "Waterscapes: Aquatic Theater and Other Floating Pleasures in Late Imperial Jiangnan." PhD diss., Harvard University, 2017.

Chang, Kang-i Sun. "Qian Qianyi and His Place in History." In *Trauma and Transcendence in Early Qing Literature*, edited by Wilt L. Idema, Wai-yee Li, and Ellen Widmer, 199–218. Cambridge, MA: Harvard University Asia Center, 2006.

Chang, Michael G. *A Court on Horseback: Imperial Touring and the Construction of Qing Rule, 1680–1785*. Cambridge, MA: Harvard University Asia Center, 2007.

———. "Historical Narratives of the Kangxi Emperor's Inaugural Visit to Suzhou." In *The Dynastic Centre and the Provinces: Agents and Interactions*, edited by Jeroen Duindam and Sabine Dabringhaus, 203–24. Leiden: Brill, 2014.

Chapman, George, Ben Jonson, and John Marston. *Eastward Ho*. Edited by R.W. Van Fossen. Manchester: Manchester University Press, 1999.

Chaves, Jonathan. "Moral Action in the Poetry of Wu Chia-chi (1618–84)." *Harvard Journal of Asiatic Studies* 46.2 (1986): 387–469.

Chen, Liana. *Staging for the Emperors: A History of Qing Court Theatre, 1683–1923*. Amherst, NY: Cambria Press, 2021.

Chikamatsu Monzaemon 近松門左衛門. *Chikamatsu jōrurishū* 近松浄瑠璃集. 2 vols. Tokyo: Iwanami shoten, 1965–67.

Chow, Kai-wing. "The Merging of *Shi* and *Shang* in Travel: The Production of Knowledge for Travel in Late Ming Book." *Frontiers of History in China* 6.2 (2011): 163–82.

———. *Publishing, Culture, and Power in Early Modern China*. Stanford, CA: Stanford University Press, 2004.

Chu Renhuo 褚人穫. *Jianhu ji* 堅瓠集. 66 *juan*. Kangxi edition (preface 1690) in *Zhongguo jiben guji ku*.

Chuanqi huikao 傳奇彙考. Shanghai: Gujin shushi, 1914.

Chuanqi huikao biaomu 傳奇彙考標目. In *Zhongguo gudian xiqu lunzhu jicheng* 中國古典戲曲論著集成, vol. 7, edited by Zhongguo xiqu yanjiuyuan 中國戲曲研究院. Beijing: Zhongguo xiju chubanshe, 1959–60.

Clunas, Craig. *Superfluous Things: Material Culture and Social Status in Early Modern China*, 2nd ed. Honolulu: University of Hawai'i Press, 2004.

Da Ming Shenzong Xian huangdi shilu 大明神宗顯皇帝實錄. 596 *juan*. Reprinted in *Ming shilu* 明實錄, vol. 112. Taibei: Zhongyang yanjiuyuan lishi yuyan yanjiusuo, 1966.

Deng Changfeng 鄧長風. "*Chuanqi huikao* tanwei" 《傳奇彙考》探微. *Hanxue yanjiu* 漢學研究 (Taibei) 17.1 (1999): 229–58.

Deng Shaoji 鄧紹基, ed. *Zhongguo gudai xiqu wenxue cidian* 中國古代戲曲文學辭典. Beijing: Renmin wenxue chubanshe, 2004.

Ding Peng 丁鵬. "Qingdai Shanzuo citan yanjiu" 清代山左詞壇研究. PhD diss., Zhongguo shehui kexue yuan 中國社會科學院, 2013.

Dong Gu 董穀. *Bili zacun* 碧里雜存. 1 *juan*. Facsimile reprint of Wanli-era *Baoyan tang miji* 寶顏堂秘笈 edition in *Siku quanshu cunmu congshu zibu* 四庫全書存目叢書子部, vol. 240. Jinan: Qi Lu shushe, 1997.

Dong Kang 董康, ed. *Quhai zongmu tiyao* 曲海總目提要. 2 vols. In *Lidai quhua huibian, Qingdai bian* 歷代曲話彙編, 清代編, edited by Yu Weimin 俞為民 and Sun Rongrong 孫蓉蓉. Hefei: Huangshan shushe, 2009.

Du, Yongtao. *The Order of Places: Translocal Practices of the Huizhou Merchants in Late Imperial China*. Leiden: Brill, 2015.

Duan Benluo 段本洛 and Zhang Qifu 張圻福. *Suzhou shougong yeshi* 蘇州手工野史. Nanjing: Jiangsu guji chubanshe, 1986.

Duan Chengshi 段成式. *Youyang zazu* 酉陽雜俎. 30 *juan*. *Sibu congkan* 四部叢刊 edition in *Zhongguo jiben guji ku*.

Ebrey, Patricia. *Women and the Family in Chinese History*. New York: Routledge, 2002.

Elman, Benjamin. *A Cultural History of Civil Examinations in Late Imperial China*. Berkeley: University of California Press, 2000.

Feng Menglong 馮夢龍, ed. *Gujin xiaoshuo* 古今小說. Facsimile reprint of 1620 Tianxuzhai 天許齋 edition in *Feng Menglong quanji* 馮夢龍全集, vols. 20–21. Shanghai: Shanghai guji chubanshe, 1993.

———, ed. *Jingshi tongyan* 警世通言. Facsimile reprint of 1624 Jianshan tang 兼善堂 edition in *Feng Menglong quanji* 馮夢龍全集, vols. 22–23. Shanghai: Shanghai guji chubanshe, 1993.

———, ed. *Mohanzhai chongding Yong tuanyuan chuanqi* 墨憨齋重訂永團圓傳奇. In *Mohanzhai dingben chuanqi* 墨憨齋定本傳奇, vol. 3. Beijing: Zhongguo xiju chubanshe, 1960.

———, ed. *Qingshi* 情史. Facsimile reprint of Dongxi tang 東溪堂 edition in *Feng Menglong quanji* 馮夢龍全集, vols. 37–38. Shanghai: Shanghai guji chubanshe, 1993.

———, ed. *Xingshi hengyan* 醒世恆言. Facsimile reprint of 1627 Ye Jingchi 葉敬池 edition in *Feng Menglong quanji* 馮夢龍全集, vols. 24–25. Shanghai: Shanghai guji chubanshe, 1993.

Feng Yuanjun 馮沅君. "Zenyang kandai *Yi peng xue*" 怎樣看待一捧雪. In *Feng Yuanjun gudian wenxue lunwenji* 馮沅君古典文學論文集. Jinan: Shandong renmin chubanshe, 1980.

Fox, Ariel. "Exit, Pursued by a Bear: *Dushu sheng* and the Limits of Community in the Early Qing." *Journal of Chinese Literature and Culture* 7.1 (2020): 149–66.

———. "Precious Bodies: Money Transformation Stories from Medieval to Late Imperial China." *Harvard Journal of Asiatic Studies* 76.1 (2016): 43–85.

———. "Southern Capital: Staging Commerce in Seventeenth-Century Suzhou." PhD diss., Harvard University, 2015.

Fu Si daqing 附四大慶. Facsimile reprint of undated manuscript of *Si daqing* in *Guben xiqu congkan wuji*, case 2, vols. 8–9.

Fu Xuancong 傅璇琮, ed. *Tang Wudai wenxue biannian shi* 唐五代文學編年史. Shenyang: Liaohai chubanshe.

Gao Yi 高奕. *Xin chuanqi pin* 新傳奇品. In *Lidai shishi changbian er ji* 歷代詩史長編二輯, edited by Yang Jialuo 楊家駱, vol. 6, 267–91. Taibei: Zhongguo xuedianguan fuguan choubeichu, 1974.

Giles, Herbert Allen. *A Chinese-English Dictionary*. 2nd ed. New York: Paragon Book Reprint Corp., 1964. First published 1912.

Goldman, Andrea S. *Opera and the City: The Politics of Culture in Beijing, 1770–1900*. Stanford, CA: Stanford University Press, 2012.

Goldstein, Joshua. *Drama Kings: Players and Publics in the Re-creation of Peking Opera, 1870–1937*. Berkeley: University of California Press, 2007.

Gu Lingsen 顧聆森. "Li Yu lun" 李玉論. *Yishu baijia* 藝術百家 5 (2011): 119–25.

———. "Lüelun 'Wumen qupai'" 略論"吳門曲派." *Suzhou daxue xuebao* 蘇州大學學報 1 (1992): 86–89.

———. "Lun kunqu Suzhou pai" 論崑曲蘇州派. *Yishu baijia* 藝術百家 1 (2011): 162–69.

Gu Yanwu 顧炎武. *Rizhi lu jishi* 日知錄集釋. 6 vols. Annotated by Huang Rucheng 黄汝成. Zhejiang: Zhejiang guji chubanshe, 2013.

Guben xiqu congkan erji 古本戲曲叢刊二集. 12 cases. Shanghai: Shangwu yinshuguan, 1955.

Guben xiqu congkan sanji 古本戲曲叢刊三集. 12 cases. Beijing: Wenxue guji kanxingshe, 1957.

Guben xiqu congkan wuji 古本戲曲叢刊五集. 12 cases. Shanghai: Shanghai guji chubanshe, 1984.

Guo, Qitao. *Ritual Opera and Mercantile Lineage: The Confucian Transformation of Popular Culture in Late Imperial Huizhou*. Stanford, CA: Stanford University Press, 2005.

Guo Yingde 郭英德. *Ming Qing chuanqi shi* 明清傳奇史. Nanjing: Jiangsu guji chubanshe, 1999.

———. *Ming Qing chuanqi zonglu* 明清傳奇總錄. 2 vols. Shijiazhuang: Hebei jiaoyu chubanshe, 1997.

———. "Xinxi shengcheng, nüxing yuedu yu yimin yishi: Zhu Suchen *Qinlou yue* chuanqi xiezuo yu kanke de qianyin houguo" 新戲生成、女性閱讀與遺民意識：朱素臣《秦樓月》傳奇寫作與刊刻的前因後果. *Xiju yanjiu* 戲劇研究 1 (2011): 37–64.

Guo, Yingde, and Xiaoqiao Ling. "Fresh Faces for Those Full of Emotions: Zhu Suchen's *Qinlou yue*." *Journal of Chinese Literature and Culture* 1.1–2 (2014): 65–89.

Handler-Spitz, Rivi. *Symptoms of an Unruly Age: Li Zhi and Cultures of Early Modernity*. Seattle: University of Washington Press, 2017.

Hardie, Alison. *The Many Faces of Ruan Dacheng (1587–1646): Poet,*

Playwright, Politician. Hong Kong: Hong Kong University Press, 2022.
Hawkes, David. *The Culture of Usury in Renaissance England*. New York: Palgrave Macmillan, 2010.
He Mengchun 何孟春. *Yudong xulu* 餘冬序錄. 3 *juan*. In *Jilu huibian* 紀錄彙編, vols. 51–53. Shanghai: Shangwu yinshuguan, 1938.
He, Yuming. *Home and the World: Editing the "Glorious Ming" in Woodblock-Printed Books of the Sixteenth and Seventeenth Centuries*. Cambridge, MA: Harvard University Asia Center, 2020.
Hearn, Maxwell. "Document and Portrait: The Southern Tour Paintings of Kangxi and Qianlong." In "Chinese Painting under the Qianlong Emperor: The Symposium Papers in Two Volumes." Special issue, *Phoebus* 6.1 (1988): 91–131.
Hegel, Robert E. *The Novel in Seventeenth-Century China*. New York: Columbia University Press, 1981.
Helmers, Helmer. "The Politics of Mobility: Shakespeare's *Titus Andronicus*, Jan Vos's *Aran en Titus* and the Poetics of Empire." In *Politics and Aesthetics in European Baroque and Classicist Tragedy*, edited by Jan Bloemendal and Nigel Smith, 344–72. Leiden: Brill, 2016.
Hevia, James L. *Cherishing Men from Afar: Qing Guest Ritual and the Macartney Embassy of 1793*. Durham, NC: Duke University Press, 1995.
Hong Mai 洪邁. *Rongzhai suibi* 容齋隨筆. 2 vols. Shanghai: Shanghai guji chubanshe, 1978.
———. *Yijian zhi* 夷堅志. Edited by He Zhuo 何卓. 4 vols. Beijing: Zhonghua shuju, 1981.
Hong Sheng 洪昇. *Changsheng dian* 長生殿. Edited by Xu Shuofang 徐朔方. Beijing: Renmin chubanshe, 1980. First published 1958.
Hu Jinwang 胡金望. *Rensheng xiju yu xiju rensheng: Ruan Dacheng yanjiu* 人生喜劇與喜劇人生：阮大鋮研究. Beijing: Zhongguo shehui kexue chubanshe, 2004.
Huang Zongxi 黃宗羲. *Mingyi daifang lu* 明夷待訪錄. Shanghai: Shanghai guji chubanshe, 1995.
Hucker, Charles O. *A Dictionary of Official Titles in Imperial China*. Taipei: Southern Materials Center, 1985.
Huntington, Rania. *Alien Kind: Foxes and Late Imperial Chinese Narrative*. Cambridge, MA: Harvard University Asia Center, 2004.
Idema, Wilt L. *Judge Bao and the Rule of Law: Eight Ballad Stories*

from the Period 1250–1450. Singapore: World Scientific Publishing, 2010.

Inglis, Alister D. "A Textual History of Hong Mai's *Yijian zhi*." *T'oung Pao*, 2nd ser., 93.4–5 (2007): 283–368.

Jiang Jurong 江巨榮 and Urabe Yoriko 浦部依子. "*Chuanqi huikao* jiqi xiangguan xiqu kaoshi shumu: Cong *Chuanqi huikao* dao *Quhai zongmu tiyao* ji *Quhai zongmu tiyao bubian*" 《傳奇彙考》及其相關戲曲考釋書目 — 從《傳奇彙考》到《曲海總目提要》及《曲海總目提要補編》. *Xiju yanjiu* 戲劇研究 3 (2009): 125–45.

Jiao Xun 焦循. *Ju shuo* 劇說. Facsimile reprint of National Library of China manuscript edition in *Xuxiu Siku quanshu*, vol. 1758.

Kang Baocheng 康保成. *Suzhou jupai yanjiu* 蘇州劇派研究. Guangzhou: Huacheng, 1993.

———. "Zhu Zuochao, Ye Shizhang pingzhuan" 朱佐朝、葉時章評傳." *Yishu baijia* 藝術百家 1 (1992): 88–94.

Kao, Karl S. Y. "Bao and Baoying: Narrative Causality and External Motivations in Chinese Fiction." *CLEAR* 11 (1989): 115–38.

Keene, Donald, trans. *Major Plays of Chikamatsu*. New York: Columbia University Press, 1990.

Keulemans, Paize. "Onstage Rumor, Offstage Voices: The Politics of the Present in the Contemporary Opera of Li Yu." *Frontiers of History in China* 9.2 (2014): 165–201.

———. *Sounds Rising from the Paper: Nineteenth-Century Martial Arts Fiction and the Chinese Acoustic Imagination*. Cambridge, MA: Harvard University Asia Center, 2014.

———. "Tales of an Open World: The Fall of the Ming Dynasty as Dutch Tragedy, Chinese Rumor, and Global News." In *The "Global" and the "Local" in Early Modern and Modern East Asia*, edited by Benjamin A. Elman and Chao-Hui Jenny Liu, 192–220. Leiden: Brill, 2017.

Kong Er 孔邇. *Yunjiao guan jitan* 雲蕉館紀談. Shanghai: Shangwu yinshuguan, 1937.

Kong Shangren 孔尚任. *Peach Blossom Fan*. Translated by Chen Shih-hsiang and Harold Acton. Berkeley: University of California Press, 1976.

———. *Taohua shan* 桃花扇. Edited by Wang Jisi 王季思, Su Huanzhong 蘇寰中, and Yang Deping 楊德平. Beijing: Renmin wenxue chubanshe, 1986. First published 1959.

Kuruppath, Manjusha. *Staging Asia: The Dutch East India Company and the Amsterdam Theatre*. Leiden: Leiden University Press, 2016.

Laing, Ellen Johnson. "'Living Wealth Gods' in the Chinese Popular Print Tradition." *Artibus Asiae* 73.2 (2013): 343–63.

Lam, Ling Hon. *The Spatiality of Emotion in Early Modern China: From Dreamscapes to Theatricality*. New York: Columbia University Press, 2018.

Leinwand, Theodore B. *Theatre, Finance and Society in Early Modern England*. New York: Cambridge University Press, 1999.

Lévi-Strauss, Claude. *The Elementary Structures of Kinship*. Translated by James Harle Bell and John Richard von Sturmer, edited by Rodney Needham. Boston, MA: Beacon Press, 1969.

Li Fang 李昉, comp. *Taiping guangji* 太平廣記. 500 *juan* in 10 vols. Beijing: Zhonghua shuju, 1961.

———, comp. *Taiping yulan* 太平御覽. 1,000 *juan*. *Sibu congkan sanbian* 四部叢刊三編 edition in *Zhongguo jiben guji ku*.

Li Jialian 李佳蓮. *Li Yu* Beici guangzhengpu *yanjiu* 李玉《北詞廣正譜》研究. Taibei: Guojia chubanshe, 2012.

Li, Kangying. *The Ming Maritime Trade Policy in Transition, 1367–1568*. Wiesbaden: Harrassowitz, 2010.

———. *Qingchu Suzhou juzuojia yanjiu* 清初蘇州劇作家研究. In *Gudian wenxue yanjiu jikan, qi bian* 古典文學研究輯刊, 七編, vol. 14, edited by Zeng Yongyi 曾永義. Xinbei: Hua Mulan wenhua chubanshe, 2013.

Li Mei 李枚. *Ming Qing zhiji Suzhou zuojia qun yanjiu* 明清之際蘇州作家群研究. Beijing: Zhongguo shehui kexue chubanshe, 2000.

Li Rihua 李日華. *Weishuixuan riji* 味水軒日記. Shanghai: Shanghai yuandong chubanshe, 1996.

Li Shizhen 李時珍. *Bencao gangmu* 本草綱目. Nanjing, 1596 edition in *Zhongguo jiben guji ku*.

Li, Wai-yee. *Enchantment and Disenchantment: Love and Illusion in Chinese Literature*. Princeton, NJ: Princeton University Press, 1993.

Li Xiusheng 李修生 et al. *Guben xiqu jumu tiyao* 古本戲曲劇目提要. Beijing: Wenhua yishu chubanshe, 1997.

Li Yu 李玉. *Beici guangzhengpu* 北詞廣正譜. 6 *juan*. Kangxi-era Qinglian shuwu 青蓮書屋 edition. University of Chicago East Asian Library Rare Book Collection.

———. *Li Yu xiqu ji* 李玉戲曲集. 3 vols. Shanghai: Shanghai guji chubanshe, 2004.

———. *Meishan xiu* 眉山秀. 2 *juan*. Facsimile reprint of Shunzhi-era edition in *Guben xiqu congkan sanji*, case 5, vols. 4–5.

———. *Qingzhong pu* 清忠譜. 2 *juan*. Facsimile reprint of Shunzhi-era edition in *Guben xiqu congkan sanji*, case 5, vols. 7–8.

———. *Renshou guan* 人獸關. 2 *juan*. Facsimile reprint of Chongzhen-era edition in *Guben xiqu congkan sanji*, case 4, vol. 8.

———., attrib. *Taiping qian* 太平錢. 2 *juan*. Facsimile reprint of undated manuscript in *Guben xiqu congkan sanji*, case 5, vol. 3.

———. *Zhan huakui* 占花魁. 2 *juan*. Facsimile reprint of Chongzhen-era edition in *Guben xiqu congkan sanji*, case 5, vol. 1.

Li Yu 李漁. *Liweng chuanqi shizhong* 笠翁傳奇十種. 2 vols. In *Li Yu quan ji* 李漁全集, vols. 4–5. Hangzhou: Zhejiang guji chubanshe, 1991.

———. *Xianqing ouji* 閒情偶寄. In *Li Yu quan ji* 李漁全集, vol. 3. Hangzhou: Zhejiang guji chubanshe, 1991.

———. "Introduction." In *The Columbia Anthology of Yuan Drama*, edited by C. T. Hsia et al., 1–13. New York: Columbia University Press, 2014.

———. *Women and National Trauma in Late Imperial Chinese Literature*. Cambridge, MA: Harvard University Asia Center, 2014.

Liang Chenyu 梁辰魚. *Huansha ji* 浣紗記. 2 *juan*. Yiyun ge 怡雲閣 edition. Taibei: Tianyi chubanshe, 1983.

Liao Ben 廖奔. *Zhongguo gudai juchang shi* 中國古代劇場史. Beijing: Zhongzhou guji chubanshe, 1997.

Liezi 列子. Annotated by Zhang Zhan 張湛. In *Congshu jicheng chu bian* 叢書集成初編, vol. 554. Beijing: Zhonghua shuju, 1985.

Ling Mengchu 凌濛初. *Erke pai'an jingqi* 二刻拍案驚奇. Facsimile reprint of 1632 Shangyou tang 尚友堂 edition. 2 vols. Shanghai: Shanghai guji chubanshe, 1985.

———. *Pai'an jingqi* 拍案驚奇. Facsimile reprint of 1628 Shangyou tang 尚友堂 edition. 2 vols. Shanghai: Shanghai guji chubanshe, 1985.

Liu Chiung-yun. "Embodied Virtue: How Was Loyalty Edited and Performed in Late Imperial China?" In *Keywords in Chinese Culture*, edited by Wai-yee Li and Yuri Pines. Hong Kong: The Chinese University of Hong Kong Press, 2020.

——— (Liu Qiongyun) 劉瓊云. "Huanguan, xiaji, he nüyi: *Xueying shi* zhong de bianyuan renwu yu yiyu xiangxiang" 宦官、俠妓和女夷:《血影石》中的邊緣人物與異域想像. *Zhengda zhongwen xuebao* 政大中文學報 24 (2015): 89–128.

Liu, Lydia. *The Clash of Empires: The Invention of China in Modern World Making*. Cambridge, MA: Harvard University Press, 2004.

Liu Qiugen 劉秋根. *Ming Qing gaolidai ziben* 明清高利貸資本. Beijing: Shehui kexue wenxian chubanshe, 2000.

Liu Sanwu 劉三吾. *Tanzhai wenji* 坦齋文集. 2 *juan*. 1578 edition in *Zhongguo jiben guji ku*.

Liu Xu 劉昫. *Jiu Tang shu*. 16 vols. Beijing: Zhonghua shuju, 1975.

Liu Yiqing 劉義慶. *Shishuo xinyu* 世說新語. In *Shishuo xinyu jianshu* 世說新語箋疏, edited by Yu Jiaxi 余嘉錫, vol. 4. Shanghai: Shanghai guji chubanshe, 1993.

Llamas, Regina. *Top Graduate Zhang Xie: The Earliest Extant Chinese Southern Play*. New York: Columbia University Press, 2021.

Lowenstein, Matthew, and Shuji Cao. "Business Accounting at Fengshengtai in Late Imperial China: Is There New Evidence of Double-Entry Bookkeeping?" *Business History Review* 97.1 (2023): 33–65.

Lü Bi 呂毖. *Mingchao xiaoshi* 明朝小史. In *Zhongguo yeshi jicheng, xubian* 中國野史集成續編, vol. 9. Chengdu: Ba Shu shushe, 2000.

Lu Eting 陸萼庭. *Kunqu yanchu shigao (xiuding ben)* 崑曲演出史稿 (修訂本). Taibei: Guojia chubanshe, 2002.

Lu Gong 路工 and Fu Xihua 傅惜華, eds. Shiwu guan *xiqu ziliao huibian* 十五貫戲曲資料彙編. Beijing: Zuojia chubanshe, 1957.

Lu, Tina. *Accidental Incest, Filial Cannibalism, and Other Peculiar Encounters in Late Imperial Chinese Literature*. Cambridge, MA: Harvard University Asia Center, 2008.

———. *Persons, Roles, and Minds: Identity in* Peony Pavilion *and* Peach Blossom Fan. Stanford, CA: Stanford University Press, 2001.

Lu Yinglong 魯應龍. *Xianchuang kuoyi zhi* 閒窗括異志. In *Yanyi zhilin* 鹽邑志林, *juan* 14. Ming-era edition in *Zhongguo jiben guji ku*.

Lufrano, Richard. *Honorable Merchants: Commerce and Self-Cultivation in Late Imperial China*. Honolulu: University of Hawai'i Press, 1997.

Ma, Ning. *Age of Silver: The Rise of the Novel East and West*. New York: Oxford University Press, 2016.

Marx, Karl. *Capital: A Critique of Political Economy*. Vol. 1. Translated by Ben Fowkes. New York: Penguin Books, 1976. First published 1867.

Meyer-Fong, Tobie. *Building Culture in Early Qing Yangzhou*. Stanford, CA: Stanford University Press, 2003.

Mige yuan gui zhengyao 秘閣元龜政要. 16 *juan*. Ming (Jiajing or later) manuscript edition in *Zhongguo jiben guji ku*.

Milburn, Olivia. "The Silent Beauty: Changing Portrayals of Xi Shi, from *Zhiguai* and Poetry to Ming Fiction and Drama." *Asia Major* 26.1 (2013): 23–53.

Niu Ruolin 牛若麟 and Wang Huanru 王煥如, eds. *Wuxian zhi* 吳縣志. 54 vols. 1642 edition in *Zhongguo fangzhi ku*.

Owen, Stephen, ed. and trans. *The Poetry of Du Fu*. 6 vols. Boston: De Gruyter, 2016.

Pei Xuelai 裴雪萊. *Qingdai qianzhongqi Suzhou jutan yanjiu* 清代前中期蘇州劇壇研究. Beijing: Zhongguo shehui kexue chubanshe, 2020.

Peng Dingqiu 彭定求, comp. *Quan Tang shi* 全唐詩. 12 vols. Beijing: Zhonghua shuju, 1960.

Pomeranz, Kenneth. *The Great Divergence: China, Europe, and the Making of the Modern World Economy*. Princeton, NJ: Princeton University Press, 2000.

Pregadio, Fabrizio. *The Encyclopedia of Taoism*. 2 vols. Abingdon: Routledge, 2008.

———. *Great Clarity: Daoism and Alchemy in Early Medieval China*. Stanford, CA: Stanford University Press, 2006.

Pu Songling 蒲松齡. *Quanben xinzhu Liaozhai zhiyi* 全本新注聊齋誌異. 3 vols. Edited by Zhu Qikai 朱其鎧 et al. Beijing: Renmin wenxue chubanshe, 1989.

Qi Biaojia 祁彪佳. *Qi Biaojia riji* 祁彪佳日記. Hangzhou: Zhejiang guji chubanshe, 2016.

Qi, Dong-fang. "Not an Ordinary Hoard: The Coins in the Hejiacun Treasure." In *The Language and Iconography of Chinese Charms: Deciphering a Past Belief System*, edited by François Thierry and Alex Chengyu Fang, 49–68. Singapore: Springer, 2016.

Qian Decang 錢德蒼. *Huibian jiaozhu Zhuibai qiu* 彙編校註綴白裘. Edited by Huang Wanyi 黄婉儀. 5 vols. Taibei: Taiwan xuesheng shuju, 2017.

Qian Zhongshu 錢鍾書. *Guanzhui bian* 管錐編. In *Qian Zhongshu ji* 錢鍾書集, vol. 4. Beijing: Shenghuo dushu xinzhi sanlian shudian, 2001.

———. *Rong'an guan zhaji* 容安館札記. Beijing: Shangwu yinshuguan, 2003.

Roy, David Tod, trans. *The Plum in the Golden Vase, or Chin P'ing Mei*. Vol. 2, *The Rivals*. Princeton, NJ: Princeton University Press, 2001.

Ruan Dacheng 阮大鋮. *Shuang jinbang* 雙金榜. 2 vols. Facsimile reprint of late Ming print edition in *Guben xiqu congkan erji*, case 10, vol. 8–9.

Sánchez, Francisco J. "The Subject of the King and a Mercantile Ideology in Early Modern Spain." *Romance Quarterly* 58.2 (2011): 81–93.

Santangelo, Paolo. "Urban Society in Late Imperial Suzhou." Translated by Adam Victor. In *Cities of Jiangnan in Late Imperial China*, edited by Linda Cooke Johnson, 81–116. Albany: State University of New York Press, 1993.

Schumpeter, Joseph A. *History of Economic Analysis*. New York: Oxford University Press, 1954.

Shang Wei. "The Making of the Everyday World: *Jin Ping Mei cihua* and Encyclopedias for Daily Use." In *Dynastic Crisis and Cultural Innovation: From the Late Ming to the Late Qing and Beyond*, edited by David Der-wei Wang and Shang Wei, 63–92. Cambridge, MA: Harvard University Asia Center, 2005.

Shanhai jing jiaozhu 山海經校注. Edited by Yuan Ke 袁珂. Chengdu: Ba Shu shushe, 1992.

Shannon, Robert M., ed. and trans. *El nuevo mundo descubierto por Cristóbal Colón: Una edición crítica y bilingüe / The New World Discovered by Christopher Columbus: A Critical and Bilingual Edition*. New York: Peter Lang, 2001.

Shao Bo 邵伯. *Shaoshi wenjian houlu* 邵氏聞見後錄. 30 *juan*. Shanghai: Shangwu yinshuguan, 1920.

Shao Jingzhan 邵景詹. *Mideng yinhua* 覓燈因話. 2 *juan*. Qing woodblock edition in *Zhongguo jiben guji ku*.

Shell, Marc. *Money, Language, and Thought: Literary and Philosophic Economies from the Medieval to the Modern Era*. Baltimore, MD: Johns Hopkins University Press, 1993. First published 1982.

Shen Deqian 沈德潛, ed. *Qing shi biecai ji* 清詩別裁集. Jiaozhong tang 教忠堂, 1760.

Shen Maoguan 慎懋官. *Huayi huamu niaoshou zhenwan kao* 華夷花木鳥獸珍玩考. 12 *juan*. 1581 edition in *Zhongguo jiben guji ku*.

Shen Shixing 申時行. *Cixian tang ji* 賜閒堂集. 40 *juan*. Wanli edition in *Zhongguo jiben guji ku*.

Shen Zhou 沈周. *Kezuo xinwen* 客座新聞. 11 *juan*. Qing manuscript edition in *Zhongguo jiben guji ku*.

Shen Zijin 沈自晉, ed. *Nanci xinpu* 南詞新譜. 26 *juan*. Facsimile reprint of 1655 edition in *Shanben xiqu congkan* 善本戲曲叢刊, vols. 29–30, edited by Wang Qiugui 王秋桂. Taibei: Taiwan xuesheng shuju, 1984.

Shih, James C. *Chinese Rural Society in Transition: A Case Study of the Lake Tai Area, 1368–1800*. Berkeley, CA: Institute of East Asian Studies, 1992.

Shisan jing zhushu (zhengli ben) 十三經注疏 (整理本). 26 vols. Edited by Li Xueqin 李學勤 et al. Beijing: Beijing daxue chubanshe, 2000.

Sibau, Maria Franca. "Maids, Fishermen, and Storytellers: Rewriting Marginal Characters in Early Qing Drama and Fiction." *CHINOPERL* 35.1 (2016): 1–27.

Sima Qian 司馬遷. *Records of the Grand Historian*. Translated by Burton Watson. New York: Columbia University Press, 1971.

———. *Shiji* 史記. Annotated by Pei Yin 裴駰, Sima Zhen 司馬貞, and Zhang Shoujie 張守節. 10 vols. Beijing: Zhonghua shuju, 1959.

Smith, Adam. *The Wealth of Nations*. New York: Modern Library Classics, 2000. First published 1776.

Sofer, Andrew. *The Stage Life of Props*. Ann Arbor: University of Michigan Press, 2003.

Song Lian 宋濂 et al. *Yuan shi* 元史. 8 vols. Beijing: Zhonghua shuju, 1976.

Stackhouse, Kenneth A., trans. and ed. *Translations of the American Plays of Lope de Vega: The Discovery of the New World, The Conquest of Araucania, Brazil Restored*. Lewiston, NY: Edwin Mellen Press, 2003.

Sun Pei 孫珮. *Suzhou zhizaoju zhi* 蘇州織造局志. Facsimile reprint in *Zhonghua zaizao shanben, Qingdai bian, Shi bu* 中華再造善本, 清代編, 史部, vol. 2. Beijing: Guojia tushuguan chubanshe, 2013.

Sun Shulei 孫書磊. *Ming mo Qing chu xiju yanjiu* 明末清初戲劇研究. Beijing: Shehui kexue wenxian chubanshe, 2007.

Suzhou lishi bowuguan 蘇州歷史博物館 et al., eds. *Ming Qing Suzhou gongshangye beike ji* 明清蘇州工商業碑刻集. Nanjing: Jiangsu renmin chubanshe, 1981.

Tan, Tian Yuan. "Prohibition of *Jiatou Zaju* in the Ming Dynasty and the Portrayal of the Emperor on Stage." *Ming Studies* 49 (2004): 82–111.

Tan Zhengbi 譚正璧, ed. *Sanyan liangpai ziliao* 三言兩拍資料. Shanghai: Shanghai guji chubanshe, 1980.

Tang Xianzu 湯顯祖. *Mudan ting* 牡丹亭. Edited by Xu Shuofang 徐朔方 and Yang Xiaomei 楊笑梅. Beijing: Renmin wenxue chubanshe, 1963.

Tao Zongyi 陶宗儀. *Nancun chuogeng lu* 南村輟耕錄. Beijing: Wenhua yishu chubanshe, 1998.

Tian Yiheng 田藝蘅. *Liuqing rizha* 留青日札. 39 *juan*. Wanli edition in *Zhongguo jiben guji ku*.

Ufer, Ulrich. "Imagining Social Change in Early-Modern Amsterdam: Global Processes, Local Perceptions." In *Imagining Global Amsterdam: History, Culture, and Geography in a World City*, edited by Marco de Waard, 27–44. Amsterdam: Amsterdam University Press, 2012.

Vogel, Hans Ulrich. "Chinese Central Monetary Policy, 1644–1800." *Late Imperial China* 8.2 (1987): 1–52.

Volpp, Sophie. "The Literary Circulation of Actors in Seventeenth-Century China." *Journal of Asian Studies* 61.3 (2002): 949–84.

———. *Worldly Stage: Theatricality in Seventeenth-Century China*. Cambridge, MA: Harvard University Asia Center, 2011.

Von Glahn, Richard. *Fountain of Fortune: Money and Monetary Policy in China, 1000–1700*. Berkeley: University of California Press, 1996.

———. "Municipal Reform and Urban Social Conflict in Late Ming Jiangnan." *Journal of Asian Studies* 50.2 (1991): 280–307.

Vos, Jan. "Vergrooting van Amsterdam." In *Alle de gedichten*, vol. 1, 809–38. Amsterdam: Jacob Lescaille, 1662.

Waltner, Ann. "Infanticide and Dowry in Ming and Early Qing China." In *Chinese Views of Childhood*, edited by Anne Behnke Kinney, 193–218. Honolulu: University of Hawai'i Press, 1995.

———. "Widows and Remarriage in Ming and Early Qing China." *Historical Reflections/Réflexions Historiques* 8.3 (1981): 129–46.

Wang Bijiang 汪辟疆, ed. *Tangren xiaoshuo* 唐人小說. Shanghai: Shanghai guji chubanshe, 1955.

Wang Chaohong 汪超宏. *Wu Qi nianpu* 吳綺年譜. Zhejiang: Zhejiang daxue chubanshe, 2011.

Wang, Cheng-hua. "One Painting, Two Emperors, and Their Cultural Agendas: Reinterpreting the *Qingming Shanghe* Painting of 1737." *Archives of Asian Art* 70.1 (April 2020): 85–117.

——— (Wang Zhenghua) 王正華. "Qingdai chuzhongqi zuowei chanye de Suzhou banhua yu qi shangye mianxiang" 清代初中期作為產業的蘇州版畫與其商業面向. *Zhongyang yanjiuyuan jindaishi yanjiusuo jikan* 中央研究院近代史研究所集刊 92 (2016): 1–54.

Wang Daokun 汪道昆. *Wuhu you* 五湖遊. In *Sheng Ming zaju chu ji* 盛明雜劇初集, *juan* 2, compiled by Shen Tai 沈泰. Facsimile reprint in *Xuxiu Siku quanshu*, vol. 1764.

Wang, Guojun. *Staging Personhood: Costuming in Early Qing Drama*. New York: Columbia University Press, 2020.

Wang Ji 汪楫. *Huizhai ji* 悔齋集. Kangxi woodblock edition in *Qingdai shiwen jihui bian* 清代詩文集彙編, vol. 140. Shanghai: Shanghai guji chubanshe, 2009.

Wang Kentang 王肯堂. *Yugangzhai bizhu* 鬱岡齋筆塵. 4 *juan*. 1602 Wang Maokun 王懋錕 edition in *Zhongguo jiben guji ku*.

Wang Shizhen 王世貞. *Xinke zengbu Yiyuan zhiyan* 新刻增補藝苑巵言. 1589 Wulin qiaoyun shushe 武林樵雲書舍 edition in *Zhongguo jiben guji ku*.

Wang Tonggui 王同軌. *Ertan* 耳談. 15 *juan*. Wanli-era Shide tang 世德堂 edition. Taibei: Weiwen tushu chubanshe, 1977.

———. *Ertan leizeng* 耳談類增. 54 *juan*. 1583 edition in *Zhongguo jiben guji ku*.

Wang Wenjun 王文君. "Guojia tushuguan suo cang *Yuefu kaolüe*" 國家圖書館所藏《樂府考略》抄本考. *Wenxue pinglun congkan* 文學評論叢刊 1 (2017): 88–96.

Wang Wenzhang 王文章 et al., eds. *Fu Xihua cang gudian xiqu zhenben congkan* 傅惜華藏古典戲曲珍本叢刊. 145 vols. Beijing: Xueyuan chubanshe, 2010.

Wang Xiangzhi 王象之. *Yudi jisheng* 輿地紀勝. 8 vols. Beijing: Zhonghua shuju, 1992.

Wang Yangming 王陽明. *Wang Yangming xiansheng quanji* 王陽明先生全集. 24 *juan*. Edited by Yu Lin 俞璘. Dunhou tang 敦厚堂, 1680.

Wang Yonghao 汪涌豪. *Zhongguo youxia shilun* 中國遊俠史論. Shanghai: Shanghai renmin chubanshe, 2016.

Wang Yongkuan 王永寬. "Mingmo Qingchu Suzhou diqu xiqu chuangzuo fanrong de shehui yuanyin" 明末清初蘇州地區戲曲創作繁榮的社會原因. *Xiqu luncong* 戲曲論叢 2 (1989): 165–86.

Wang Yongkuan 王永寬 et al. *Zhongguo gudai xiqu wenxue cidian* 中國古代戲曲文學辭典. Beijing: Renmin wenxue chubanshe, 2004.

Wang Zhonghan 王鍾翰. *Qingshi liezhuan* 清史列傳. Beijing: Zhonghua shuju, 1987.

Watson, Burton, trans. *Chuang Tzu: Basic Writings*. New York: Columbia University Press, 1996.

West, Stephen H. "Playing with Food: Performance, Food, and the Aesthetics of Artificiality in the Sung and Yuan." *Harvard Journal of Asiatic Studies* 57.1 (1997): 67–106.

Widmer, Ellen. *The Margins of Utopia:* Shui-hu hou-chuan *and the Literature of Ming Loyalism*. Cambridge, MA: Harvard University Asia Center, 1987.

Wilkinson, Endymion P. "Chinese Merchant Manuals and Route Books." *Ch'ing-shih wen-t'i* 2.9 (1973): 8–34.

Woodbridge, Linda, ed. *Money and the Age of Shakespeare: Essays in New Economic Criticism*. New York: Palgrave Macmillan, 2003.

Wu Jiaji 吳嘉紀. *Wu Jiaji shijian jiao* 吳嘉紀詩箋校. Edited by Yang Jiqing 楊積慶. Shanghai: Shanghai guji chubanshe, 1980

Wu Shuyin 吳書蔭, ed. *Suizhong Wushi cang chaoben gaoben xiqu congkan* 綏中吳氏藏抄本稿本戲曲叢刊. 48 vols. Beijing: Xueyuan chubanshe, 2004.

Wu Qi 吳綺. *Linhui tang ji* 林蕙堂集. 26 *juan*. *Wenyuan ge Siku quanshu* 文淵閣四庫全書 edition in *Zhongguo jiben guji ku*.

Wu Xinlei 吳新雷. "Li Yu shengping, jiaoyou, zuopin kao" 李玉生平、交游、作品考 (1961). In *Wu Xinlei kunqu lunji* 吳新雷崑曲論集. Taibei: Guojia chubanshe, 2009.

———. "Lun Suzhou pai xiqu dajia Li Yu" 論蘇州派戲曲大家李玉. In *Zhongguo xiqu shilun* 中國戲曲史論, 175–84. Nanjing: Jiangsu jiaoyu chubanshe, 1996.

———. "Shilun Li Yu de daibiao zuo *Qingzhong pu* chuanqi" 試論李玉的代表作《清忠譜》傳奇. In *Zhongguo xiqu shilun* 中國戲曲史論, 165–74. Nanjing: Jiangsu jiaoyu chubanshe, 1996.

Wu, Yenna. *A Chinese Virago: A Literary Theme*. Cambridge, MA: Harvard University Asia Center, 1995.

Wujiang zhi 吳江志. 22 *juan*. 1488 edition in *Zhongguo fangzhi ku*.

Xiaoxiaosheng 笑笑生. *Jin Ping Mei cihua jiaozhu* 金瓶梅詞話校註. 5 vols. Annotated by Bai Weiguo 白維國 and Bu Jian 卜鍵. Changsha: Yuelu shushe, 1995.

Xie Kun 謝堃. *Chuncao tang ji* 春草堂集. Quyi: Kuiwenzhai, 1845.

Xie Zhaozhe 謝肇淛. *Wu zazu* 五雜組. 16 *juan*. 1616 Ruwei guan 如韋館 edition in *Zhongguo jiben guji ku*.

Xu Fuzuo 徐复祚. *Yi wen qian* 一文錢. In facsimile reprint of *Sheng Ming zaju* 盛明雜劇, vol. 8. Beijing: Zhongguo shudian, 1980.

Xu Jiankun 許建崑. *Cao Xuequan yu wan Ming wenxue shi* 曹學佺與晚明文學史. Taibei: Wanjuan lou, 2014.

———. "Wanli guimao nian Fuzhou shitan shengshi kao" 萬曆癸卯年福州詩壇盛事考. *Wenxue xinyao* 文學新鑰 18 (2013): 87–116.

Xu Min 許敏. "Shangye yu shehui bianqian" 商業與社會變遷. In *Wan Ming shehui bianqian wenti yu yanjiu* 晚明社會變遷問題與研究, edited by Wan Ming 萬明, 85–142. Beijing: Shangwu yinshuguan, 2005.

Xu Shiqi 徐石麒. *Tan'an Fu Xi Shi zaju* 坦庵浮西施雜劇. Shunzhi-era Nanhu xiangshu tang 南湖享書堂 edition in *Zhongguo suwen ku* 中國俗文庫. Beijing: Beijing Airusheng shuzihua jishu yanjiu zhongxin, 2017.

Xu, Yinong. *The Chinese City in Space and Time: The Development of Urban Form in Suzhou*. Honolulu: University of Hawai'i Press, 2000.

Xue Yongruo 薛用弱. *Jiyi ji* 集異記. Beijing: Zhonghua shuju, 1980.

Xunzi xinzhu 荀子新注. Edited by Beijing daxue Xunzi zhushi zu 北京大學荀子注釋組. Beijing: Zhonghua shuju, 1979.

Xuxiu Siku quanshu 續修四庫全書. 1800 vols. Shanghai: Shanghai guji chubanshe, 1995–1999.

Yan Changke 顏長珂 and Zhou Chuanjia 周傳家. *Li Yu pingzhuan* 李玉評傳. Beijing: Zhongguo xiju chubanshe, 1985.

Yang Jialuo 楊家駱, ed. *Lidai shishi changbian erji* 歷代詩史長編二輯. Taibei: Zhongguo xuedianguan fuguan choubeichu, 1974.

Yang Shen 楊慎. *Yang Sheng'an congshu* 楊升庵叢書. 6 vols. Chengdu: Tiandi chubanshe, 2002.

Yang Xunji 楊循吉. *Su tan* 蘇談. 1 *juan*. In *Jilu huibian* 紀錄彙編, vol. 69. Shanghai: Shangwu yinshuguan, 1938.

Yao Xie 姚燮. *Jinyue kaozheng* 今樂考證. In *Zhongguo gudian xiqu lunzhu jicheng* 中國古典戲曲論著集成, vol. 10, edited by Zhongguo xiqu yanjiuyuan 中國戲曲研究院. Beijing: Zhongguo xiqu chubanshe, 1980. First published 1959.

Ye Chengzong 葉承宗. *Luo han* 濼函. Facsimile reprint of 1660 Yousheng tang 友聲堂 edition in *Siku weishou shu jikan* 四庫未收書輯刊, ser. 7, vol. 21. Beijing: Beijing chubanshe, 1997.

Ye, Xiaoqing. *Ascendant Peace in the Four Seas: Drama and the Qing Imperial Court*. Hong Kong: Chinese University of Hong Kong Press, 2012.

Yin Yun 殷芸. *Yin Yun xiaoshuo* 殷芸小說. Edited by Zhou Lengjia 周楞伽. Shanghai: Shanghai guji chubanshe, 1984.

Yu, Pauline. *The Poetry of Wang Wei: New Translations and Commentary*. Bloomington: Indiana University Press, 1980.

Yü Ying-shih (Yu Yingshi) 余英時. *Rujia lunli yu shangren jingshen* 儒家倫理與商人精神. Guilin: Guangxi shifan daxue chubanshe, 2004.

Yuan Dong 袁棟. *Shuyin congshuo* 書隱叢說. 19 *juan*. Qianlong-era edition in *Zhongguo jiben guiji ku*.

Yuan Min 袁敏. "An Zhiyuan wenji diaoban yicun kaolüe" 安致遠文集雕版遺存考略. *Weifang xueyuan xuebao* 濰坊學院學報 14.3 (2014): 25–26.

Zang Maoxun 臧懋循. *Yuanqu xuan* 元曲選. 100 *juan*. Wanli edition in *Zhongguo jiben guji ku*.

Zeitlin, Judith T. "The Cultural Biography of a Musical Instrument: Little Hulei as Sounding Object, Antique, Prop, and Relic." *Harvard Journal of Asiatic Studies* 69.2 (2009): 395–441.

———. *Historian of the Strange: Pu Songling and the Chinese Classical Tale*. Stanford, CA: Stanford University Press, 1993.

———. *Phantom Heroine: Ghosts and Gender in Seventeenth-Century Chinese Literature*. Honolulu: University of Hawai'i Press, 2007.

Zeng Guoguo 曾果果. "*Rushi guan* wei Zhang Dafu suo zuo xianyi" 《如是觀》為張大復所作獻疑. *Hainan daxue xuebao renwen shehui kexue ban* 海南大學學報人文社會科學版 30.5 (2012): 49–53.

Zeng Zao 曾慥. *Leishuo* 類說. 5 vols. Beijing: Wenxue guji kanxingshe, 1955.

Zhang Dafu 張大復, attrib. *Dushu sheng* 讀書聲. 2 *juan*. Facsimile reprint of undated manuscript in *Guben xiqu congkan sanji*, case 10, vol. 9.

———. *Hanshan tang Xinding jiugong shisan diao nanqupu* 寒山堂新定九宮十三調南曲譜. Facsimile reprint in *Xuxiu Siku quanshu*, vol. 1750.

———, attrib. *Kuaihuo san* 快活三. 2 *juan*. Facsimile reprint of manuscript dated 1635 in *Guben xiqu congkan sanji*, case 10, vol. 6.

Zhang Dai 張岱. *Tao'an mengyi; Xi Hu mengxun* 陶庵夢憶; 西湖夢尋. Beijing: Beijing Zhonghua shuju chubanshe, 2007.

Zhang Hongxia 張紅霞. "Zhu Suchen chuanqi yanjiu" 朱素臣傳奇研究. PhD diss., Henan daxue 河南大學, 2012.

Zhang Tingyu 張廷玉 et al. *Ming shi* 明史. 28 vols. Beijing: Zhonghua shuju, 1974.

Zhanguo ce zhushi 戰國策注釋. 3 vols. Edited and annotated by He Jianzhang 何建章. Beijing: Zhonghua shuju, 1990.

Zhao Jingshen 趙景深 and Zhang Zengyuan 張增元, eds. *Fangzhi zhulu Yuan Ming Qing qujia zhuanlüe* 方志著錄元明清曲家傳略. Beijing: Zhonghua shuju, 1987.

Zhao Yuan 趙園. *Ming Qing zhiji shidafu yanjiu* 明清之際士大夫研究. Beijing: Beijing daxue chubanshe, 1999.

Zheng Qian 鄭騫, ed. *Jiaoding Yuankan zaju sanshi zhong* 校訂元刊雜劇三十種. Taibei: Shijie shuju, 1962.

Zheng Zhenduo 鄭振鐸. *Chatuben Zhongguo wenxue shi* 插圖本中國文學史. 4 vols. Beijing: Zuojia chubanshe, 1957.

Zhongguo fangzhi ku 中國方志庫. Beijing: Beijing Airusheng shuzihua jishu yanjiu zhongxin, 2017. http://server.wenzibase.com.

Zhongguo jiben guji ku 中國基本古籍庫. Beijing: Beijing Airusheng shuzihua jishu yanjiu zhongxin, 2017. http://server.wenzibase.com.

Zhou Gongping 周鞏平. "Zhang Dafu xiqu zuopin kao ban" 張大復戲曲作品考辨. *Xiqu yanjiu* 戲曲研究 19 (1986): 113–32.

Zhou Qin 周秦. *Suzhou kunqu* 蘇州崑曲. Suzhou: Suzhou daxue chubanshe, 2007.

Zhou Zhilian 周稚廉. *Yuanbao mei* 元寶媒. Facsimile reprint of Shudai caotang 書帶草堂 edition in *Guben xiqu congkan wuji*, case 6, vol. 2.

Zhu Guozhen 朱國禎. *Yong chuang xiaopin* 湧幢小品. Beijing: Wenhua yishu chubanshe, 1998.

Zhu Suchen 朱素臣, attrib. *Jinyi gui* 錦衣歸. 2 *juan*. Facsimile reprint of undated manuscript in *Guben xiqu congkan sanji*, case 9, vol. 1.

———, attrib. *Jubaopen* 聚寶盆. Facsimile reprint of undated manuscript in *Guben xiqu congkan sanji*, case 8, vol. 6.

———, attrib. *Jubaopen* 聚寶盆. Facsimile reprint of undated manuscript in *Suizhong Wushi cang chaoben gaoben xiqu congkan* 綏中吳氏藏抄本稿本戲曲叢刊, 12:344–491. Beijing: Xueyuan chubanshe, 2004.

———, attrib. *Longfeng qian* 龍鳳錢. Facsimile reprint of undated manuscript in *Guben xiqu congkan sanji*, case 8, vol. 7.

———. *Qinlou yue* 秦樓月. 2 *juan*. Facsimile reprint of Wenxi tang 文喜堂 edition in *Guben xiqu congkan sanji*, case 8, vols. 8–9.

———, attrib. *Shiwu guan* 十五貫. 2 *juan*. Facsimile reprint of manuscript dated 1650 in *Guben xiqu congkan sanji*, case 8, vols. 4–5.

———, attrib. *Wenxing xian* 文星現. 2 *juan*. Facsimile reprint of undated manuscript in *Guben xiqu congkan wuji*, case 2, vol. 6.

Zhu Yunming 祝允明. *Zhuzi zhiguai lu* 祝子志怪錄. 5 *juan*. Facsimile reprint of Ming edition in *Xuxiu Siku quanshu*, vol. 1266.

Zhu Zuochao 朱佐朝, attrib. *Jiqing tu* 吉慶圖. 2 *juan*. Facsimile reprint of undated manuscript in *Guben xiqu congkan sanji*, case 7, vols. 9–10.

———, attrib. *Yujia le* 漁家樂. In *Kunju shouchao quben yibai ce* 崑劇手抄曲本一百冊, vol. 27. Edited by Zhang Zhonglai 張鐘來. Yangzhou: Guangling shushe, 2009.

Zhuangzi jishi 莊子集釋. 4 vols. Edited and annotated by Guo Qingfan 郭慶藩. Beijing: Zhonghua shuju, 1961.

Index

Harvard-Yenching Institute Monograph Series

24. *Population, Disease, and Land in Early Japan, 645–900*, by William Wayne Farris
25. *Shikitei Sanba and the Comic Tradition in Edo Fiction*, by Robert W. Leutner
26. *Washing Silk: The Life and Selected Poetry of Wei Chuang (834?–910)*, by Robin D. S. Yates
28. *Tang Transformation Texts: A Study of the Buddhist Contribution to the Rise of Vernacular Fiction and Drama in China*, by Victor H. Mair
30. *Readings in Chinese Literary Thought*, by Stephen Owen
31. *Remembering Paradise: Nativism and Nostalgia in Eighteenth-Century Japan*, by Peter Nosco
33. *Escape from the Wasteland: Romanticism and Realism in the Fiction of Mishima Yukio and Oe Kenzaburo*, by Susan Jolliffe Napier
34. *Inside a Service Trade: Studies in Contemporary Chinese Prose*, by Rudolf G. Wagner
35. *The Willow in Autumn: Ryutei Tanehiko, 1783–1842*, by Andrew Lawrence Markus
36. *The Confucian Transformation of Korea: A Study of Society and Ideology*, by Martina Deuchler
37. *The Korean Singer of Tales*, by Marshall R. Pihl
38. *Praying for Power: Buddhism and the Formation of Gentry Society in Late-Ming China*, by Timothy Brook
39. *Word, Image, and Deed in the Life of Su Shi*, by Ronald C. Egan
41. *Studies in the Comic Spirit in Modern Japanese Fiction*, by Joel R. Cohn
42. *Wind Against the Mountain: The Crisis of Politics and Culture in Thirteenth-Century China*, by Richard L. Davis
43. *Powerful Relations: Kinship, Status, and the State in Sung China (960–1279)*, by Beverly Bossler
44. *Limited Views: Essays on Ideas and Letters*, by Qian Zhongshu; selected and translated by Ronald Egan
45. *Sugar and Society in China: Peasants, Technology, and the World Market*, by Sucheta Mazumdar
49. *Precious Volumes: An Introduction to Chinese Sectarian Scriptures from the Sixteenth and Seventeenth Centuries*, by Daniel L. Overmyer
50. *Poetry and Painting in Song China: The Subtle Art of Dissent*, by Alfreda Murck

51. *Evil and/or/as the Good: Omnicentrism, Intersubjectivity, and Value Paradox in Tiantai Buddhist Thought*, by Brook Ziporyn
53. *Articulated Ladies: Gender and the Male Community in Early Chinese Texts*, by Paul Rouzer
55. *Allegories of Desire: Esoteric Literary Commentaries of Medieval Japan*, by Susan Blakeley Klein
56. *Printing for Profit: The Commercial Publishers of Jianyang, Fujian (11th–17th Centuries)*, by Lucille Chia
57. *To Become a God: Cosmology, Sacrifice, and Self-Divinization in Early China*, by Michael J. Puett
58. *Writing and Materiality in China: Essays in Honor of Patrick Hanan*, edited by Judith T. Zeitlin and Lydia H. Liu
59. Rulin waishi *and Cultural Transformation in Late Imperial China*, by Shang Wei
60. *Words Well Put: Visions of Poetic Competence in the Chinese Tradition*, by Graham Sanders
61. *Householders: The Reizei Family in Japanese History*, by Steven D. Carter
62. *The Divine Nature of Power: Chinese Ritual Architecture at the Sacred Site of Jinci*, by Tracy Miller
63. *Beacon Fire and Shooting Star: The Literary Culture of the Liang (502–557)*, by Xiaofei Tian
64. *Lost Soul: "Confucianism" in Contemporary Chinese Academic Discourse*, by John Makeham
65. *The Sage Learning of Liu Zhi: Islamic Thought in Confucian Terms*, by Sachiko Murata, William C. Chittick, and Tu Weiming
66. *Through a Forest of Chancellors: Fugitive Histories in Liu Yuan's* Lingyan ge, *an Illustrated Book from Seventeenth-Century Suzhou*, by Anne Burkus-Chasson
67. *Empire of Texts in Motion: Chinese, Korean, and Taiwanese Transculturations of Japanese Literature*, by Karen Laura Thornber
68. *Empire's Twilight: Northeast Asia Under the Mongols*, by David M. Robinson
69. *Ancestors, Virgins, and Friars: Christianity as a Local Religion in Late Imperial China*, by Eugenio Menegon
70. *Manifest in Words, Written on Paper: Producing and Circulating Poetry in Tang Dynasty China*, by Christopher M. B. Nugent
71. *The Poetics of Sovereignty: On Emperor Taizong of the Tang Dynasty*, by Jack W. Chen
72. *Ancestral Memory in Early China*, by K. E. Brashier
73. *'Dividing the Realm in Order to Govern': The Spatial Organization of the Song State*, by Ruth Mostern
74. *The Dynamics of Masters Literature: Early Chinese Thought from Confucius to Han Feizi*, by Wiebke Denecke
75. *Songs of Contentment and Transgression: Discharged Officials and Literati Communities in Sixteenth-Century North China*, by Tian Yuan Tan
76. *Ten Thousand Scrolls: Reading and Writing in the Poetics of Huang Tingjian and the Late Northern Song*, by Yugen Wang
77. *A Northern Alternative: Xue Xuan (1389–1464) and the Hedong School*, by Khee Heong Koh

78. *Visionary Journeys: Travel Writings from Early Medieval and Nineteenth-Century China*, by Xiaofei Tian
79. *Making Personas: Transnational Film Stardom in Modern Japan*, by Hideaki Fujiki
80. *Strange Eventful Histories: Identity, Performance, and Xu Wei's* Four Cries of a Gibbon, by Shiamin Kwa
81. *Critics and Commentators: The* Book of Poems *as Classic and Literature*, by Bruce Rusk
82. *Home and the World: Editing the Glorious Ming in Woodblock-Printed Books of the Sixteenth and Seventeenth Centuries*, by Yuming He
83. *Courtesans, Concubines, and the Cult of Female Fidelity*, by Beverly Bossler
84. *Chinese History: A New Manual, Third Edition*, by Endymion Wilkinson
85. *A Comprehensive Manchu-English Dictionary*, by Jerry Norman
86. *Drifting among Rivers and Lakes: Southern Song Dynasty Poetry and the Problem of Literary History*, by Michael Fuller
87. *Martial Spectacles of the Ming Court*, by David M. Robinson
88. *Modern Archaics: Continuity and Innovation in the Chinese Lyric Tradition, 1900–1937*, by Shengqing Wu
89. *Cherishing Antiquity: The Cultural Construction of an Ancient Chinese Kingdom*, by Olivia Milburn
90. *The Burden of Female Talent: The Poet Li Qingzhao and Her History in China*, by Ronald Egan
91. *Public Memory in Early China*, by K. E. Brashier
92. *Women and National Trauma in Late Imperial Chinese Literature*, by Wai-yee Li
93. *The Destruction of the Medieval Chinese Aristocracy*, by Nicolas Tackett
94. *Savage Exchange: Han Imperialism, Chinese Literary Style, and the Economic Imagination*, by Tamara T. Chin
95. *Shifting Stories: History, Gossip, and Lore in Narratives from Tang Dynasty China*, by Sarah M. Allen
96. *One Who Knows Me: Friendship and Literary Culture in Mid-Tang China*, by Anna Shields
97. *Materializing Magic Power: Chinese Popular Religion in Villages and Cities*, by Wei-Ping Lin
98. *Traces of Grand Peace: Classics and State Activism in Imperial China*, by Jaeyoon Song
99. *Fiction's Family: Zhan Xi, Zhan Kai, and the Business of Women in Late-Qing China*, by Ellen Widmer
100. *Chinese History: A New Manual, Fourth Edition*, by Endymion Wilkinson
101. *After the Prosperous Age: State and Elites in Early Nineteenth-Century Suzhou*, by Seunghyun Han
102. *Celestial Masters: History and Ritual in Early Daoist Communities*, by Terry F. Kleeman
103. *Transgressive Typologies: Constructions of Gender and Power in Early Tang China*, by Rebecca Doran
104. *Li Mengyang, the North-South Divide, and Literati Learning in Ming China*, by Chang Woei Ong

105. *Bannermen Tales (Zidishu): Manchu Storytelling and Cultural Hybridity in the Qing Dynasty*, by Elena Suet-Ying Chiu
106. *Upriver Journeys: Diaspora and Empire in Southern China, 1570–1850*, by Steven B. Miles
107. *Ancestors, Kings, and the Dao*, by Constance A. Cook
108. *The Halberd at Red Cliff: Jian'an and the Three Kingdoms*, by Xiaofei Tian
109. *Speaking of Profit: Bao Shichen and Reform in Nineteenth-Century China,* by William T. Rowe
110. *Building for Oil: Daqing and the Formation of the Chinese Socialist State,* by Hou Li
111. *Reading Philosophy, Writing Poetry: Intertextual Modes of Making Meaning in Early Medieval China,* by Wendy Swartz
112. *Writing for Print: Publishing and the Making of Textual Authority in Late Imperial China,* by Suyoung Son
113. *Shen Gua's Empiricism,* by Ya Zuo
114. *Just a Song: Chinese Lyrics from the Eleventh and Early Twelfth Centuries,* by Stephen Owen
115. *Shrines to Living Men in the Ming Political Cosmos,* by Sarah Schneewind
116. *In the Wake of the Mongols: The Making of a New Social Order in North China, 1200–1600,* by Jinping Wang
117. *Opera, Society, and Politics in Modern China,* by Hsiao-t'i Li
118. *Imperiled Destinies: The Daoist Quest for Deliverance in Medieval China,* by Franciscus Verellen
119. *Ethnic Chrysalis: China's Orochen People and the Legacy of Qing Borderland Administration,* by Loretta Kim
120. *The Paradox of Being: Truth, Identity, and Images in Daoism*, by Poul Andersen
121. *Feeling the Past in Seventeenth-Century China*, by Xiaoqiao Ling
122. *The Chinese Dreamscape, 300 BCE–800 CE*, by Robert Ford Campany
123. *Structures of the Earth: Metageographies of Early Medieval China*, by D. Jonathan Felt
124. *Anecdote, Network, Gossip, Performance: Essays on the* Shishuo xinyu, by Jack W. Chen
125. *Testing the Literary: Prose and the Aesthetic in Early Modern China*, by Alexander Des Forges
126. *Du Fu Transforms: Tradition and Ethics amid Societal Collapse*, by Lucas Rambo Bender
127. *Chinese History: A New Manual (Enlarged Sixth Edition)*, Vol. 1, by Endymion Wilkinson
128. *Chinese History: A New Manual (Enlarged Sixth Edition)*, Vol. 2, by Endymion Wilkinson
129. *Wang Anshi and Song Poetic Culture*, by Xiaoshan Yang
130. *Localizing Learning: The Literati Enterprise in Wuzhou, 1100–1600*, by Peter K. Bol
131. *Making the Gods Speak: The Ritual Production of Revelation in Chinese Religious History*, by Vincent Goossaert
132. *Lineages Embedded in Temple Networks: Daoism and Local Society in Ming China*, by Richard G. Wang

133. *Rival Partners: How Taiwanese Entrepreneurs and Guangdong Officials Forged the China Development Model*, by Wu Jieh-min; translated by Stacy Mosher
134. *Saying All That Can Be Said: The Art of Describing Sex in* Jin Ping Mei, by Keith McMahon
135. *Genealogy and Status: Hereditary Office Holding and Kinship in North China under Mongol Rule*, by Tomoyasu Iiyama
136. *The Threshold: The Rhetoric of Historiography in Early Medieval China*, by Zeb Raft
137. *Literary History in and beyond China: Reading Text and World*, edited by Sarah M. Allen, Jack W. Chen, and Xiaofei Tian
138. *Dreaming and Self-Cultivation in China, 300 BCE–800 CE*, by Robert Ford Campany
139. *The Painting Master's Shame: Liang Shicheng and the* Xuanhe Catalogue of Paintings, by Amy McNair
140. *The Cornucopian Stage: Performing Commerce in Early Modern China*, by Ariel Fox